IRONY
in the
FOURTH GOSPEL

Paul D. Duke

John Knox Press
ATLANTA

Library of Congress Cataloging in Publication Data

Duke, Paul D., 1953-
  Irony in the Fourth Gospel.

  Bibliography: p.
  Includes indexes.
  1. Bible. N.T. John—Criticism, interpretation, etc.
2. Irony in the Bible. I. Title.
BS2615.2.D85   1985   226'.5066   85-42822
ISBN 0-8042-0242-7

© copyright John Knox Press 1985
10 9 8 7 6 5 4 3 2 1
Printed in the United States of America
John Knox Press
Atlanta, Georgia 30365

ACKNOWLEDGMENTS

To write, as to have faith, is both the loneliest of pursuits and the richest in grateful dependence upon community. It gives pleasure to confess that the private labors issuing in this work were both heartened and helped by an exceptionally generous community of friendship and faith. I gladly acknowledge my debts to many, and especially to the following incarnations of encouragement.

Walter J. Ong, S. J., opened for me the door of literary criticism. He taught me how to read, and pointed me toward worthy reading, some of it his, which sharpened my hearing and seeing of words. Under his instruction I first dived with delight into the large literature on irony. Professor Ong's work will continue to have widening impact upon the field of biblical studies, and I remain appreciative of its impact on me.

John B. Polhill, Wayne E. Ward, and D. Moody Smith offered critically sensitive readings of my work in its earlier stages. For the clarifications offered by them, and especially for Professor Smith's encouragement toward publication, I am most thankful. Highest praise, too, for Jacque Culpepper, who retyped my poor pages with competence, efficiency, and a graciousness which considerably brightened my way.

My deepest debt is to R. Alan Culpepper. With incomparable intrigue he first opened to me the suggestive riches of John's Gospel. Since that introduction I have experienced an expanding delight both in the knowledge of this Gospel and in the friendship of my teacher. In many ways my work is an expansion and elaboration upon one facet of his much broader pioneering work on the literary character of John's Gospel. For his generous sharing of unpublished manuscripts I am especially thankful. For every nudge of encouragement, every caution of criticism and every smiling silence of one who knows his irony, I offer my thanks.

This work would never have seen the light of day were it not for the strengthening, lively nurture of three overlapping communities of faith: the Southern Baptist Theological Seminary; the Highland Baptist Church of Louisville, Kentucky; and my family, most notably my wife, to whom this book is dedicated with profoundest admiration and gratitude.

CONTENTS

To Cathy Chandler Duke
best friend, full partner,
pure joy

INTRODUCTION

The eagle has long been considered by the church to be a profoundly appropriate symbol of the Fourth Gospel. The thought of this Gospel reaches dizzying heights, its majestic language spirals and soars, presenting a Christ "lifted up" to a glory more elevated than we might otherwise have seen. It is altogether understandable then that this writing, perhaps more than any other ancient Christian document, makes constant use of irony. For irony is a voice calling from great distance. It is an elevated perspective from which the initiated may view a world of rejected meanings and values far below. Irony, in Søren Kierkegaard's words, "looks down, as it were, on plain and ordinary discourse."[1] So irony in the Fourth Gospel, with discourse splendidly extraordinary, invites the reader to abide with an ascended Christ and to see from that height what a world that loves darkness will not see.

It is hardly a new discovery that John's Gospel abounds in irony.[2] Though there are places in which the author touches his text with irony so subtle we might not catch it in a hundred readings, there are other places in which the device is employed with such a heavy hand no reader can fail to notice. Until recently, however, very little separate attention was given to this phenomenon. Now we have R. Alan Culpepper's splendid analysis of the literary features of this Gospel, including a survey of Johannine irony.[3] Before his work we had only a handful of essays with limited scope, written prior to the publication of some outstanding recent critical examinations of irony.[4] The purpose of the present work is to do what these earlier works could not do and what Culpepper's survey could only begin: to clarify the substance and method of Johannine irony, to delineate its forms in this Gospel, to ascertain its functions for John's readers and to ask why the Fourth Gospel makes such consistent use of this literary device.

The workings of irony are decidedly difficult to comprehend. Insight has been recently gained, however, on the perspective and techniques of authors who use irony, and on the effects upon readers who perceive it. Thus, given the presence of irony in John and given the present concern in biblical scholarship with the shape and function of texts, a study probing the ironic method of the Fourth Gospel seems well in order, if not curiously overdue.

Before setting out upon this study, a word or two of qualification may be helpful. D. A. Carson has recently leveled some criticism against those who would apply the label "literary device" to certain recurring phenomena in the text of a Gospel.[5] His point is this: the phrase *literary device* tends to reduce these patterns of biblical expression to mere techniques of writing and so to undercut their pervasive theological import and historical foundation. Such justifiable protest makes it necessary to explain our designation of irony as a literary device. That phrase does not refer merely to a particular technique of literary expression. Certainly this sense of the phrase is included, but much more is intended. Behind the particular instances of ironic expression examined in these pages runs the deep rhythm of the ultimate irony that spawned them all: the Word became flesh, was rejected by his own, yet forged from that rejection a new community of light. Thus, the aim of this study is not to eclipse but to illumine this Gospel's larger proclamation of ironic truth by probing particular instances of its ironic expression and particular patterns of its literary technique.

Why then do we call Johannine irony a *literary device*? Aside from the fact just mentioned—that we are indeed concerned with irony as a stylistic technique—two other factors have influenced the use of this designation. There is first the issue of control. Scholars and critics who quest after ironies in a text are prone, once they have caught the thrill of the hunt, to become downright intoxicated—not only bagging their limit, so to speak, but opening fire on everything in the text that moves. Numerous undisciplined discussions of how this or that development in a story might be viewed as ironic reveal more creativity from the critic than from the author. Though the issue of authorial intent remains difficult (a problem to be taken up later), and though this study will inevitably make an unapologetic foray or two into the heady clime of subtleties intended or not, the emphasis here will consistently be upon those ironies which seem clearly present in the text. The term *literary device* reinforces the primary focus of this study upon those ironies that appear to be intended.

The second reason for focusing on Johannine irony as a literary device has to do with the quality of irony present in this Gospel. One way of distinguishing the various uses of irony is by the ironist's posture in life. While some writers employ irony as a strategic element toward some end, others use it to express their fundamental detachment from life, their permanent bemusement, their love of irony for irony's sake. This latter kind of ironist, however, is a creature of the modern era and bears no resemblance to the author of the Fourth Gospel.[6] John's irony is employed only to serve a larger purpose. This point might seem overly obvious, but many recent discussions about ironists do not seem to recognize such a distinction. Let it be clear then that we speak of Johannine irony as a *literary device,* distinct from any philosophical stance, that is used not purely for pleasure of negation but for positive purpose.[7]

Having clarified our purpose, it now remains to unfold the course to be traveled on this venture. Chapters 1 and 2 are devoted to the task of understanding irony itself. Inquiry is made into the origin of the idea and how it developed its different contemporary meanings. Various types of irony are delineated, and some central features unifying these subgroupings are isolated. No neat definition is achieved, but sufficient criteria are established through which irony can be recognized in John's Gospel. Of special interest in the second chapter is an exploration of the roles of author and reader in ironic communication. What can be said of the ironic author's perspective? How does he or she shape the irony and signal its presence? What is assumed about the readers and what demands are placed on them? What happens when we perceive an author's irony? These questions will have obvious import in the significance and intent of the Fourth Gospel's irony.

Chapters 3 through 6 turn to the text of the Gospel itself. Chapters

3 and 4 examine those particular texts which contain clear and pointed ironies occurring more or less at a given instant in the narrative. These "local" ironies are studied in relation to their methods, themes, presuppositions concerning the reader, and effects upon the reader. The forms of these ironies are probed in relation to analogous forms elsewhere in ancient literature and to the themes they express in John. Chapters 5 and 6 address the same questions with respect to the broader, more extended ironies in the Fourth Gospel. How does John weave the shorter ironies into sustained narrative irony? What can be said of the subtle ironic developments in plot and characterization? In what sense can it be said that the Gospel's larger proclamation functions ironically? It must be made clear that this writer has no illusions about cataloguing in these chapters every instance of Johannine irony. Certainly the obvious ironies are presented. Even a host of irony hunters in John's Gospel, however, could produce no definitive list. The subject simply will not stop moving. Irony, it should be remembered, laughs at all pretensions, especially the pretension of claiming to have grasped irony.

The last chapter seeks to relate the Johannine irony to the total context of the Gospel. Does the use of irony give any clue to the influences behind the Gospel or to its genre? What does the use of irony say about the Johannine worldview? How does irony relate to the other Johannine literary devices and to the total proclamation of this Gospel? Does an understanding of the Fourth Gospel's irony bring any insight to recent reconstructions of a Johannine community? Scholars speak of such a community's war with the synagogue (and later with itself), and argue about who it is that the Gospel seeks to address. Our findings about the effects of irony, its use as weapon and witness, may offer a constructive word here. Again, however, a disclaimer is needed. It is dangerous business to move from literary analysis to historical judgment. This study does not claim to reach any historical probabilities; such conclusions are simply not derivable from the study of a literary device. Nevertheless, where others have raised the historical issues, and where the use of a literary device is seen to have certain universal functions and effects, it is entirely within reason to lay those functions and effects alongside the various historical reconstructions and see how they do or do not relate. With considerable caution, therefore, the literary findings of this study will be brought into interface with the questions of history raised by the Gospel of John.

The historical issues, however, are penultimate. Our search is for what John's irony wants to do with the readers of this Gospel. The deeper question then is: what does it want with us? That issue remains the underlying force behind this study. But such a posture is not grounded in the hyper-subjectivity of pop-existentialism or the "New Criticism." It is based rather on the conviction that certain shapes of language have certain timeless functions and that biblical language in particular is designed to accomplish something timeless in its readers. Irony is language shaped both for judgment and invitation.

The Johannine eagle is fierce, but occasionally he startles us with what appears to be a smile or a wink. A sensitivity to how his irony hooks us, corrects us, leads us, and shapes us will be instructive not only for understanding this Gospel but for understanding ourselves and the Christ to whom this Gospel points us.

1

THE MEANING
OF IRONY

It is best to confess at the outset of this venture that no complete and satisfying grasp of the subject awaits us at the end of this book. Ground will be gained, to be sure; but some mysteries will persist. Such is bound to be the outcome when a journey is made in the company of two such intriguing and elusive companions. The first of these is the Fourth Gospel itself, so simple and cordial on the surface, and yet so awesome in its depth that the student of John "will not be true to the book he is studying if, at the end, the gospel does not remain strange, restless, and unfamiliar."[1] The second companion is Irony, the well-named "mother of confusions." She is beautiful, brilliant, inviting, sometimes comic, sometimes cruel, always enigmatic. As one ironologist has put it, "Getting to grips with irony seems to have something in common with gathering the mist; there's plenty to take hold of if only one could."[2] There are no illusions here about achieving a firm hold on this cloudy couple, the Beloved Disciple's book and the Irony with which it dances. Still, there is much about the marriage of these two which invites patient study with the promise of great reward. Rich ground has been gained in Johannine studies during the last two decades. During the same period literary critics and ironologists were making considerable headway toward clarifying and delineating the varied shapes and functions of irony. Bringing the results of these literary inquiries to bear on the text of John's Gospel offers the possibility of further insight into the meaning of this portion of Scripture. It remains true, of course, that in spite of the hundreds of articles and books devoted to the explication of irony (and because of some of them), the subject is still a slippery one. Nevertheless, if one

7

will follow the more sensible critics and be armed with caution and courage, a profitable exploration may proceed.

Origin and Development of Irony

Irony is not only as mysterious as love, but almost as ancient and universal as well. It has been said that irony is virtually as old as speech itself,[3] and experts claim it has been present in all cultures, at least in its oral form. To be sure, there is a marked difference between the ironic expression of a fundamentally oral culture and one with a more literary consciousness. The distancing provided by writing lends the perspective from which sophisticated and subtle ironies are made possible. The ironic parlance of a purely oral culture tends to be more heavy-handed, trading in riddles, double meanings, and jolting twists of fate, or in reversals of fortune. Typically the agent of such irony is that ancient and popular character, the wily trickster: Odysseus, Jacob, and in the African-based Remus tales, Br'er Rabbit.

It is in this figure of the clever trickster that the word *irony* has its root. The Greeks gave the name *eirōn* to that person who slyly pretended to be less than he really was. The etymology of the word is uncertain, though it seems related to *eirein,* to say or speak, or perhaps more closely to the Ionic *eirōmai,* to ask questions.[4] The word is rather late, first appearing in the comedic dramatists of the fifth century B.C.[5] At that time it was a vulgar word, used with overtones of contempt. The *eirōn* wore a mask of goodwill which concealed enmity. He was a grinning fox, a scoundrel not to be trusted. It was precisely with this sense of disdain that the epithet, *eirōn,* was hurled at the man who came to typify (and later to dignify) the term—Socrates. Quintilian summed up Socrates in this way: "he was called *eirōn* because he assumed the character of an ignorant man, and affected to be the admirer of other men's wisdom."[6]

Socrates' method of questioning his opponents with apparent innocence and admiration while ultimately intending to prove them fools was not an endearing technique. Plato presents an illustrative account of one victim's outrage in *The Republic,* when Thrasymachus speaks these words:

What folly, Socrates, has taken possession of you all? And why, sillybillies, do you knock under to one another? I say that if you want really to know what justice is, you should not only ask but answer, and you should not seek honor to yourself from the refutation of an opponent, but have your own answer . . . this sort of nonsense will not do for me; I must have clearness and accuracy.——336c–d.

When Socrates answers with a wordy apology and a plea for mercy ("you clever people should pity us and not be angry with us"), Thrasymachus is indignant.

How characteristic of Socrates! he replied, with a bitter laugh;—that's your ironical [eirōneia] style! Did I not foresee—have I not already told you, that whatever he was asked he would refuse to answer and try irony [eirōneusoio] or any other shuffle, in order that he might avoid answering?——337a.[7]

Of course Socrates engaged in such fun for good purpose. When confronting the highbrow Sophists, his ironic needle was for bursting bubbles of conceit. When with his students, irony was more gently employed in playful earnest, to nudge and agitate them into new vision. As played by Socrates, the character of the *eirōn* was both assassin of pretension and midwife of truth.

It is this first, more negative function of the *eirōn* that was emphasized in Greek comedy. The *eirōn*'s counterpart and enemy in the drama was the *alazōn*. While the *eirōn* presented himself as less than he really was, the *alazōn* vaunted himself as more. As the classic distinction has it, the *eirōn* dissimulates, the *alazōn* simulates. In the Greek comedies *alazōnes* were invariably swaggering imposters in one of two ways. Either they claimed honorable positions or professions which in fact were not theirs, or they claimed privileges and pleasures which they did not deserve. The result was usually some hilarious disaster in which the pompous quack was exposed for the pretender he was. Alazony in comedy is the exact counterpart of hubris in tragedy: downfall follows.[8] The agent of this downfall, the wily one who triumphs over the pretender, is the character who seemed so little and emerges so large—the *eirōn*.[9]

Philosophers and rhetoricians of the ancient world generally commended irony with reservation. In his *Nicomachean Ethics* (IV, 7), Aristotle indicates that the ideal mode of life is a truthful mean between the two extremes of the boasting *alazōn* who pretends toward excess, and the evading *eirōn* who pretends toward "the underside of truth." Still he made it quite clear that boastfulness is worse than self-depreciation. Pointing to Socrates as an admirable example, Aristotle claims "a moderate use of self-depreciation [*eirōneia*] in matters not too commonplace and obvious has a not ungraceful air."[10] Demosthenes and Theophrastus had a more negative evaluation, focusing more on irony as a social vice by which dissimulating persons try to shirk responsibility. It was not until Cicero that the word *ironia* was granted complete dignity. He praised Socrates' "accomplished wit in this strain of irony or assumed simplicity." Irony was, in Cicero's mind, "a choice variety of humor and blended with austerity . . .," an example of an "excellent sauce."[11]

In none of these examples is irony regarded strictly as a rhetorical device. Irony as the Greeks understood it was primarily a mode of behavior. In time, however, it became associated more and more with the verbal deceptions by which the dissimulation was effected. In particular, irony came to signify saying one thing and meaning another—understating, overstating, praising in order to blame, blaming in order to praise. Aristotle, and to a much greater extent Cicero, viewed irony at least partially as this kind of rhetorical device. But by the time of Quintilian this rhetorical element was primary; irony had become a figure of speech.

The above is a brief sketch of the origin and development of the word *irony (eirōneia, ironia)* in the ancient world. Unfortunately, such a survey of word usage still leaves us largely in the dark about the actual application of irony in ancient times. The surprising truth is that the use of irony in antiquity far outstripped any conscious concept of it. The Greeks' use of the words *eirōn* and *eirōneia* touches only the tip of a massive mountain of ideas, assumptions, and styles which the ancients did not call irony but which properly deserves the name. In the modern era we employ the Greek word *irony* in ways the Greeks never did—to describe broad or subtle contrasts between appearance and reality. However, when the roots of those broader perceptions and devices of modern irony are explored, it is discovered that they are firmly planted in ancient soil, especially in Greek and Semitic soil, deep in that great mountain of ideas, assumptions, and style that for centuries was unnamed, unconceptualized—irony.

Such irony is manifest in the sensitivity of most ancient peoples to the unexpected reversal of fate and fortune. Aristotle called it *peripeteia,* the jolting turn of events that forms the foundation of both tragedy and comedy, wherein the mighty are brought low and the humble exalted. Euripides often concluded his plays with these lines:

> Many things not looked for the gods bring about
> The things that seemed likely are not brought to pass
> And for the unlikely things heaven finds a way.[12]

Though the whole ancient world was fascinated with the possibility that present appearance might not be identical with present or future reality, no people were quite so inclined to step back and make an obvious art of enjoying it as were the Greeks. Their literature loves to tell of a character whose demise is brought about by his own hubris or by some cruel twist of fate; furthermore, as the story unfolds, the victim's unwitting march to destruction is drawn out deliciously by underlining the fact that his own blind confidence or his own efforts to escape his fate are precisely the deeds that bring about his destruction.

The Greeks were particularly taken with this perspective of life, but it was not uniquely theirs. Such a stance was at the very center of Israel's faith in a vindicating God and in the Christian proclamation of a crucified Savior. So when one scholar asserts of irony, "You may fairly call it a Greek thing,"[13] sensibility is offended. He might more correctly have said, artful extravagance in heightening irony is generally a Greek thing. For the ancient Israelite saw clearly enough the ironies of history, telling the tales with subtly engaging economy and praise to Yahweh (e.g., the Song of Moses, Exod. 15:1–18; the triumph of Joseph over his brothers, Gen. 37, 39–45). The ancient Greek saw the same patterns but with marvelously meticulous art proceeded to expose every thought, word, and action that might heighten the inevitable irony.[14]

This particular way of highlighting the irony of a character or situation came later to be called *dramatic irony.* The definition by M. H. Abrams is useful:

> *Dramatic Irony* involves a situation in a play or narrative in which the audience shares with the author knowledge of which a character is ignorant: the character acts in a way grossly inappropriate to the actual

circumstances or expects the opposite of what fate holds in store, or says
something that anticipates the actual outcome, but not at all in the way he
means it.[15]

This kind of irony was quite popular with the Greek tragedians. Bishop
Connop Thirlwall, perhaps the first to use the term *dramatic irony,*
equated it with *tragic irony* or *Sophoclean irony.*[16] Many would object
to these latter names, not only because Sophocles was neither the
inventor nor the chief user of dramatic irony (Homer used it earlier,
Euripides, as much), but also because it was a device of comedy as
well. Furthermore, dramatic irony was native to Israel as well as to
Greece. Even so, tragedians like Sophocles and Euripides were
antiquity's most obvious dramatic ironists. Their technique of sharply
underlining the irony of a character's situation for an audience is quite
like that of the Fourth Evangelist and employs certain principles to
which this chapter will return.

All the shades of irony's meaning discussed thus far have existed
both in ancient times and in recent centuries. As already intimated,
however, there are some perspectives on irony that are peculiarly
modern and, unlike those ironic forms which the ancients used but did
not name, are beyond the philosophical framework of antiquity.
Consequently these perspectives are not within the purview of this
study. Nevertheless, because the distinction has sometimes been
blurred, and in order to avoid anachronism, let us briefly note these
modern modes of irony and be done with them.

It was the German Romantics of the eighteenth and nineteenth
centuries who transformed irony from a rhetorical device to "a grand
Hegelian concept, with its own essence and necessities; or a synonym
for romanticism; or even an essential attribute of God."[17] Romantic
Irony is indefinable, for its proponents (Schlegel, Tieck, Goethe,
Heine, Brentano) were in disagreement as to precisely what it was; but
it bespoke the godlike freedom of authors who with boundless
detachment can manipulate their characters like puppets. A
perspective related to Romantic Irony and growing out of it was
Cosmic Irony, a movement which has had even more influence in
modern literature. Cosmic irony points to the unresolvable conflicts in
the universe, to the hopeless tedium of life, to a cosmos in which,
act or believe as they will, human beings are inevitably micro-

cosmic victims on a small planet adrift in meaningless, empty space. That this kind of ironic vision has permeated our time hardly needs illustration.

To this grim philosophical kind of irony may be added a particular literary-critical view, totally unrelated, but certainly supplementing the twentieth-century confusion about what is and is not ironic. The American "New Critics," writing at the midpoint of the century, had hypersensitive eyes for irony. Cleanth Brooks was typical.[18] For him irony occurs whenever one part of a text qualifies another part; irony is "pressure" or opposition in a context. Obviously, such a definition is tremendously wide, making ironic almost anything that is literary. The problem with such an understanding of the word is that it robs us of a meaningful term with which to describe the particular literary phenomenon that is at issue here.

Some people, therefore, see an awful irony in every rising of the sun; some see a constructive, balancing irony in virtually every poem and story. As has already been made clear, however, irony as used in the first century is something quite different from these recent views. Having set these aside, and having surveyed something of the historical development of the concept of irony, it is now possible to take a further step toward clarifying, for the present context at least, what irony is.

Toward a Definition

Lexicographers do not do especially well with irony. There is, according to D. C. Muecke, "no brief and simple definition that will include all kinds of irony while excluding all that is not irony."[19] Still, certain elements do seem basic, and by coming to terms with these something at least resembling a definition might be reached. It is Muecke who gives what some judge to be the best list of formal criteria of irony. He notes that all irony (1) is a double-layered or two-storied phenomenon, (2) presents some kind of opposition between the two levels, and (3) contains an element of "innocence" or unawareness.[20] An explication of these three elements will be helpful in understanding the essence of irony.

(1) Irony Is Double-layered

Every irony presents two levels of meaning. In *Julius Caesar* Mark Antony refers repeatedly to Brutus as "an honorable man." The ostensible meaning of the words, perhaps consonant with Brutus' estimation of himself, is quite different from Antony's meaning, forcefully communicated to the audience. "Brutus is an honorable man" is therefore a two-storied utterance. Because the literal meaning is incongruous with what we know of Brutus and the speaker's opinion of him, we translate into another level of meaning: Brutus is not honorable at all. Something of this process occurs in every ironic utterance; consequently, one frequently found definition of verbal irony is "saying one thing and meaning another." The problem with such a definition is that it is far too broad, for it equally well defines both metaphor and allegory. Mark Antony, for example, might simply have said, "Brutus is a snake in the grass." He would have been "saying one thing and meaning another," but he would not have been ironical. For irony to exist, the double-layered statement must be of a particular type.

(2) Irony Presents Opposition

Here is perhaps the most distinctive aspect of irony. All ironic communication contains some incongruity or clash of meaning. The two layers of meaning are not consistent with each other or built upon each other, as is the case with metaphor or allegory; instead they oppose each other in some way. The level of meaning settled upon by the perceptive reader in some way negates the ostensible level of meaning. Thus, if there is irony in a remark about the honor of Brutus, our reconstruction of meaning will necessarily negate or qualify Brutus' honor.

Ironic opposition occurs when a statement says less than it means (understatement) or more than it means (overstatement). The opposition may consist in a kind of double meaning in which what is said is precisely what is meant but in a sense unexpected by the hearer. An example is furnished in the book of Judges 3:20, where Ehud tells Eglon, "I have a *dabar* (word) from God for you." Eglon interprets in the natural sense and rises, expecting a word, but receiving an altogether unexpected "message"—a dagger.

Another method of ironic incongruity employs an opposition of tone against content, as when the speaker in Swift's "Modest Proposal" argues with cool gentility for the benefits of eating Irish children. Or the discord may lie simply in the presentation of two conflicting images or ideas which in juxtaposition are obviously ironic. "Woe to heroes—at drinking wine," says Isaiah; "valiant men—at mixing liquors!" (Isa. 5:22). Sometimes the irony growing out of opposition can be supremely subtle, existing "somewhere between the literal meaning and its logical opposite, in a no-man's-land where we feel our way deliciously and sensitively, among many puzzling nuances of mood and tone."[21]

One helpful way to summarize this aspect of opposition in irony is to say with Haakon Chevalier that "the basic feature of every Irony is a contrast between a reality and an appearance."[22] A glance at some ironies already noted is illustrative. Antony appears to praise Brutus; *dabar* appears to mean a spoken word; the *eirōn* appears to be a fool; the *alazōn* appears to have great knowledge; ancient ironists often open their tragedies with the appearance of smiling fate; modern ironists often begin with the appearance of a meaningful universe. In each case the irony emerges when the appearance is corrected or exploded by the contrasting reality perceived by the ironist and perceptive audience. Irony, then, is a leap from what seems to be to what is.

So essential is this element of opposition, so necessary is it that the perception of irony begin with a resounding no, some critics have judged irony to be essentially negative. Indeed it is possible for the love of irony to lead one into what Kierkegaard called "infinite absolute negativity."[23] German Romantic Irony was precisely this, a sweeping attempt to undercut every foundation, to oppose all values against each other until only nothingness was left. So the ironist is one who comes to destroy, according to Kierkegaard.[24] He was, however, not altogether correct, for not every ironist is without positive purpose.

Nonetheless there is more than a measure of truth in Kierkegaard's analysis. Even when irony seeks to create new meaning or new community, it begins in negation. From the school of Speech Act Theory has come the hypothesis that the linguistic process dominating every ironic utterance is negation, expressed either with lexical negatives on the surface or with more covert "deep structure negation" absorbed into the language.[25] This verdict from linguistics is matched by the verdict of experience. When readers witness irony they witness opposition. Ostensible meanings of language, assumptions of fact, expectations of outcome, or outward appearance of circumstance are negated to some degree. In irony a new vision of things is gained, and the newness springs from the clash of opposition. Thus, irony is a double-layered phenomenon presenting some degree of discord between the two levels. This description, however, is still not narrow enough, for through this door could pass other literary devices such as contrast or paradox. At least one other criterion is needed to isolate irony from these others.

(3) Irony Contains an Element of Unawareness

Every ironic communication seems to make its play by virtue of some lack of understanding, either real or pretended. Just as one person's skepticism has little meaning apart from someone else's credulity, so the "punch" of irony depends in part upon some failing to see it. Irony, particularly dramatic irony, often operates on some unwitting victim. One character will be unaware that his or her actions are leading to tragic consequences; another will cling to assumptions that are utterly false, or speak words that have meaning quite different from the meaning intended, or hear words with a tragic (or comic) misunderstanding of their intended meaning. Usually another character is quite aware of the real situation or meaning, and smiles or laments as the victim is taken in. Even when no character has sufficient knowledge to see the irony, the author knows, as does that portion of the audience which shares in the author's perspective. This kind of irony is realized when we who are aware observe the inappropriate assumptions, words, and deeds of those who are unaware. The more obvious their unawareness, of course, and the more confidence exhibited by them, the richer is the irony.

Sometimes the element of innocence in irony consists of no actual ignorance of characters or even of the audience. Some ironies depend on a feigned innocence on the part of a speaker. In most verbal irony, for example, the speaker communicates more than he pretends to say. With or without the desire to make victims of others, he becomes his own "pseudo-victim."[26] The truth is, every ironist who uses any degree of subtlety engages in some level of feigned unawareness. This is because, as will be seen, virtually all irony is indirect communication, inviting the observer into some initiative of perception. Provided that an author refrains from blatant intrusions, blaring out, "Look here, this is ironic," some illusion of authorial unawareness will be maintained. Consequently, some critics will speak of irony as being a deception.[27] It is, after all, in the very nature of the *eirōn* to be self-effacing.

Beyond these three formal criteria for irony, little can be added toward a helpful definition of irony, though some critics have suggested other elements. Of particular interest is the assertion that all irony entails some clash of the painful with the comic. One writer has said that the effect of all irony "is the emotional discord we feel when something is both funny and painful . . . to feel it one must be pained for a person or ideal gone amiss. Laughter rises but is withered on the lips."[28] There does indeed seem to be a general relationship between comedy and tragedy and irony. Northrop Frye has placed irony on a kind of continuum between the two, pointing out that tragedy moves toward comedy and comedy moves toward tragedy, both by way of irony.[29] Nevertheless, even if it could be shown that irony always evokes some degree of "painful laughter," such a claim presents an affective quality of irony, not a formal one, and so offers limited help in definition. The same is true concerning the element of "detachment" sometimes included in descriptions of irony.[30] Detachment is always present in the author and audience of irony; but because such an element describes the participants more than the device itself, it is omitted here and reserved for the discussion of author and audience.

Formally, then, what is irony? The impossibility of concise and comprehensive definition has already been confessed. Nonetheless, for the present purposes irony may be loosely described as follows: irony as a literary device is a double-leveled literary phenomenon in which two tiers of meaning stand in some opposition to each other and in which some degree of unawareness is expressed or implied.

The preceding paragraphs have attempted to explicate the criteria

of irony. What follows is an attempt to understand how this broadly
defined phenomenon manifests itself in so many distinctive and
diversified ways.

Some Types

If definitions of irony are difficult, taxonomies of irony are
impossible. No one, to the knowledge of this writer, has ever been
deluded enough to charge into the mists of irony in hopes of emerging
with a complete catalogue of types; and this is certainly no place to
begin. Such an endeavor would be absurd, not only because the types
and shades of irony are countless, but because they fade in and out of
each other like colors of a spectrum. Still, there are certain fundamental delineations of irony that stand out rather clearly. Some of
these have been touched upon already. It is necessary now to take
more careful stock of some significant variations of irony.

Stable and Unstable Irony

One of Wayne Booth's real gifts to ironology is his discussion of
irony in terms of stability and instability. By stable irony Booth means
irony that is intended, covert, fixed, and finite.[31] It will be helpful to
clarify the meaning of these categories and to note their boundaries
and flexibilities in ironic communication.

Intended and unintended irony. It is said that the phrase *"Arbeit
macht frei"* was inscribed over the entrances to some Nazi concentration camps. It is difficult to miss the irony, but we can be rather
certain that the official who chose those words did not intend them
ironically. The irony rises out of the horror of subsequent events, our
knowledge that these events formed a ghastly contradiction to the
slogan, and our perception that anyone committing such crimes under
such a banner was morally destitute. So we call that slogan tragically
and pathetically ironic. We may not say, however, that the ones who
wrote it were being ironical. The irony lies in the events, in the perception of the victims and the observers, but not in the intention of the
authors.

The difference is in some respects a crucial one. It was noted in the

Introduction that discussions of irony in literature are sometimes prone to lose all connection with the apparent intention of the text. Ironies are found which are real enough, but whose reality is more in the mind of the critic than that of the author. Now it should be clear that speaking of ironies unintended by the author is a totally valid enterprise. The point here, however, is that irony conceived by an author, structured into a text, and somehow signaled for perception (assuming the goal is not a private irony) is not quite the same thing as irony that is exclusively in the eye of the beholder. For in discussing the former, we must speak of techniques and strategies; in speaking of the latter, the subject must be changed to address the observer's sense of irony, and his or her responses and attitudes about what constitutes an ironic situation.

There is no desire here to undercut the complexity of the intentionality issue. Since the work of Wimsatt and Beardsley, the problem of "intentional fallacy" has been much discussed in literary circles. Their contention was that "design or intention of the author is neither available nor desirable as a standard for judging the success of a work of literary art;"[32] and by this they mean two things. In the first place, no interpreter has the capacity to probe an author's psyche and expose his or her intentions. In the second, even when an author gives overt explanations of intention, there is a degree to which the work is not bound by them. Authors, like the rest of us, are incredibly complex creatures, and may consciously or subconsciously express more than they see or profess to see. Intentionality is indeed elusive, and no easy equation can be drawn between intention and meaning.[33] Consequently, when one seeks out "purposeful" ironies, the lines will sometimes be fine; some intended ironies will be missed, some ironies not consciously intended will be "caught," all quite within the boundaries of a text's ironic meaning.

Nevertheless, a basic distinction between irony *communicated* and irony *perceived* must be recognized. Absolute certainty concerning the intentionality behind an irony perceived in a text may not always be possible. Still there are instances of irony about which there can be little doubt of intent, and many others in which there seems to be at least the probability of such intention. As we shall see, this is because authors generally signal their irony in some way. It is this more or less clearly signaled irony that gives solid ground on which the interpreter of a text may stand—stability, as Booth has it. Such is not the case with purely subjective readings. Though all irony entails a demanding degree of subjectivity, when there is no ground at all for suspecting an ironist's intention our claims about irony become so subjective that we no longer interpret meaning so much as create it.

Covert and overt irony. Overt irony, according to Booth, occurs when an ironist relinquishes all subtlety and tells us forthrightly, "This is ironic."[34] Such an obvious intrusion is the mark of what has been called the "naïve" ironist. The "sophisticated" ironist, on the other hand, has no need to announce that he is being ironic, and allows the reader to catch or miss the meaning. When a reader is robbed of all participation in discovering the irony, in a rather important sense the communication ceases to be ironic. That is to say, rather than accomplishing an ironic insight with an audience, overt irony merely describes this insight. In Booth's words, when we have to be told that something is ironic, the utterance has moved "from dance to assertion."[35] For ironic communication to *happen,* some degree of silence must be kept by the author. The degree to which the author's voice is heard or not heard is a matter of substance to which we will later return.

Fixed/finite and unfixed/infinite irony. An irony is fixed when "once a reconstruction of meaning has been made, the reader is not then invited to undermine it with further demolitions and reconstructions."[36] That is to say, once we have made the leap to higher meaning, we stay there. The author does not shake the new foundation and send us scurrying about in search of radical reinterpretations. We may indeed be invited to explore successive levels of meaning within a fixed irony; but these levels move in one direction, are aligned with each other, and grounded in each other also. Fixed irony is stable. It is solid ground on which author and sound reader can stand together with common and consistent perception.

For this shared confidence to be possible, the irony must also be "finite." When Kierkegaard spoke of the irony of his day as "infinite absolute negativity," he explained: "It is negativity because it only negates; it is infinite because it negates not this or that phenomenon;

and it is absolute because it negates by virtue of a higher which is not."[37] By finite irony, then, is meant irony that directs its negation (or qualification) toward a specifiable position rather than undercutting everything in general. For this reason Muecke's terms may be more helpful. Instead of finite and infinite irony, he speaks of "specific" and "general" irony.[38] Specific, finite irony tends to be purposive, often corrective; general, infinite irony offers only a dirge.

If irony, then, is finite, we are given some place of meaning on which to stand. If it is fixed, that place is solid enough that we can pitch our interpretive tents there. If it is covert, we have freely made the journey without having been forced at swordpoint by the author. If it is intended, we have some degree of confidence that we have not made the move alone. Added together, these variables of ironic method comprise stable irony. It is this irony that moves and rewards us. It is this irony that permeates the Fourth Gospel. Consequently, the remaining categories to be considered here are all subspecies of stable irony.

Verbal Irony

Writers on the subject of irony sometimes differ in what they mean by a given term. *Verbal irony* is one of those terms that is not used with consistency. Some critics use this designation for any intended irony conveyed through language. In this study, however, the issue of intentionality is treated on its own terms. *Verbal irony* will be used in a narrower sense, that of a "statement in which the implied meaning intended by the speaker differs from that which he ostensibly asserts."[39] Excluded from this definition are those instances of irony in which an author shows us ironic events, situations, and characters. Excluded also is that dramatic device by which words carry more or different import than the speaker knows. The present focus is on that type of spoken irony which is intended to be ironic.

The simplest and crudest form of verbal irony is sarcasm. Though not all sarcasm is ironic, much of it is, taking the form of an ostensibly good word that must be reinterpreted as not good at all. Sarcasm's most obvious feature is that its "higher" level of meaning is hardly covert at all. The listener, particularly the victim, is left in no doubt at all as to the speaker's meaning. The reason for the immediacy of perception is evident in the meaning of the word *sarcasm* itself—i.e., *flesh-tearing.*

The sarcastic one means to inflict a wound that the victim cannot possibly miss.[40] The Apostle Paul was not lacking in sarcastic skill, particularly with the Corinthians.[41] In the Old Testament a beleaguered Job blasts his wordy counselors with sarcasm from the dungheap ("No doubt you are the people and wisdom will die with you!" Job 12:2), but is later humbled when sarcasm interrogates him from the whirlwind in the well-known "Can *you* . . .?" (Job 38 & 39). This final instance, incidentally, is a supreme example of one of the primary features of sarcasm: it seldom leaves room for reply.

Understatement and overstatement are two other forms of verbal irony, though either can be used without irony. When the angel of the Lord finds Gideon hiding in a wine press and hails him, "You mighty man of valor," what he is smiling with, among other things, is ironic overstatement (Judg. 6:12). Far more common is ironic understatement, which should be no surprise since the ancient *eirōn* was understatement incarnate. Euripides puts some wonderfully understated lines on the lips of the female chorus in *Medea:*

> I have often engaged in arguments,
> And become more subtle and perhaps more heated,
> Than is suitable for women;
> Though in fact women too have intelligence,
> Which forms part of our nature and instructs us—
> Not all of us, I admit; but a certain few
> You might perhaps find, in a large number of women—
> A few not incapable of reflection . . .[42]

The last line is an example of a particular kind of understatement called *litotes,* the denial of a contrary. The remark of the preceding paragraph that Paul was not lacking in sarcastic skill is also litotes. One occasionally finds this device in Scripture, as evidenced in Isaiah 10:7 and Acts 21:39.[43]

There are numerous other ways in which verbal irony might be accomplished. A speaker might give praise in order to blame (as is often the case in sarcasm and overstatement), or blame in order to praise. There might be pretended agreement with a victim or pretended advice or encouragement to a victim. Rhetorical questions may be employed ironically, as may ambiguity, analogy, parody, insinuation, incongruity, pretended error, pretended doubt, and other dissimulating devices.[44] These techniques comprise for the warrior of words both fortress and arsenal, both shield and sword. The speaker engaged in verbal irony stands protected behind the screen of ostensible meaning, while the silent intent of the word shoots beyond to do its piercing work.

Dramatic Irony

When the roles of verbal irony are reversed, the result is dramatic irony. While verbal irony is achieved by an intentional speaker who knows more than may be apparent, dramatic irony employs a speaker (or actant) who knows less than is apparent and whose involvement in the irony is quite unintentional. While in verbal irony the real meaning may be momentarily or indefinitely hidden from a "victimized" audience, the audience of dramatic irony sees the irony clearly, and the real meaning is hidden from the victimized speaker or actant. As its name implies, dramatic irony is preeminently the irony of theater, where spectators from good seats "on high" view an illusory world of characters and events in which they may not interfere, but over which they exercise a kind of omniscience. The characters seem powerless in comparison, and the possibilities of irony-observed become endless. That does not mean, of course, that dramatic irony is restricted to the theater, for it is abundantly present in any narrative in which the author invites us to compare what the characters say and do with what we know to be true.

This aspect of audience knowledge is absolutely crucial to the workings of dramatic irony. Like the proverbial tree whose falling in the deep forest is unheard and thus is said to make no sound, dramatic irony makes no music apart from the engagement of an audience that knows and understands. As one writer puts it, dramatic irony presupposes "a vital relationship between actors and audience. What is being performed is not independent of the spectators but depends on their involvement as witnesses."[45] Or as Chevalier says, "This spectator becomes a vital factor. He is not, it must be observed, a mere casual bystander. Nor is he an observer in the strict sense. . . . He thus enjoys an intimate and exclusive complicity with the action."[46] This

complicity derives from the essential fact that the audience knows
what the character does not.

There are numerous ways by which this superiority of knowledge
is gained by the audience. Often in the ancient Greek theater the
myths and legends portrayed were already so well known to the
audience that the author needed no device to fill them in. This is
the case with Sophocles' *Oedipus the King*. Everyone in the theater
knows from childhood what poor Oedipus does not: that he has killed
his father and married his mother. The irony plays off this prior
knowledge without resorting to any explanatory devices in the play
itself. Most of these plays, however, made some effort to insure that
even the least informed spectator was not left behind; the authors
resorted to certain stock methods of communicating the knowledge
necessary for the irony to work. One favorite technique was the
"omniscient prologue," in which a character, usually a god, related to
the audience the events leading up to the story's beginning and
foreshadowed or even foretold the events that were about to unfold.[47]
Such a device was crucial when the irony revolved around some
hidden or mistaken identity. When the omniscient prologue was not
used, however, the playwright had at his disposal the devices of
prophecies, oracles, and soliloquies of various kinds. In narrative this
function is often fulfilled more simply by the use of a reliable,
omniscient narrator. Regardless of the technique employed, however,
it cannot be overstressed that for dramatic irony to function the
audience must know more than the characters. This knowledge is
usually divulged early, and the result is a constant interplay in the
observers' minds between anticipation and reminiscence—the two
steadfast companions of dramatic irony.[48]

Dramatic irony is expressed in a number of ways. The definition
offered by M. H. Abrams has already been given, but an examination
of it will be instructive here in understanding the various possible
layers of dramatic irony.[49] Abrams' definition begins: "*Dramatic Irony*
involves a situation in a play or narrative in which the audience shares
with the author knowledge of which a character is ignorant." This
principle in conjunction with the other criteria of irony already
given—two layers of meaning in opposition—produces dramatic
irony. It may be present in a rather generalized sense, being only, as

one description puts it: "the sense of contradiction felt by spectators of a drama who see a character acting in ignorance of his condition."[50]

This "sense of contradiction," however, may be focused to a sharp point by which dramatic irony is underlined. Abrams' definition continues by offering three variations of this underlining. (1) "The character acts in a way grossly inappropriate to the actual circumstances." Such is the case in Euripides' *Bacchae,* in which crazed Agave, when she has killed and mutilated her son Pentheus, parades madly with his head on a stick, gloating because she thinks what she has killed barehanded is a lion. (2) "Or expects the opposite of what fate holds in store." In the *Oedipus,* the king and his mother/wife are confident both that old oracles about Oedipus' killing his father have been safely averted and that by ridding Thebes of the mysterious offender happiness will be restored. Likewise in Esther 5:14 Haman builds gallows intended for Mordecai, not himself. (3) "Or says something that anticipates the actual outcome but not at all in the way he means it." So Jonah predicts, "Yet forty days and Nineveh will be turned upside down" (Jon. 3:4), not knowing that indeed the city will be changed, but not as he foresees. Likewise Oedipus swears that he will maintain the cause of his wife's deceased husband, "as if he were my father," intending a simile, but bearing unwitting witness to the literal truth. This kind of double entendre is especially common in dramatic irony and is the particular effect generally meant by the term *Sophoclean irony.* It may also function in reverse. That is, dramatic irony may surface when a character wrongly interprets someone else's verbal irony, rather than unintentionally speaking it himself. It is dramatic irony, for instance, when Croesus hearing from the Delphic oracle that "Croesus, if he cross the Halys, shall undo a mighty realm," proceeds to cross the Halys and discovers too late that it is *his* mighty realm that is undone.[51] An example that includes both kinds of double entendre is found in Genesis 22:8. As Abraham and Isaac make their way to the mountain of sacrifice, Isaac inquires as to the whereabouts of the offering. Abraham answers, "God will provide himself the lamb for a burnt offering, my son." On one level this is a sorrowful verbal irony by which a father seeks by double meaning to delay his doomed son's anguish. Isaac assumes there will be a lamb. Abraham knows the grim truth that God has provided a different "burnt offering, my son." If we have never before heard this story, we still see this irony, for we have already been informed of God's ghastly command. If, on the other hand, the story is already familiar to us, as it would have been to its Hebrew readers, we know that there is a richer, deeper irony at work. The double entendre swings two ways. Abraham will be the happy victim of his own irony. He has blindly prophesied the truth.

These examples of methods by which dramatic irony is underlined have been given here because of the importance of dramatic irony in this study. It must be made clear, however, that these devices do not actually constitute the irony; they only give it fine focus. *General* dramatic irony is at work when an audience observes characters acting in ironic ignorance of their situation. The phenomenon becomes *specific* dramatic irony, however, only when authors draw out their characters' ignorance through actions that are glaringly inappropriate, expectations that are obviously ill-founded, or a use of language that is freighted with hidden meaning.

Situational Irony

Dramatic irony is one form of ironic situation, but it is by no means the only one. It is possible for characters and situations to develop ironically without an absolute dependence on the superior foreknowledge or memory of the audience. Some other types of situational irony appropriate to this study are listed briefly here.

Irony of Events explores the particular incongruity arising when events bring the unexpected, especially when the means sought to avoid an occurrence turn out to be the very means of bringing it about. Amos' picture of fleeing a lion, only to be met by a bear employs such irony (Amos 5:19). *Irony of Self-betrayal* occurs whenever the words or deeds of a person clearly divulge a different character than he or she claims to be. Such inadvertent self-disclosure might be accomplished by means of some secretive action, a soliloquy, a letter, or, as in the case of a certain Pharisee, a prayer: "God, I thank thee that I am not like other men" (Luke 18:11). Sometimes situational irony is grounded in *imagery* which seems somehow in opposition to the action which it accompanies. In *Agamemnon,* for example, the king arrives with great flourish and all the accoutrements of the victorious warrior riding toward a triumphal welcome; but the action shortly makes it clear that he is riding toward nothing but the axe of his own wife. Irony may also be achieved through *characterization*. Characters may be developed in such a way that their ultimate behaviors or personalities turn out to be in ironic contrast to what they have previously displayed. The exposure of the *alazōn* and the triumph of the *eirōn* are obvious types of ironic characterization.

Further classifications, examples, tones, and half-tones of irony could be catalogued, *ad infinitum*. Those types given here are fundamental, however, and reflect the necessary delineations for the study of irony in the Fourth Gospel. They also raise further questions about how authors of irony accomplish their subtle work, how the audience of irony reconstructs meaning, and what effects emerge in the process.

2
THE FUNCTIONS
OF IRONY

The Author and Audience of Irony

It has already been made clear that all stable irony, and especially dramatic irony, requires a shared sense of understanding between author and audience. Irony is a kind of fellowship into which author and sound reader or spectator enter in silence. Together they watch, wink, and smile, because together they share the perspective that blinded characters and perhaps less adept observers do not share. They form a community of superior knowledge.

Reliability

In order for this partnership of perspective to take place there must be reason for the reader to trust the writer. If the reader of a narrative is to have any confidence in making the leap to higher, ironic levels of meaning, there must be a sense that whatever clues the author has given toward irony are trustworthy. We must find it believable that the "lower" structure of meaning as portrayed is truly undesirable and that the "higher" structure to which we are invited is sound. We must have confidence that the shape of the narrative world is accurately conveyed, that characters and events have been presented "as they are."

Now in much modern literature, the narrator does precisely the opposite, relating characters and events through biased or ill-informed eyes. In this kind of writing the readers can pick their way through what is ironic and what is not only if the implied author has given reliable clues that the narrator is unreliable and therefore the chief victim of the irony. Where both narrator and implied author are

unreliable, however, the reader becomes the victim, for all foundations are shaken and the irony becomes unstable. But, once again,
such a convention is confined to our own unstable age. In all classical
irony and especially in first-century irony, the reader's perception of
irony is firmly grounded in the confidence that the teller of tales is a
good guide. The fellowship of irony is founded upon the bond we feel
with a narrator who is reliable.[1]

Voice

The reader's dependence on a reliable narrator or author does not
mean that the writer is relied upon to spoon-feed the ironies. For the
process of ironic communication to be operational, the writer must not
only be trustworthy, but discrete, treading lightly, knowing when to
keep silent. As already suggested, the most genuine irony is covert,
allowing the observer the freedom to choose one structure of meaning
over another. The success of irony, according to Booth, depends on
"swift communion of meanings that make the reader himself feel
clever for seeing so much in so little, the less the better."[2] The author of
irony, then, must generally exercise considerable economy and
restraint, speaking in hushed tones, if speaking at all. Booth again
says:

> In short, even when the ironist in this mode must nudge—and he
> frequently must—he must not be *thought* to nudge. Recognizable
> nudging, anything that might be seen as increased bustle on the author's
> part, decreases the active role of the reader. In the language of J. L. Austin,
> the speech act moves from being a performative—"*do* something for or
> with me"—to descriptive, from dance to assertion. Since irony "claims" to
> be performative, nudging contradicts its claims.[3]

Ironic utterance, then, is preeminently an indirect form of discourse. It
is frequently, to be sure, a forceful form of commentary upon the
situations and characters which the ironic author presents; but it is
commentary only implied.[4] Indeed the power of irony, as is the case
with symbolism, imagery, and metaphor, lies in the eloquent
implicitness of its silence.

Still, there are various ways in which the ironist's voice is heard,
and various levels at which authorial presence is apparent. Muecke
lists four modes of irony in which the ironist's voice is heard in

diminishing degrees.[5] (1) *Impersonal Irony* (which includes most verbal irony) occurs when we hear the voice of the ironist but are more or less unaware of him or her as a person. The irony lies "more in what is said than who said it." (2) *Self-disparaging Irony* includes those particular kinds of verbal irony in which the ironist's real opinion is in critical opposition to what is expressed by his *persona*. Under this rubric is found understatement, overstatement, and other forms of clear dissimulation. The voice of the ironist is hidden behind the pretended character of the ironist. (3) *Ingénu Irony* is a mode in which the author withdraws behind a particularly innocent character who is used as a mouthpiece for ironic truth. The *ingénu* differs from the *eirōn* in that he or she is not especially sly, but simply honest. Some well-known examples include Huck Finn, Lear's fool, Don Quixote (though he is more than an *ingénu*), Uriah the Hittite (2 Sam. 11:11; cf. 11:1–5), and the little child in "The Emperor's New Clothes," who simply says what he sees. Such an innocent clear-sightedness is obviously a happy screen behind which an ironist can artfully speak. (4) *Dramatized Irony* is that mode in which the author presents only ironic circumstances and people, leaving all the detective work to the audience. Though Muecke's claim—that in dramatized irony the ironist tends to "withdraw completely"—has been contested,[6] it remains true that this mode of irony shows the least evidence of the ironist's whispered presence.

Detachment

If the author's voice is truly muted *behind* the surface of the ironic story or discourse, it is also true that the author's stance lies well *above* the ironic story or discourse. We have already mentioned the distancing which is central to the ironic perspective. Such detachment is essential not only for the author but also for the audience of irony, who are invited to join the author on his lofty perch. Inherent in the ability to see things ironically is the capacity to become removed from the surface level of action or words, and from that elevated standpoint to observe with a mixture of pity and amusement the folly of those who do not see. Indeed one finds it impossible to speak of irony without reference to words such as *see, observe, spectator, perspective, point of view,* and *appearance.* Seeing is the most distanced of the human senses, and seeing is precisely what must happen in irony. That, incidentally, is why the more literary a culture is, the more sophisticated are its ironies.[7] It is also why the theater is such a suitable image and archetype of the ironic experience. At the same time, however, the distance of the ironic point of view should by no means be infinite. Total detachment would reduce the ironic response to mere ridicule. The combination of pity and amusement would be impossible were the observers of irony still unable to identify to some degree with those who do not see. So the opposition at the heart of irony makes its home in those who are above, but not beyond it. Though "he who sits in the heaven laughs," the ties to the world below are strong enough to keep his laughter ever on the edge of tears.

Clues

Face-to-face verbal irony is usually not difficult to decipher. The ironic speaker may wink or smile, exaggerate her tone or quite subtly modify her manner in countless ways in order to signal us that her words do not themselves speak the whole truth. The strictures on writing, however, do not permit such immediate indicators. The writer of irony is faced with the challenge of trying to transmit the wink to paper, and the reader is given the detective's task of discovering it. Though the task of rightly reading the clues is not always simple, it is both profitable and inevitable. When we "feel" as if a certain line or work is ironic it is generally because the author has planted some subtle signal which we may not consciously recognize as such, but which has hooked us nonetheless. As slippery as irony is, it must like all other language be law-abiding. Certain identifiable factors in particular conjunction will usually constitute the irony, and we tend to recognize it by these factors. Very few authors truly wish to be misunderstood. Where there is ironic intent, and especially where there is purposive ironic intent, we may be assured that the author will leave a trail sufficiently clear for the sensitive reader to follow.

Quintilian, speaking of the orator's art, addresses the ways by which irony may be signaled.

> [Irony] is made evident to the understanding either by the delivery, the character of the speaker or the nature of the subject. For if any of these

three is out of keeping with the words, it at once becomes clear that the speaker is other than what he actually says.[8]

Throughout the following centuries rhetoricians have echoed Quintilian's triad of delivery, speaker, and subject as key factors in the perception of irony. Aside from the fact that this rule applies more to oral than to written discourse, it is an oversimplification; for any one of these three factors might well be out of kilter for reasons other than irony.[9] Still, it cannot be denied that this triad broadly covers all possibilities; all signals to irony's presence will fall under one of these three categories.

Booth suggests a system of five ways by which an author may signal irony.[10] (1) Straightforward warnings may be given in the author's own voice, as in an incongruous title or epigraph, or a simple announcement that irony is present. (2) Known error may be proclaimed, as when a speaker shows incredible ignorance of what most readers would commonly know to be true. The knowledge violated in this case is external to the text itself. The botching of popular expressions, historical facts, and conventional judgments are all examples of this kind of clue. (3) A conflict of facts may occur within the work, as when, for example, the author presents a position in one part of a work and the opposite position elsewhere. This is especially a device of dramatic irony, where we learn the truth from one character or event and later witness another character who in ignorance acts or speaks as if the opposite were true. (4) A clash of style may arise. There are numerous ways in which this sort of subtle discrepancy between what is ostensibly said and the language employed to express it may occur. The incongruity between Swift's tone and theme in "A Modest Proposal" has already been mentioned as a clue to his irony. Subtle degrees of overstatement or understatement may fall under this heading as well, as does the use of inappropriate modifiers or metaphors, or the presence of conflicting tones or styles within the work. (5) A conflict of belief may signal irony, as when a piece expresses a conviction which is not held by most people, or which is not held by those people likely to read that work, or which is suspected not to be held by the author. Here, to be sure, a subjective element has entered in, but one which is both necessary and entirely justifiable. The reader's judgment about irony may often come down, then, to

asking such questions as these: what has been my past experience
with the position expressed here? what do I know or suspect about the
beliefs of the one who wrote this work?

In addition to these five broad categories of clues to irony, an
author may employ some smaller verbal techniques to underline
irony. In cases where the irony hinges on some kind of overstatement
or understatement, there may be a particular use of "lexical
intensifiers." Words like *rather* (a "compromiser"), *indeed* (a
"booster"), *hardly* (a "diminisher"), and *a bit* (a "minimizer") are the
kind of expressions that irony often uses.[11] Another type of linguistic
intensification often employed ironically is repetition. When a word,
phrase, or image is often repeated, its importance is stressed, and its
ironic content may be heightened. The presence of irony may also be
indicated by a substantial usage of the definite article or demonstrative
pronoun, words which are generally expressive of distance.[12] It should
also be recalled that silence itself, the refusal of an author to comment
on a particular incongruity, may be a clue in itself to ironic intent.

Reconstruction

The choice of words such as *clue* and *signal* implies the centrality
of the reader's response to irony. The process of that response needs
now to be considered step by step. Throughout this and the preceding
chapter the image of "reconstruction" has been used to indicate the
reader's process of grasping an author's irony.[13] In using irony an
author invites the reader to reject an ostensible structure of meaning.
The meaning to be rejected is often far more than the literal meaning
of a particular sentence or expression, but rather a whole structured
"world" of meanings or values which the author spurns. Those who
do not share the author's perception may choose to remain in such a
structure. The perceptive reader, however, will abandon this house of
meaning, mentally demolishing it, and from its rubble leap to the new
structure on a higher site where the author and all sound readers dwell
together. From this new house of meaning the author and perceptive
reader can view the rejected structure and its uninformed inhabitants
at a pleasurable distance.

The process by which the reader accomplishes this "adventure in moving" may be outlined in four steps. (1) The reader rejects the literal meaning. Because of internal or external clues, the ostensible sense of the words is met with a resounding no. (2) Alternative interpretations or explanations are attempted. The reader might quickly consider some of the following possibilities: maybe the author slipped or is crazy; maybe I missed something earlier; maybe the words do not mean what I think; or maybe in this or that sense the words are ironic. (3) A decision is made about the author's knowledge or beliefs. The reader here evaluates what is known or suspected of the author's convictions and competence, and asks if this information sheds light on interpretation. The conclusion may be, for example, something like this: given what I know about this writer, she simply cannot have written this way and not have meant it ironically. (4) A choice is made for a new meaning or cluster of meanings, based upon the conclusions reached in the previous steps. To be sure, this process is rarely as laboriously methodical as this outline seems to suggest. Most often the insight flashes into the reader's mind in an instant in what has been called a "delightful leap of intuition."[14] The speed of the process notwithstanding, however, these four elements will be present if not as sequential steps then as decisive vectors in the reader's intuition of irony.

Despite the apparent simplicity of these four steps, this whole process is extraordinarily complex. It is based upon the author's inferences about the readers and their experience of language and culture, their convictions about meaning and value, and their experience of literature, particularly the genre at hand. The readers are presented with a series of implied choices made by the author on the basis of these inferences; and reciprocally, they must make countless inferences about him, his experience, and his convictions. That such a procedure so often yields a deep and widely shared understanding of what an author literally did *not* say is baffling testimony to the power of human communication. The fact that this miracle usually occurs with lightning speed may explain why irony is such a universally satisfying and powerful instrument of speech. As Booth says, "Perhaps no other form of human communication does so much with such speed and economy."[15]

Uses of Irony

When the issue of irony's function is raised, the relationship of the audience to the author is still largely in view. Nevertheless, it seems wise to treat function separately, because the function of irony may range beyond the immediate impact on those who read and perceive it, and because function is an issue of singular importance to this study.

D. C. Muecke speaks of three unexceptionable uses of irony.[16] It may be used as a *verbal device* whereby a speaker underlines intended meaning; it may be used as a *satirical device* to attack some point of view or to expose someone's ignorance or folly; finally, irony may be used as a *heuristic device,* employed "to lead one's readers to see that things are not so simple or certain as they seem, or perhaps not so complex or doubtful as they seem." These three functions rarely appear separately. The ironist may use verbal irony to underline the folly of one he is exposing, or he may attack one point of view in order to lead readers to the discovery of some alternative. The following discussion of irony's functions does not follow Muecke's outline, but rather divides the issue into its two more elemental components: irony's positive appeal to its readers and irony's negative function with its victims, who may be readers, or characters in the narrative world, or real people to whom the text directly or obliquely refers.

Irony as Appeal

Mention was made earlier of the satisfaction rendered by irony. This theme is not new. Goethe observed, "Irony is that little grain of salt which alone renders the dish palatable."[17] Likewise Anatole France, complaining that "martyrs are lacking in irony," goes on to say that such a fault is unpardonable, "for without irony the world would be like a forest without birds; irony is the gaiety of meditation and the joy of wisdom."[18] What does one make of such claims? In what does the pleasure of irony consist?

It might first be said that the process of reconstruction discussed above is itself gratifying. Provided the ironist is not trading in obscurities, readers are generally delighted to discover that they have been entrusted with the task of rising above a rejected surface of meaning in search of a better one. One writer has said, "Such irony always rests on implicit flattery, enhanced by an earned 'do it yourself' quality. We pat ourselves on the back for recognizing that this is *not* a truth."[19] Part of the agreeableness found in this process stems from the fact that initially, if only for an instant, the real meaning is not readily apparent. Thus, like the sequence of tension and release inherent in laughter itself, irony leads us away from an initial anxiety about an unreliable meaning to a leap toward new meaning and finally to a sense of confirmation that we are now indeed on solid ground.[20] The thrill stems both from the "danger" and from the sense of accomplishment when such a leap has been successfully completed.

The appeal of irony does not end here, however; for readers may find themselves not only relieved and flattered, but also remarkably immersed in new depths of insight. A critic once called irony "the shoe-horn of new ideas,"[21] for in the indirect whispering way of irony there is both a gentle beckoning and a powerful persuasion. Perhaps it is in irony's silence that this power resides. For precisely in its restraint from dictation of a literal meaning to its readers, irony is able to move those minds to an intensely active state and to engage them in an open search for solid ground that will make them grateful when they find it. On one level the reader's search is a literary one. A structure of verbal meaning is rejected and the search begins for another. If ultimate meaning or values are at stake in the irony, however, then when the literary search is over and the higher structure has been discovered, the excitement of that interpretive leap is easily transferred to the possibility of a more ultimate leap. Particularly when irony is artfully done, the choice to share the author's perspective on a narrative world may become a decisive step toward dwelling with that author in a deeper sense and embracing a new perspective on the real world. Having already danced with the author, the reader is much more prone to consider marriage.

Wayne Booth is particularly intrigued with this winsome aspect of irony. He notes that irony is far richer in expressive and emotive power than any non-ironic translation could be. He illustrates, interestingly enough, with an example from the New Testament. Mark 15:18 reports that Jesus was mocked with the words "Hail, king of the Jews." Mark's restrained report of this mockery renders the words doubly ironic: the soldiers' verbal irony is turned back on them by the awesome and ultimate irony that Jesus is indeed the King. Booth's point is that, by presenting this truth ironically, Mark is engaging in a maximally effective form of witness:

> But it seems clear that Mark's irony builds a larger community of readers than any possible literal statement of his beliefs could have done. If he had said simply, "Those who gathered to mock Jesus did not know that he was in fact King, king not only of the Jews but of all mankind, quite literally the Son of God," a host of unbelievers would draw back, at least slightly. But the ironic form can be shared by everyone who has any sympathy for Jesus at all, man or God; even the reader who sees him as a self-deluded fanatic is likely to join Mark in his reading of the irony, and thus to have his sympathy for the crucified man somewhat increased.[22]

Irony, then, exercises a peculiar power over those who perceive it. Of course, such a statement requires some qualification. Inasmuch as irony does not coerce, it has its greater power among those who are at least somewhat open to its message. In the passage just quoted, Booth restricts the irony's appeal to "everyone who has any sympathy for Jesus at all." Irony's function is to deepen such existing sympathies or inclinations. When its message is in stark contradiction to the reader's own convictions, however, it will have limited effect, and indeed may not even be perceived as irony. In this connection, irony is sometimes a decided risk, courting the possibility of complete misunderstanding or angry rejection. Purposive irony, however, may well take such risks, for when it does succeed, it achieves a stronger success than any literal statement can assure. Kierkegaard's summary of the strength of irony is typically rich:

> As there is something forbidding about irony, so also it has some extraordinarily seductive and enchanting moments. The disguise and mysteriousness which it entails, the telegraphic communication which it initiates, inasmuch as the ironist must always be understood at a distance, the infinite sympathy it assumes, the elusive and ineffable moment of understanding immediately displaced by the anxiety of misunderstanding—all this captivates with indissoluble bonds. Should the individual feel himself emancipated and enlarged under the first moment of contact with the ironist, inasmuch as the ironist opens himself to this individual, at the next moment he has fallen into his power.[23]

If irony has this power to win people more fully into the ironist's camp, it has another agreeable effect as well: irony rewards its followers with a sense of community. This is true in a number of ways. First there are the elements just discussed: irony has a way of slipping its readers gently into new insight or strengthened convictions, thus offering to its readers the sense of a community of like-mindedness. Though irony often functions as a sharp, polemical device that makes victims and outcasts of some, its more native function seems to be constructing a partnership of perspective. As Booth says:

> . . . the building of amiable communities is often far more important than the exclusion of naïve victims. Often the predominant emotion when reading stable ironies is that of joining, of finding and communing with kindred spirits. . . . every irony inevitably builds a community of believers even as it excludes.[24]

This sense of finding and joining is several-sided. It involves not only positions and values, but the interpretive act itself, which as we have seen draws the reader into an impression of belonging to a privileged minority who see the irony that uninitiated, ordinary eyes do not.

Also present in the common bond may be a shared love for irony itself. The fellowship may thus be grounded in more than common convictions about the world, and in more than common literary insights, but in the warm and welcomed feeling that the one who wrote this way and the ones who understand it are all people who think as I do. The fact that irony with all its subtleties, inferences, and indirections can be grasped with common understanding by a number of individuals gives testimony to the workings of kindred minds. Some people can catch irony's peculiar accent and converse in it; others cannot. The voice of irony whispers its invitation to any who will come and join the party, but obviously those who hear it best are the ones already there. As we will see, then, irony's relation to community is circular. It aims at drawing people more fully into its camp, but its fullest force is with those already within. Indeed irony may often be not so much a call to community as the sure sign of its presence.[25]

Irony as Weapon

While Irony has her allurements and richly rewards those who dance with her, she can be positively cruel to her enemies. It has been clear throughout this chapter that one of the functions of irony is the making and the mocking of victims. While irony is a witness to those who will see, it is a weapon against those who will not see.

Such a weapon is double-edged. Irony may single out certain persons, attitudes, beliefs, social customs, philosophical systems, or even life itself as targets for its scorn. The one who writes or speaks ironically about such matters is indirectly presenting at least the possibility of an alternative view of things. We may speak of these targeted entities as *objects* of irony. On the other hand, and often simultaneously, the element of "unawareness" that is present in all irony may be brought to particular focus, and one who claims to know or ought to know is mocked by the ironical vision of those who do know. We can speak of such persons as *victims* of irony. Obviously, these categories frequently overlap, and the one whose position is being assaulted may also be mocked as hopelessly enslaved in ignorance.

We may remember that the favorite victim of the ironist is the *alazōn*, the one who pretends to more knowledge, more power, or more privilege than he really has. Particularly as the *alazōn* is confident or serenely unaware in his claims does irony have its fun. The more he swaggers or sings in his ignorance, the harder he will fall. As Muecke remarks, "Simple ignorance is safe from irony, but ignorance compounded with the least degree of confidence counts as intellectual hubris and is a punishable offence."[26] The victim need not have made any verbal claim to confidence for the irony to work, however; he may simply be in a position in which he *ought* to know more than he does, and so is convicted of a kind of imputed confidence. As Muecke again reminds us, it is not especially ironic when a man dives into an empty swimming pool thinking it to be full; but when the man is the diving instructor, the irony is wonderful.[27]

Irony's method of attack is indirect, though that does not mean its blade can never be obvious. In sarcasm and some other forms of verbal irony, the assault is made unmistakably clear to the victim, though of course the speaker still says one thing and means another. At other times the indirect arrows of irony may repeatedly go undiscovered by the victim until he becomes a Saint Sebastian look-alike—in which case if he is still smiling, the irony is all the richer. Obvious or not, however, the tact of nonsarcastic irony is, rather than aggressively pursuing a victim, to heighten the possibility of self-betrayal and destruction. Its aim is not so much to vanquish as to expose. As in its more positive aspect, irony seeks to be a catalyst of revelation. So it asks questions, raises possibilities, then steps back to watch the show. As Kierkegaard said of irony, "It does not destroy vanity, it is not what punitive justice is in relation to vice. . . . On the contrary, it reinforces vanity in its vanity and renders madness more mad."[28]

When irony wages its warfare the issues are seldom frivolous. It is no mere trifling vanity or minor stupidity at which irony usually laughs. Rather, irony wants to be the tearful laughter of a liberated few who are spectators of a more fundamental enslavement. As Booth says, irony "demands that we look down on other men's follies or sins; . . . accuses other men not only of wrong beliefs but of being wrong at their very foundations and blind to what these foundations imply."[29] It must be remembered, however, that irony is usually not the manner of outright ridicule. There remains in irony, if not always the hope of correction, at least a touch of identification with the victim, and so quite often an element of sorrow. From such a mixture of mirth and sadness can stem a degree of redemption. Anatole France's justification is worth quoting.

> Irony and Pity are two good counselors; the one, by smiling, renders life lovable; the other, that weeps, renders it sacred. The Irony which I invoke is not cruel. It mocks neither love nor beauty. It is gentle and kindly. Its laughter calms anger, and it teaches us to make fun of scoundrels and fools whom we might otherwise have the weakness to hate.[30]

Conclusion

Perhaps the only certainty to have emerged from these pages is the certain truth that irony is not simple. Its method, as it turns out, seems merely to reflect its essence: irony is itself alive with the clash of opposition. It is a forceful voice that speaks best in silence; a detachment from the world that will not let the world go; a figure dancing everywhere and grasped nowhere; an invitation brandishing a sword; the ring of laughter choked with tears. Irony is a device; and irony is the truth.

It is a fascinating prospect to consider irony's remarkable power in the content of that baffling and infinitely inviting document we call John's Gospel. The Fourth Gospel makes frequent and artful use of irony. Readers who know this Gospel will already have made numerous connections between the ways of irony and the ways of John. A careful reading of the Fourth Gospel in view of what has been discussed here would seem to be most promising. It is to that task that our attention now turns.

3

LOCAL IRONY:
The Socratic Christ
and His Little Children

Irony not only appears in various moods, forms, and functions, it comes in an assortment of sizes and shapes. In one work the irony is compact, tightly compressed and quite sharp; in another it appears in a broad, long-curved arc; in still another it may show itself in some combination of the above—smaller, pointed ironies punctuating the longer, larger ones. In this study the smaller, punctual ironies are designated *local;* the longer, larger ones are called *extended.*[1]

Local irony occurs at a given point in a text. Though its punch may depend upon knowledge gained by the reader elsewhere, either in the text or outside it, this kind of irony does its work quickly, and its parameters can be drawn rather narrowly. Extended irony demands more development and employs scattered hints and devices throughout an episode or an entire work. It is often more subtle than local irony, though its effect in the end is frequently just as sharp and may be considerably more forceful.

This spatio-temporal way of looking at irony has an uneven correspondence with the types of irony discussed in the previous chapter. Verbal irony, for example, is almost always local. Though occasionally the true intent of a statement is left unrevealed for quite some time, the typical usage of verbal irony will have a much more immediate effect; the reader makes the ironic leap from a rather narrow springboard of words. Dramatic irony, on the other hand, as well as other forms of situational irony, can be either local or extended. Ironic images and situations can be presented in an isolated context, and dramatic irony, particularly when it is underlined by double

43

entendre can be more or less self-contained. Quite often, however, ironic images, situational irony, and dramatic irony are employed with a much broader stroke, with the effect depending upon a total narrative structure. In such a case, the reader must make an extended series of little jumps before the ironic leap is complete, though such reading may be less like leaping and more like embarking upon a transtextual flight.

The Gospel of John draws its irony small and large—local and extended. The approach of examining local ironies separately from extended ones is not an entirely satisfactory one, for the themes treated by the two are often the same, and, in fact, the larger irony of the Fourth Gospel sometimes emerges from the sum of related local ironies. The two styles will nevertheless be considered separately here because there are crucial differences of form and technique, if not always of general type and theme. It is not merely a matter, then, of looking at the "little" ironies and then at the "big" ones. Our approach is rather an acknowledgment that in biblical literature, as in all worthy art, substance and function are inseparable from form.[2] The various forms and techniques of John's irony deserve careful and separate attention, for they bear revealing witness to the several-shaded purpose of this Gospel.

The present chapter and the one following will consider John's local ironies on the basis of who utters them: first Jesus and the disciples; then the other respondents to Jesus. Such an arrangement allows us to see that in the Fourth Gospel a different kind of irony proceeds from each of these sources. Ironies deriving less from dialogue and more from character, image, and situation will be reserved for subsequent chapters. Though some of these may be considered local, their impact seems more generally tied to the larger movement of the narrative. The texts discussed here will not be examined in the order of their textual appearance but according to the logic of their mutual relationships.

In each text where irony is at work, four questions will guide our discussion: (1) technically, how is the irony achieved? (2) what is the theme of the irony? (3) what knowledge in the audience of the Gospel does the irony seem to presuppose? (4) what effect does the irony seem to have on the reader? Similar passages from the Synoptics will be examined where elucidating, as well as parallel ironic forms from other ancient sources.

Irony of the Johannine Jesus

Jesus is the only character in the Fourth Gospel who utters irony without being the victim of it. It is intentional, verbal irony he speaks, often saying subtly less or more than he ostensibly means. Other characters may attempt verbal irony in this Gospel—his opponents often trade in sarcasm—but their intended cleverness always misfires in view of the Truth. In this Gospel only Jesus knows whereof he speaks (7:15–17; 8:27; 12:49). The first instance of Jesus' irony illustrates the point by way of dramatic contrast.

3:10 "Are you the teacher of Israel and do not understand this?" Nicodemus has come at night, initiating conversation with these words, "Rabbi we know that you are a teacher come from God." Jesus abruptly issues a solemn pronouncement: "Amen, amen." Nicodemus' reply is a question revealing total incomprehension. Jesus responds by solemnly repeating the pronouncement, rephrasing it, adding both explication and enigma; and again Nicodemus can only counter with a bewildered question, this time just four exasperated words: "How can this be?" Jesus makes a third pronouncement, this one issuing in an eleven-verse monologue. Before he takes up the chant, however, he pauses to ask the asker of dumbfounded questions a question of his own, a question that will effectively sweep Nicodemus back into darkness for another four chapters: *Su ei ho didaskalos tou Israēl kai tauta ou ginōskeis?* The emphatic use of the pronoun *su* draws out the irony more clearly: "*You* are the teacher of Israel and do not know these things?"

Jesus here seems to be feigning surprise at Nicodemus' bewilderment. A classic Socratic pose is struck in such a question, and the subtle, needling word-play is exquisite.[3] Nicodemus began by hailing Jesus as *didaskalos*—teacher. Jesus here may be deferring by returning the title, as if to say, "Aren't you, not I, supposed to be *ho didaskalos?*"[4] The addition of the definite article is significant, ascribing to Nicodemus a representative role, distancing him from Jesus, and heightening the position from which he is to fall.[5] Jesus not only repeats Nicodemus' word "teacher," he goes on to recall this Pharisee's claim to knowledge: "We know *[oidamen]* that you are a teacher come from God" (3:2)/"You do not know *[ginōskeis]* these things?" The phrase also parrots as well as puns upon the man's second baffled question: "How can these things be *[tauta genesthai]?*" (3:9)/"You do not know these things *[tauta ou ginōskeis]?*"[6] Further, there is evidence that in the Fourth Gospel the word *Israel* is always used in a deeper theological sense than may appear on the surface (cf. 1:31, 49; 12:13)—that, in fact, some readers of the Gospel know *Israel* to mean "the true Israel," God's new people through Jesus Christ.[7] So there is irony in the fact that while Nicodemus may be "a ruler of the Jews," he is by no means "a teacher of Israel."

In short, there are overtones of irony in virtually every word of this piercing question. The irony is achieved by word position *(su, ginōskeis)*, by repetition and near-repetition of Nicodemus' words *(didaskalos, tauta, ginōskeis)*, by use of the definite article, and by use of theological double meaning *(tou Israēl)*. The remark poses two elements incongruous with each other, the second effectively negating the first. Jesus appears to offer deference, but in fact he offers judgment. He is here the classic *eirōn,* "praising in order to blame," raising his eyebrows as he raises a question.

10:32 "I have shown you many good works from the Father; for which of these works do you stone me?" Here the irony is both more simple and more blunt. For the second time "the Jews" have heard Jesus claim his oneness with God and taken up stones to kill him (see 8:58–59). Where earlier Jesus hid himself, he now lays before them the absurdity of their rage before eluding them once again. It is an irony of simple incongruity. Jesus presents two images: here are my good works—noble, beautiful *(kala)* works,[8] works clearly from the Father; and there are the stones in your hands. "For which of these works"—*ergon* is repeated for emphasis, and *poion* stresses the quality of the works—"do you stone me?"[9]

The question is not intended to stop the stoning, but serves to force "the Jews" into a particular confession. Throughout chapter 10 there is an emphasis on response both to Jesus' works and to his words. In verses 1–18 he speaks, and the response is a division "because of these words" (vs. 19). Those who defend his words, however, do so on the basis of his *works* (vs. 21). Then in verse 24 "the Jews" insist that Jesus tell them plainly if he is the Christ. His response is that he has told them and that, in particular, his *works* in the Father's name have borne witness to him. Twice we have been told that the proof of Jesus' word is his work. When, in response to Jesus' word, "the Jews" move to kill him, Jesus corners them with the issue of his good works. Now they must reveal themselves, and they gladly comply. The stones are for blasphemy—words—and "for no good work." So set are they against the words that they dismiss the evidence of his works out of hand. The irony of Jesus' question succeeds in illustrating his earlier remark, "that those who see may become blind" (9:39). Their deafness to his word has induced a terrible blindness to his work.[10]

7:23 "If on the sabbath a man receives circumcision, so that the law of Moses may not be broken, are you angry with me because on the sabbath I made a man's whole body well?" This question has a kinship with the previous one. It juxtaposes Jesus' cure of a sick man and the anger of "the Jews." The irony of their hostility is underlined with the typical *a minori ad maius* argument. "The Jews," after all, make perfect one part of a man on the sabbath. How much better that Jesus heal a whole person on the sabbath? For this, he asks, "Are you angry with me?" While the irony of the question itself may end there, it is suggestive of a larger context.

We have just seen an instance in which "the Jews'" hostility toward Jesus is expressly not at his works but at his scandalous words. The question of 7:23 recalls the miracle performed in chapter 5, in which the timing of a work did indeed anger "the Jews." Following that controversy, however, is Jesus' discourse concerning his voice and his word. Then chapter 6 (whether in its original position or not) climaxes in the fact that though his miracles have drawn large crowds, his hard words have driven them away. It will also be recalled that in 5:18 "the Jews" sought to kill him, not simply because of the sabbath sign, but because he called God his Father. Could the irony of 7:23 go deeper than a mere presentation of incongruity? Perhaps the question "Are you so angry that I heal on the sabbath?" invites the answer no. The anger behind the anger is that this one who commandeers the sabbath speaks so outrageously of his identity with God.

7:28 "You know me and you know where I come from." The words of the Jerusalemites in verses 25–27 are heavy with irony to which we shall return in the next chapter. And Jesus' reply intentionally ironizes their unintentional irony. The words may be punctuated as a question—"So you know me, do you?"—in which case the irony is obvious enough.[11] There is no indication in the Greek, however, that a question is intended; and, in fact, the irony becomes stronger if we read it as declaration. The repetition in the Greek forms a little chiasm which almost carries the rhythm of a taunt: *Kame oidate kai oidate pothen eimi.* As he had done with Nicodemus, Jesus echoes their claim of knowing, here twice. The double usage of the conjunction, *kai,* as Bultmann says, "gives [a] certain ring to the sentence. 'Certainly! You know me and know. . . .'"[12] The New English Bible captures the same tone: "No doubt you know me; no doubt you know where I come from." The point is clear enough. The people have claimed to know Jesus' origin, and so deny that he can be the Christ. Jesus' reply is a confirmation that ironically refutes them. Of course they know where he is from; and precisely in that knowledge are they ignorant of his origin—*ho pempsas mē, hon humeis ouk oidate.* Bultmann's analysis is worth quoting:

> The irony of Jesus' observation that they know him and his origin does not lie in the suggestion that their knowledge is based on faulty information. No, they are quite right; people know very well who his parents are (6:42). Yet in a paradoxical way this is at the same time the proof of their ignorance. Their knowledge is unknowing; for they use their knowledge, which in itself is perfectly correct, to conceal the very thing which it is important to know. Their knowledge serves only to prevent them from recognizing Jesus; he cannot be the Messiah because they know where he comes from (v. 27)! Thus in truth they do not know him, for they do not know who sent him.[13]

16:31 "Do you now believe?" As in the last case it is not certain whether these words are declarative or interrogative. Most commentators and translators, however, punctuate the verse as a question. There seems to be no doubt that our next example, 13:38, a verse in several ways parallel to this one, *is* interrogative; and even if 16:31 is intended as a declaration, it is a declaration raising doubt, posing a question.[14] The disciples have just made an enthusiastic profession of faith that is unwittingly ironic. They claim at last to have understood Jesus! "Ah, now you are speaking plainly, not in any figure! Now we know that you know all things, and need none to question you; by this we believe that you came from God." Jesus' first response to this rather wordy profession is only two words, *arti pisteuete*—Do you now believe?

As in 3:10 and 7:28, Jesus echoes his interlocutors, here taking up both the verb, *believe,* and the theme of *now.* The disciples have twice used the word *nun* in their confession. Jesus uses the word *arti,* a synonym for *nun.*[15] It is emphatic: "*Now* you believe?" As we shall see, there is evidence in the disciples' profession itself that their faith is less than solid; but Jesus' words shift the focus to what will be the proof of their failure. "The hour is coming and has come" when the disciples will be scattered each to his own, leaving Jesus alone. Such is the extent of their belief. Now in the sweet glow of supper, cleansed feet, and gorgeous discourse they believe; but soldiers, swords, and a great darkness will shortly surround them and crowd out all belief. Between their bright profession and Jesus' dark prediction stand those two ironic words—*arti pisteuete.* Jesus' question is what all purposeful irony strives to be: an open door from appearance to reality.[16]

13:38 "Will you lay down your life for me?" In exasperation at his master's elusiveness, Peter has promised, "I will lay down my life for you." Jesus' reply returns the words for reconsideration. The repetition, even the word order, is exact; only the pronouns are transposed. As in 16:29–32, 13:37–38 contain the following elements: (1) a rash pledge of loyalty, (2) Jesus' question, which ironically echoes the pledge, (3) Jesus' prediction which solemnly cancels the pledge.[17] The irony of Jesus' question here is richer than that of 16:31. His words not only call Peter's present courage into doubt, they also imply the question of who will die for whom in that hour; and, for the reader who knows the outcome, they point to the distant day when this disciple will indeed lay down his life for Jesus. The full sweep of this "irony of character," however, will be explored in chapter 6.

Other sayings. The irony of the sayings above seems clear enough, but other sayings of the Johannine Jesus which are sometimes called "ironic" are far more problematical. One complicated instance is John 2:19. Bultmann refers to the phrase, *destroy this temple,* as an *ironic imperative,* in the style of the prophets.[18] Amos 4:4–5, for example, hurl this invitation:

> "Come to Bethel, and transgress;
>   to Gilgal, and multiply transgression; . . .
>   for so you love to do, O people of Israel!

Like Amos, Jesus presents the ironic incongruity of the people of God undoing the house of God and sarcastically entreats them to continue their present course toward destruction. His next utterance, "and I will raise it up in three days," relocates "temple" as the body of Jesus and mocks their worst destructive capacities with the ease of his power. On its own merits the sentence has a double edge, on the one hand drawing an equation between the rejection of Jesus and the destruction of the temple, and on the other replacing that temple with the exalted Christ. The irony of the first clause is severely weakened, however, by the narrator's emphasis on the second aspect of Jesus' pronouncement (vss. 21–22).[19] It later becomes clear that "the Jews" will indeed lose their holy place, ironically, as they seek to keep it safe from Jesus (11:48). The narrator's interpretive intrusion here, however, so underscores Jesus' hidden reference to resurrection and the Jews' failure to grasp it that the destruction of the actual temple fades deep into the shadows. Local irony *per se* is lost, although the seed is quietly planted for the tragic irony of Israel's doom that will burst into view as the Passion unfolds.

Some writers interpret any enigmatic utterance of Jesus as ironic. Irony is used by some to dismiss difficulties or to blur theological nuances. An example is 2:4. When the mother of Jesus remarks, "They have no wine," he responds, "What is this to you and me, woman? My hour is not yet come." There is enigma here, but hardly verbal irony.[20] While the words Jesus speaks seem incongruent with what he will shortly do, he seems to be feigning nothing here at all. This question seems to reflect a genuine dissociation of interest in the issue of wedding wine and shifts the focus to a recurring theme of this Gospel: this Jesus will be motivated by no human concern; he will act only on his own purpose, at his own time.[21] The same is certainly true when Jesus refuses his brothers' suggestion to go to Jerusalem, then goes to Jerusalem (7:6–10; cf. 11:6–7). This is sovereign evasion, not irony.[22]

In other cases commentators on the Fourth Gospel have simply chosen to use the term *irony* in a way very different from our use of it here. François Vouga, for example, in a work that is often insightful, applies the word *ironie* to the broad theme of Jesus' incomprehensibility. Jesus speaks ironically when he says to Nicodemus, "You must be born from above" or when he engages the Samaritan woman in dialogue about living water.[23] According to Vouga, the ironic method of the Johannine Jesus employs a series of "enigmatic affirmations," so that his interlocutors doubt of their certitudes one by one, until finally their own existence is questioned and they are led to despair. Once they are stripped of all certainty Jesus reveals himself, for only then can he be received. Vouga thus speaks of the "infinite negativity" of Jesus' irony, a phrase which, it will be recalled, was used by Kierkegaard to describe Socrates' irony. The problem with Vouga's terminology, aside from the fact that it imports more of Kierkegaard, existentialism, and Neo-orthodox language than these texts can easily bear, is that it leaves us no meaningful word with which to distinguish the rhetorical device which concerns us here. It seems best, then, to place Vouga's suggestive discussion under the related heading of Johannine *misunderstanding,* and to employ the word *irony* only in its sharper, more usable sense.

Summary. We have discussed six sayings of Jesus in which irony is clearly present, in varying degrees of strength (3:10; 7:23, 28; 10:32; 13:38; 16:31). A few other sayings, to be considered in the course of chapters 5 and 6, might be called ironic (9:41; 13:36; 18:34; 19:28); but in these texts the irony seems either so faint or so tied to the broader context that they hardly have the character of local or verbal irony.

The six sayings before us present some rather consistent patterns of ironic technique. (1) Five of the six are questions, and the exception (7:28) is an ironic declaration raising so much doubt that it is often punctuated as a question. (2) All but one of these queries (10:32) go unanswered, an unsurprising feature in view of the fact that verbal irony—particularly that of the heavenly Word—is essentially unanswerable.[24] (3) In four of the six the most obvious technique is that of repetition; Jesus pointedly, wearily echoes their promises and claims, and the echo is hollow indeed. (4) The point of reference for the irony is usually self-contained. That is, the irony swings upon an incongruity presented in the question itself (3:10; 7:23; 10:32) or in remarks which immediately follow (7:28–29; 13:38; 16:31–32). Only in one case might the irony partially depend upon knowledge extraneous to the immediate context; 13:38 will have extra ironic import if the reader knows Peter will one day be martyred.

The themes of these ironies are various. Twice the subject is "the Jews'" hostility in view of Jesus' good works; twice it is the disciples' failure in view of their promises; twice it is someone's claim to knowledge which in fact is ignorance. These themes correspond to three types of "victim": hostile opponents ("the Jews" and the accusing crowd), the disciples (Peter and the group), and the uncommitted curious (Nicodemus and Jerusalemites).

Is the verbal irony of Jesus in John consistent with his way of speaking in the Synoptics? The irony of the Synoptic Christ has often been noted,[25] but tends to manifest itself in different ways. In one sense it is more permeating. Jesus' understanding of the kingdom of God has at its heart an irony of reversal that is constantly proclaimed (e.g., in the Beatitudes and many of the parables). Like the prophets he delivers scathingly ironic denunciations (Mark 7:9; Matt. 23:13–39). He occasionally responds with sardonic resignation when God's people display hopeless wickedness: "it cannot be that a prophet should perish away from Jerusalem" (Luke 13:33); or misunderstanding, as when at the Last Supper his disciples proudly announce, "Look, Lord, here are two swords," and Jesus sighs, "It is enough" (Luke 22:38).[26]

Jesus also makes ironic use of particular words, such as the word *righteous:* "I came not to call the righteous, but sinners" (Mark 2:17;

cf. Matt. 5:20; Luke 15:7). Only rarely, however, does the Synoptic Jesus ask ironical questions, and when he does, it is never in the context of a dialogue, as in the Fourth Gospel, but in response to actions—to Judas at Gethsemane: "Friend, why are you here?" and to his captors: "Have you come out as against a robber?" (Matt. 26:50, 55).

This difference is rather striking when one realizes that in the Synoptic dialogues Jesus asks far more questions than he does in the Johannine dialogues.[27] These questions, quite often counter-questions, are used to probe, to expose, to clarify issues, to turn the tables on his opponents—functions, in other words, compatible with irony, but where verbal irony itself is absent. There is certainly nothing in the Synoptics to compare with the question that nudges the teacher of Israel about his ignorance, nor with the quizzical, grand concession that the crowd knows him after all. All sources seem to agree that Jesus was an ironist;[28] but as with metaphor, parable, antithesis, and other forms of speech, the Fourth Gospel manages to preserve the general form of irony, while filling it with an idiom, a technique, a theme that is radically different.

The Johannine Jesus is a different sort of ironist than we meet in the other Gospels. He is more Socratic,[29] more the interrogator bemused at the foolishness before him and seeking to expose it. While the Synoptic Jesus is not without humor, his irony is spoken with fire in his eyes. The heavenly revealer of John's Gospel speaks irony too, but his eyebrows are raised, and there is the trace of a smile on his lips.

Irony of the Disciples

The disciples in the Fourth Gospel tend to stand in the middle, between Jesus and the world.[30] Those who do not defect (6:66) abide with Jesus and are not of the world as he is not of the world (17:14). Yet they are in the world (17:11), the realm of darkness; and particularly before the resurrection they are subject, even while they believe, to the grossest misunderstandings of Jesus. They are, therefore, the occasional victims of irony. Because of their belief, however, and because their false assumptions and claims are not generally made with the same degree of arrogance displayed by the other respondents, this Gospel's irony is rather gentle with them.[31] Though their verbal errors are often similar to the misstatements of others, the irony is usually underlined with a much lighter touch (gentler, for example, than Mark's treatment of them). Those texts that ironize the disciples, however sympathetically, are grouped here according to the types of expression by which their "innocent unawareness" is exposed: false assumption, misunderstanding, superficial confession, or false promise.

False Assumption

1:46: "Can anything good come out of Nazareth?" There is one instance in which a disciple gives voice to an assumption about Jesus which is manifestly not true; and the remark is made just prior to that disciple's coming to faith. In John 1:46 a cynical Nathanael replies to Philip's breathless testimony about having found the Messiah, "Can anything good come out of Nazareth?" Nathanael himself intends a tone of irony. The word order of his overstated question stresses the incongruity of this little town spawning the Messiah: "From Nazareth is it possible for anything good to come?" There is little point in asking whether this derision is rooted in a popular proverb, an ongoing rivalry between neighboring Cana and Nazareth, or some tradition of Nazareth's bad reputation.[32]

The saying forms part of an ironic motif in this Gospel concerning the "whence" of Jesus, and particularly his Galilean heritage (cf. 6:42; 7:41, 52). Here as elsewhere, the one who disparages Jesus' origin becomes the victim of his own irony. A good thing has indeed come from Nazareth; and the overstatement is now transformed into ironic understatement: not just "anything good," but the Christ. Of course, the irony does not end there. For the reader already knows from the prologue, and will know more forcefully in later chapters, that in fact Jesus has not come from Nazareth but from above, from God (1:1; 8:23). Thus, in a sense Nathanael is right, even as he is wrong. The "good thing" does not have its origin in Nazareth.

Two matters of comparison are worth noting here. First, this disciple's false assumption is laced with less ironic force than the false assumptions of Jesus' other interlocutors. In virtually every such question posed about Jesus in this Gospel the negative particle *mē* is present to underline the speaker's certainty that Jesus cannot be who he claims to be.[33] Here the particle is absent. This disciple is allowed to be wrong, but he is spared the dead-wrong presumption of the *alazōn*. Secondly, it is instructive to observe John's way of dealing with doubts about Jesus compared with the method of Matthew. Apparently the fact of Jesus' rootage in Nazareth was problematic in more than one Christian community. Matthew, after locating Jesus' birth in Bethlehem, explains his later home in Nazareth by a rather strained reference to fulfilled prophecy (2:23).[34] The Fourth Evangelist, however, neither hides the question about Jesus' origin, nor engages in proof-texting. His method is to assign the question to one of his characters, who will ask loudly and with sarcasm—and then to leave the question unanswered. That silence is the method of irony. The speaker is given all the verbal rope needed to hang himself. No rebuttal is required. The silence becomes an invitation to the reader to weigh the unlikely probability of the speaker's assumptions. Here it also becomes an invitation to Nathanael. "Come and see," says Philip. Echoing the words of Jesus himself (vs. 39), this invitation is implicit in all the ensuing silences of this beckoning Gospel.

Misunderstanding

Like virtually everyone else in the Fourth Gospel, the disciples have difficulty understanding Jesus. Their misunderstanding is not always described with irony, but in at least two texts the author seems at pains to underline their slowness in such a way that the reader who knows better will find these miscues painfully comic.

16:16 "*A little while and you will see me no more; again a little while and you will see me.*" The reference is to death and resurrection. Jesus has made the same prediction before (cf. 7:33; 12:35; 13:33; 14:19; 16:10). The reader is expected to know what the prediction means, if not by prior knowledge, then by the fact that both death and resurrection have been clearly alluded to by the narrator (11:51; 12:33; 2:22). The striking feature of the disciples' misunderstanding here is not so much that the disciples cannot grasp the mystery—though we who do "grasp" it may feel that they should. Nor

is it in their pretending to know more than they do, for indeed, what
they confess is precisely their ignorance. The remarkable aspect of
that confession is its exasperated length, its interminable reiterative
asking. They turn to each other saying, "What is this he says to
us?"—and they repeat the entirety of Jesus' remark in verse 16; they
reach back to verse 10 to reiterate and inquire of his phrase, "because
I go to the Father"; they repeat the phrase "a little while" and ask its
meaning. Then they conclude (all out of breath?), "We don't
understand!" *(ouk oidamen)*. If that were not enough, following this
triple repetition, and confession of utter ignorance, Jesus acknowl-
edges their confusion and actually repeats their repetition of his
original remark in verse 16. Aside from the monotony, this repetition
has other effects. The replay of the words underscores the significance
of the misunderstood mystery and the importance of the one who
uttered it.[35]

The reader who knows the meaning of Jesus' prediction hears
these endless echoes of the disciples' confusion and feels confirmed
that the knowledge he holds is both privileged and crucial. What else
can all the asking mean but that here is *the* question on which all else
depends—a question resoundingly answered for those abiding with
the glorified Christ. The elongated "we don't understand" of the
disciples provides a dramatic irony to which informed readers can
reply, "But we do!" For any who have failed to accept the previous
allusions to death and resurrection for any reason, the irony is lost; but
the extended repetition may yet have the effect of signaling the
presence of something crucial, not yet grasped, but soon to be
revealed. Thus, what is irony for enlightened readers may function for
those still in the dark as a clue.

16:29 "Ah, now you are speaking plainly, not in any figure!" The
disciples give utterance to another expression of misunderstanding
which provides a clearer example of irony. In their first speech since
confessing total ignorance in verse 18, they respond to Jesus'
renewed announcement that he is going to the Father, "Ah, now you
are speaking plainly *(en parrēsia),* not in any figure *(paroimian)!"* The
problem is that Jesus has only just told them that he has been speaking
in figures *(en paroimiais)* and that the hour for plain speaking

(parrēsia) is yet to come (vs. 25).[36] Their overeager ignorance is painfully obvious, a mistake akin to one made by the crowd in 6:30. There, Jesus has no sooner performed a sign than the people ask him to perform one. Here, Jesus has no sooner said that clarity is yet to come than the disciples claim clarity, a sure sign that he was right! The author effects this irony not only by the obvious incongruity, but by making the disciples' language a bit overblown. *Ide*—Look! There! ("Ah"—RSV). *Ide* is a favorite dramatic word in this Gospel, often used with utter seriousness, but employed at least five times in association with irony (7:52; 12:19; 16:29; 19:5, 14). The word *nun* is in emphatic position, stressing the disciples' claim to clarity *now*, precisely when Jesus has promised it later. The superficial faith they confess in the next verse is an extension of this irony and builds upon it.

Superficial Confession

16:29-30 *"Now you are speaking plainly, not in any figure! Now we know that you know all things, and need none to question you; by this we believe that you came from God."* These words form an ascending parallelism, almost in a jaunty rhyme and rhythm, whereby the disciples build faulty confession upon faulty claim upon faulty assumption. The process can be set out as follows:

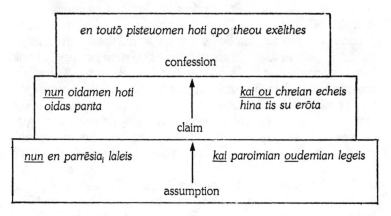

The second line (cf. 2:25) repeats the form of the faulty first line, and so is already suspect; and though its content states no untruth, there are hints that not all is as it should be. The *oidamen,* particularly in conjunction with *nun,* smacks of ironic overconfidence, as it often does in this Gospel.[37] The reference to Jesus' knowing all things is unassailable, of course, but it hardly seems to be a momentous insight, since it only reiterates the Samaritan woman's claim to faith in chapter 4 (cf. 4:25, 29, 39).

The remark about Jesus needing no one to question him is also adequate. It probably makes reference to verse 23a, in which he says, "In that day you will ask me nothing." As in verse 29, however, the disciples have shifted Jesus' meaning from a promise of the future into a declaration about the present. The necessary death and resurrection are neatly swept away. This is even more apparent in the ensuing confession of faith: "by this we believe that you came from God." Again, they are repeating the words of Jesus, but again they choose to omit a crucial element, for Jesus has spoken both of coming and of *going* (vs. 28).[38] The disciples once again remain blind to the harder half of his truth. Thus, Jesus can meet their enthusiasm with a skeptical question and the prediction of a dark hour that will prove just how full their faith is (vss. 31–32).

There are other instances in John's Gospel where scholars have spoken of irony in the disciples' superficial statements of faith. One instance is 1:45, where Philip refers to "Jesus of Nazareth, son of Joseph."[39] Elsewhere this Gospel will indeed make ironic play upon the claim of some to know Jesus' parentage; but the fact that Philip's remark is allowed to stand without correction need not signify ironic intent. Upon reading and rereading this Gospel, one could become sensitized enough to the author's ironic method that "son of Joseph" might evoke a smile. But there are no grammatical or contextual clues that Philip's testimony is in question. Were irony intended so early in the narrative, such clues would be indispensable. "Son of Joseph" stands, then, as a rather colorless and quite natural ascription, locating for the reader, as for Nathanael, the historical coordinates of the Word made flesh. It is likewise doubtful that Nathanael's reference to Jesus as "Rabbi" should be read ironically, as some others have done.[40] The fact that Nathanael couples that ascription with "Son of God" and "King of Israel" should be sufficient clue that the author intends no denigration of the term *Teacher.* While, as verse 51 indicates, the disciples and readers will be met with an expanding christology as events unfold, the acclamations of chapter 1 will be enlarged and never negated.

False Promise

11:16 "Let us also go, that we may die with him." We have already noted and will note again the ironic falsehood and truth of Peter's promise to die for Jesus in 13:37. A similar event occurs in 11:16. Thomas, who with the other disciples has just reminded Jesus of the dangers of Judea, responds to Jesus' determination with the words above. Such a remark is typical of Thomas' character. He is the one with an eye for the grim facts, but no perception of the glory that will infuse and transform these facts.[41] His prediction that the journey will result in death is true enough (11:53), but he is ironically wrong in presuming that the disciples will have any share in that death. Jesus will die alone (16:32), in their behalf (15:13), but not in their company. None of this has been spelled out in the text up to this point, though 2:22 implies it clearly enough, and the whole texture of this Gospel intimates that Jesus does all his work alone. Readers unfamiliar with the outcome might not catch the irony of Thomas' bravado until the Passion narrative, though 11:16 is not without clues to irony's presence. These are as follows: (1) Thomas' little speech recalls the disciples' warning of verse 7, giving no sign of having understood Jesus' intervening answer; (2) the disciples have just voiced a gross misunderstanding of Jesus' reference to "sleep," thus setting a context that casts doubt on Thomas' perception; (3) in the preceding verse Jesus has expressed gladness at Lazarus' death and the upcoming journey "so that you may believe" *(hina pisteuete)*. The stark contrast of Thomas' pessimistic resolve, "so that we may die" *(hina apothanōmen),* seems clue enough that all is not as it seems. Some interpreters have read into this passage the deeper irony that Thomas, like Peter in 13:37, was correct in a way he did not know, that this journey to Judea would indeed issue in his "dying with Christ" in the Pauline sense of commitment.[42] While it is possible that the ultimate martyrdom of some of the disciples is operative in the larger irony of this text, it is doubtful that any spiritualizing of death is intended.

Summary. The verbal devices by which the author of John's Gospel places irony on the lips of the disciples are much the same as the ironic devices employed by Jesus; in particular, there are questions (1:46; 16:17–18) and repetitions of Jesus' words (verbatim repetition, 16:17–18; repetition with crucial omission, 16:29–30; repetition of *hina* clauses, substituting an opposing verb, 11:16). The effect of these devices is the obverse of their effect when used by Jesus—exposing the speakers' own ignorance or inconsistency.

It is also instructive to consider the themes of the disciples' irony. In one instance (1:46) the theme is Jesus' origin, a subject upon which the author will cast an ironic eye throughout his Gospel. All other instances of the disciples' irony, however, are concerned with their failure to understand Jesus' death. Individual disciples twice claim a willingness to die with or for Jesus (11:16; 13:37), thus displaying both a comic overestimation of themselves and a total oblivion to Jesus' purpose and power. When the eleven become supremely confused and wonder out loud for two verses what Jesus means, the subject is Jesus' leaving them (16:17–18); and again, when they make their premature profession of understanding and belief, the crucial element not grasped is Jesus' imminent departure (16:29–30). Jesus' opponents also misunderstand his death (cf. 7:35; 8:22), but their misunderstanding tends to be expressed by unconsciously prophesying its meaning; the disciples' misunderstanding is more simply a blindness to its necessity. Significantly, this is the target of Mark's ironic treatment of the disciples as well. The Fourth Gospel expands its treatment of this theme through its portrait of Simon Peter, an instance of extended irony to be examined in chapter 6.

As lethal as John's irony can be, he is fairly gentle with the disciples. They are portrayed as hopelessly bewildered by Jesus, of course, but so is everyone else in this Gospel, except the Beloved Disciple. They do not become the outsiders as do Mark's disciples; there are no Gentile witnesses to see what they refuse to see.[43] They do not so much forsake Jesus as they are dismissed by him (18:8); and though a devil is in their ranks, he is neatly sundered from the group (6:70–71; 13:30). When the disciples do fall prey to irony, John's grammatical signals of *alazōny* (e.g., *hēmeis oidamen,* and the confident use of *mē* in questions) are absent. In their representative function for the reader, therefore, they present a sober reminder of the limits of human understanding and commitment, while at the same time offering hope that if such blundering flesh will only abide with Jesus, he will keep them (17:12) and overcome their worldly testing (16:33).

4

LOCAL IRONY:
Words from the Dark

Though the texts considered above bear witness to the ironic vision of the Fourth Gospel, only now do we enter fully into what is generally called "typical Johannine irony." When non-believers respond to Jesus in John's Gospel, particularly when his opponents speak, they are prone to speak volumes more than they know. They intend to question him, to mock him, to discredit him, and finally to destroy him; but the words they choose and the steps they take inevitably have the reverse effect. The knowledge of which they are most certain turns out to be false; the accolades they would never dream of giving to Jesus pour from their lips when they least expect it; and, more tragically, when they set out to preserve themselves by destroying this blasphemer, it is they who perish along with all they hold dear. They never know, of course. But the author and readers exchange glances as these respondents speak and move upon the stage—glances caught between tears and laughter. It is our purpose here to freeze the action at such moments, to note the posture of the actors, to study their lines, word by loaded word, and to discern the silent communication of the author/director toward us, the readers. How do the signals work? What patterns emerge? What seems to be the purpose? We begin to address these questions by considering one at a time the several types of their ironic speech: false claims to knowledge, false assumptions, accusations, suggestions of belief, and unconscious prophecy or testimony.

False Claims to Knowledge

Oddly enough, the opponents of Jesus are constantly claiming to have expertise on the subject of his origin—his parentage and place of birth. Such claims are so central to this Gospel and are so tied to popular messianic expectations, it seems likely they reflect some genuine issues of debate between early church and synagogue. The historical question will be set aside for now, however, as we examine the texts themselves.

6:42 "Is not this Jesus, the son of Joseph, whose father and mother we know? How does he now say, 'I have come down from heaven'?" Jesus has claimed to be the bread of life come down from heaven (vss. 35, 38). On hearing this, "the Jews" murmur at him. Their reasoning is straight-forward: because they know Jesus' parents, he is obviously not from heaven. The language in which they express themselves is typical of John's irony. The demonstrative pronoun *houtos* is used of Jesus with a kind of distancing contempt: *this* fellow, the one who is apart from us, *this* one, whom we can locate, fix, examine, and be rid of.[1] Similarly the definite article is used with *huios,* which was anarthrous in 1:45, again distancing Jesus and emphasizing just whose son they know him to be. Their confidence in that knowledge is stressed by the emphatic pronoun with the verb, *hēmeis oidamen,* "*we* know!" On the basis of this knowledge they ask their question, "How does he now say 'I have come down from heaven'?" How *(pōs)* is the typical earthly, literal, superficial question invariably asked by Jesus' interlocutors.[2] The repetition of Jesus' words, a feature we have already recognized as typical of John's ironic style, shifts *en tou ouranou* to the beginning to emphasize their dismissal of that realm as Jesus' home.

What is the locus of this irony? Some have said the unspoken subject is the virgin birth.[3] This could be the case, for a reader's knowledge of that tradition certainly sharpens the irony; the crowd would be dead wrong in their claim to know Jesus' father. There is no evidence, however, that the author has this tradition in mind. The irony is present regardless, for whether or not Jesus' biological paternity is at issue, John is quite clear that God is the true Father of Jesus. On this level, in fact, the irony is actually deeper (if not sharper) than it would be if Mary's virginity were the point. For the point is that the crowd can be both utterly correct in the natural sense and utterly mistaken in the important sense.[4] This Gospel reveals their blindness again and again by having Jesus say precisely this: you do not know my Father (cf. 8:19, 55; 15:21; 16:3; 17:25). The irony is all the deeper in view of the surrounding discussion of the crowd's fathers, who ate manna and died (vss. 31, 49), and Jesus' living Father, who has given him as the living bread (vss. 32, 35, 40, 51, 57). Jesus knows their fathers far better than they know his. That they still bear the blindness of their fathers to the true Father is clear from the designation of their unbelief as "murmuring" (vss. 41, 43)—a deliberate echo of the murmuring which surrounded the first gift of manna.[5]

It is often noted that 6:42 echoes a remark about Jesus found in the other three Gospels. Only in John, however, is this objection dressed in irony. In the Synoptics the context is the hometown preacher who speaks powerfully (Luke 4:22), or scandalously (Mark 6:33; Matt. 13:55). The feeling in the first case is pride (Can you believe Joseph's boy can speak so well?), and in the second, contempt (This is just Mary's boy, just the carpenter—where does he come off with all this?). Only John makes "the Jews'" claim to know him so confident and places it so squarely in a high christological context, contrasting his paternity with their own.

7:27 *"Yet we know where this one comes from; and when the Christ appears, no one will know where he comes from."* Here is a group of Jerusalemites who say, "we know." The emphatic pronoun is absent, perhaps because these respondents are more open to Jesus than those in 6:42 (cf. vs. 26). Again, however, they use the demonstrative pronoun in a belittling sense; and again they claim knowledge of Jesus' origin, here not his parents but his "whence" *(pothen).* "We know whence this fellow is: but when the Christ comes, no one will know whence he is." This view expresses a popular apocalyptic expectation that the Messiah's presence would be unknown, perhaps even to himself, until Elijah came to anoint him.[6] Jesus cannot be the Christ since he does not meet this necessary condition.

The broader irony here lies in the rather common dramatic device of speakers emphasizing the difference between a party who is present but not recognized (Jesus), and a party thought to be absent (the Christ), when in fact the two are one and the same.[7] The more specific irony works in a kind of progression in which the speakers undo their own assertion by virtue of their own expectation, thus transforming the expectation from condition unmet to prophecy fulfilled. To say, "We know whence this one is," is true enough, until another truth is added—that the Christ's origin is unknown. The reader who believes Jesus is the Christ is now provoked to reevaluate the first assertion, which promptly crumbles. Though the speakers know well enough that Jesus is from Nazareth, they do not know "whence he is." The Christ's origin *is* unknown. These citizens of Jerusalem have in one breath set out a condition for Christ's coming and unwittingly testified that, just so, he has come.[8] In the process, the prophecy cited to negate Jesus' messiahship has only served to negate their claim to know him.

7:41b–42 "Is the Christ to come from Galilee? Has not the scripture said that the Christ is descended from David, and comes from Bethlehem?" In 7:40–52 various parties speak to each other in response to Jesus, while he himself disappears from the stage.[9] His absence from these verses is conspicuously appropriate, for it is quite clear that many who argue about him are utterly blind to who he is. Likewise, his silence in these verses is heavy with significance, for in the hush of his voice, the clamoring questions and claims of his enemies are allowed to ring out into their own emptiness; and for those with ears to hear, the reverberating irony is thunderous. The first of several ironies in this passage, and one of the two "false claims" to be considered in this section, appears in 7:41b–42.

Two confessions of faith are made by different factions of the crowd in 7:40–41a. Some say, "This is really the prophet," while others exclaim, "This is the Christ!" The first confession is shelved by the author until the end of this section (vs. 52b). The second, hailing Jesus as Davidic Messiah, is more promptly refuted by the antagonists.[10] They raise a question allowing only one answer: *mē gar ek tēs Galilaias ho christos erchetai?* The particle *mē* expects only a negative reply, and the following verse presents unarguable scriptural evidence for such confidence: the Christ comes from David and Bethlehem. Ergo, Jesus, the Galilean, cannot be the Christ.

Though no one doubts irony's presence here, scholars debate its actual locus. Some say the author has in mind the tradition of Jesus' birth in Bethlehem. Others say John neither knows nor cares about that tradition, the ironic point being that Jesus is the Christ precisely in *spite* of his Galilean origin, because he is really from God.[11] Though certainty is impossible, the ironic technique already established favors John's knowing the Bethlehem tradition and expecting his readers to know it. While this Gospel reports accusations made against Jesus that are totally, outrageously false, *no other* instance of claimed knowledge is without some unexpected element of truth. That is how John's irony usually works. Unwitting speakers utter testimony that is false where they think it is true, but true in ways they had not imagined. So it is here. The falsehood is that Christ is truly "from Galilee"; the redefined truth is that the Christ—and Jesus!—is from Bethlehem. Besides, if the author wished to break his pattern of emphasizing Scripture's witness to Jesus, it seems unlikely that his method would be the silence of irony. The ironic silence of this Gospel most often conceals not just negation but the smiling nod of unforeseen agreement.[12]

Although the irony of 7:42 presupposes a Bethlehem tradition, it is important to stress that a Bethlehem birth is neither the end of this irony nor its most crucial point. Yes, nods the author, Jesus the Christ is, as Scripture says, from David's line and David's town; and yes, he nods to the earlier doubtful question, Jesus the Christ is from Galilee too, spurned by opponents and disciples alike (cf. 1:46). But once the witness of Scripture and the facts of history are affirmed, the larger interest and the larger irony emerge: the Christ is in fact from none of these places so much as he is from above.[13] That is the whole point of the now-enriched irony of the Jerusalemites' remark in 7:27: *no one* knows the origin of the Christ. Jesus' bemused reply to that group who claimed to know him is just as applicable to those believers who, upon reading 7:42, smile with the knowledge that he was born in Bethlehem: "No doubt you know me, and you know where I come from" (7:28).

7:52b "Search and you will see that the prophet is not to arise from Galilee." The first words of verse 52, implying that Nicodemus too is a Galilean, are reserved for later discussion, for they touch upon a different issue. The Pharisees' rather sarcastic challenge to their colleague to read his Bible, however, is based upon their confident claim that the Scriptures do not predict a Galilean origin for the Mosaic Prophet. We follow here the reading of p⁶⁶ and p⁷⁵ᵛⁱᵈ *(ho prophētēs),* which has good probability of being the earlier reading.[14] If the broader, later textual tradition is followed—"no prophet is to arise from Galilee"—there is still irony; for in this case these experts in Scripture would simply have been wrong about their sacred writings. The Old Testament does tell of prophets rising from Galilee (specifically Jonah and Nahum, and see the messianic prediction of Isa. 9:1). Furthermore, rabbinic sources view prophets as coming from every tribe and town in Israel *(Sukkah* 27b; *Seder Olam* R. 21).[15]

It seems more likely, however, that the Pharisees make reference to the Mosaic Prophet. If such is the case, they are, as in verse 42, technically correct about Scripture. They embarrass themselves at two points, however. First, they are in fact stretching the witness of Scripture, for the Old Testament prescribes *no* specific origin of the Prophet.[16] More importantly, the point again seems to be that ultimately Jesus is not from Galilee anyway. If our reading of verse 42 is correct, the Bethlehem tradition could still be in mind here; but more to the point is the Gospel's continuing affirmation that Jesus is from God. The Pharisees would know this were it not for their blindness. In the only other Johannine use of the verb *eraunaō* Jesus accuses them of searching the very Scriptures that bear witness to him, yet refusing to come to him (5:39–40).[17] In 7:52 there is proof of such searching-without-seeing. In the Fourth Gospel one can rightly "search and see" in the Scriptures only when one will "come and see" Jesus (cf. 1:39, 47).

9:29 "We know that God has spoken to Moses, but as for this one, we do not know where he comes from." The pattern repeated here is now a familiar one. The opponents negatively compare sacred tradition with their knowledge of Jesus. Again the stress is on their overconfidence *(hēmeis oidamen);* and again they reduce Jesus to "this one" *(touton)*. Their knowledge of the tradition is once more technically correct, supportable this time with specific scriptural references (Exod. 33:11; Num. 12:2–8). They are perfectly correct in asserting that God has spoken to Moses. Likewise they are perfectly correct—delightfully so—in complaining that the "whence" of Jesus is beyond them, though ironically enough, they had earlier claimed precisely the opposite (7:27). But now in the heat of their growing anger, and no doubt intending to insult him, the truth leaps from their oblivious tongues, proving again the doctrine of the unknown Christ. In addition, as before, the first part of their claim is now called into question. Do they really know that God has spoken to Moses? Only the fact of it, apparently, nothing of the content, for they have already been told Moses spoke of Jesus and so accuses them (5:45–47). In 9:29 the Pharisees claim knowledge of two figures, God and Moses, and ignorance of a third. "Why this is a marvel!" replies a man with remarkable sight (vs. 30). For this unknown source of light is he to whom Moses only pointed and in whom God has made his Word become flesh.

It is notewothy that every instance of this particular type of irony in John is concerned with the issue of the origin of Jesus. In each of these "false claims to knowledge" the opponents juxtapose what they think they know of Jesus with what they think they know of the Christ (6:42; 7:27, 42) or the Prophet-like-Moses (7:52; 9:29). In every case their claims prove to be both resoundingly false and peculiarly true, though in ways never known to them. Their assertions are met either with silence (7:42, 52) or with mocking reply ("Stop murmuring," 6:43; "No doubt you know me," 7:28; "What a marvel!" 9:30). Author and reader share the wink, and the actors are none the wiser.

False Assumptions

The categories of "false assumptions" and "false claims to knowledge" might seem to overlap somewhat, but the type of irony isolated here is distinct. While the speakers are still confident, they do not emphasize their knowledge as before. As sure of themselves as they are, these respondents shape their ironic utterance in a form that is more open. Incredulous questions are asked of Jesus, always based upon assumptions about him that are negative. By this form, however, the author manages to signal a silent answer which turns on its head every negative assumption about the man from Nazareth.

4:12 "Are you greater than our father Jacob, who gave us the well, and drank from it himself, and his sons, and his cattle?" The entire scene of 4:4–42 is rich with irony, some of which will be noted in the following chapter. Verse 12, however, is a choice ironic moment which stands on its own. The woman addresses the magisterial stranger sitting beside Jacob's well and asks him if he is greater than Jacob: *mē su meizōn ei tou patros hēmōn Iakōb.* The pronoun *su* is emphatic; the particle *mē* signals negative expectation: *You* aren't greater than Jacob, are you? That would be irony enough, but the woman's every word heightens the hidden meaning of the question. That Jacob is "our father" will shortly be undercut by the reminder of another Father who calls his children to move beyond this venerated site and all others to the realm of spirit and truth. Jacob is defined as the one "who gave us the well"; but "the gift of God," Jesus has already said, is "living water," a gift the woman will shortly ask to be given her. The superiority of Jesus as gift and giver is unconsciously emphasized further when the woman elaborates upon the sufficiency of the well, which satisfied Jacob, "and his sons, and his cattle"—a bountiful well indeed![18] "*You* aren't greater than such a provider, are you?" she asks the stranger—whose own gift is a spring of water "welling up to eternal life" (vs. 14).[19]

8:53 "Are you greater than our father Abraham, who died?" The words of "the Jews" are exactly parallel to 4:12. Again, *mē* leaves no doubt as to their opinion. Their "our father Abraham" has an emptier ring than the woman's "our father Jacob," for Jesus has just met their claims to be sons of Abraham with the news that their father is the devil (8:33–44). The issue at stake in their question is Jesus' relation to death. In verse 51 he has claimed that those who keep his word will not taste death. Upon hearing this, "the Jews" are certain he has a demon, for everyone dies, even Abraham and the prophets. Their question therefore springs from a typical misunderstanding. Jesus speaks spiritually, they hear literally. The resulting query, far more penetrating than their surface minds can know, probes deeper than Jesus' relation to the patriarchs. At its heart is *this* question, "You aren't greater than death, are you?"[20] Small wonder that their next incredulous question is "Who do you claim to be?" The enlightened reader, knowing the timeless beginning of the Logos and the coming exaltation that will lift him through death and far above it, quietly smiles with the answer.

8:57 "You are not yet fifty years old, and have you seen Abraham?" Jesus has indirectly responded to their question about being greater than Abraham, concluding with the provocative word, "Your father Abraham rejoiced that he was to see my day; he saw it and was glad" (vs. 56). It is to this seemingly preposterous claim that "the Jews" retort with a tiresomely earthbound reference to Jesus' age. As in their claims to know his origin and his parentage, of course, there is a sense in which on the literal level they are quite correct. The same literal level has fascinated commentators, for whom this verse was fodder to speculate upon the age of Jesus. But had "the Jews" said "not yet ninety" the author's point would be the same, and their assumption would be no more absurd. In the opening lines of the Gospel, readers receive the privileged information that renders 8:57 ironic. This not-yet-fifty flesh is the Word that "was in the beginning with God" (1:1–2). "The Jews" have not only quite naturally assumed otherwise, they highlight their accidental irony by the ensuing question. Jesus has said Abraham saw *him;* they reverse the perspective in their repetition and ask if the young Jesus has seen Abraham.[21] The change probably signals their misunderstanding, and again presupposes Abraham's superiority: "Have you seen *Abraham?"* Ironically, however, it sets things in even truer perspective. For though, as Jesus had said, Abraham saw Jesus and rejoiced, we know who first saw whom. Jesus shortly breathes the startling word that will complete the reversal begun by his opponents: "Before Abraham was, I AM" (vs. 58).

7:15 "How is it that this fellow has education, when he has never studied?" In the Synoptics, too, people marvel at the audacious power of Jesus' teaching compared with that of the scholastic scribes (cf. Mark 1:22 par.; 6:2 par.). Only in John, however, is it so flatly stated, "he has never studied." It is an assumption which, like that of 8:57, is true enough in one sense, but is fantastically wrong in another. It is well to understand the particular reference of their remark. The first clause asks how (*pōs*) "this" fellow (once again with contempt) "knows letters." On a literal level the question could be about Jesus' literacy; but far more probably, as the context indicates, the reference is to the skill of his teaching.[22] Whether or not their question is tinged with sarcasm is not certain. At particular issue is probably Jesus' nimble use of Scripture and his high claims to authority, both explicit and implicit. The point of amazement or sarcasm is that Jesus engages in such teaching without having "learned" or "studied" (*memathē-kōs*). He has no accreditation, no diploma; he is as suspect as the "accursed" crowd "who do not know the law" (7:49). Only forty verses previous, however, Jesus addressed this very issue of where one gets learning. "It is written in the prophets, 'And they shall be taught by God.' Everyone who has heard and learned (*mathōn*) from the Father comes to me" (6:45).

It has already been established, then, first, that true learning is not derived humanly but only from God, and second, that all who have this learning will come to Jesus. John 7:16–17 reiterates that Jesus' teaching is from God and that godly people will be in no doubt of this. To say that such a one "has never learned" is both true and hilariously, tragically false. He has already been hailed as the supreme Teacher both by the first disciples (1:38, 49) and by the alleged teacher of Israel (3:2).[23] He will say in 8:28, "the Father taught me." He has been with God from the beginning. He is therefore more than learned, and even more than Teacher. He is according to John the Subject, the very substance and end of all true learning. When those who disobey their own teaching (7:19) point to the poor schooling of the Logos of God, the irony of their ignorance becomes tragic indeed.

Four false assumptions of Jesus' opponents come under the author's ironic scrutiny: Jesus is not greater than Jacob nor greater than Abraham; he is not fifty and so cannot have seen Abraham; and he has not "studied." Each is framed as a negative question. The first two, in exactly the same form, contain no element of truth. The second two are grounded in literal facts but are utterly negated by Truth. As in other types of Johannine irony there emerges here remarkable consistency of theme. In three of the four texts the subject is specifically Jesus' relationship to the patriarchs. In all four the theme is the sovereignty of Jesus extending into the past, whether his preeminence over Israel's fathers or his living, learning, and seeing with the eternal Father.

Accusations

On a number of occasions in John the opponents of Jesus make outright accusations against him. The author does not generally present these charges with heavy irony, but in several of them there may be to the perceptive reader the suggestion, at least, of a wink.

Charges of demon possession. In the Synoptics Jesus casts out demons; in John's Gospel he is accused of having one (7:20; 8:48, 52; 10:20). The parallel in Mark 3:21-27 is often cited; but the similarity is by no means exact. The scribes there charge that Jesus "has Beelzebul," meaning that his exorcisms must be in league with the devil. The accusation in John is more direct: "You have a demon"; and, typically, it is not the deeds but the words of Jesus that precipitate the charge. A connecting thread naturally runs through these several texts, but each has an ironic edge of its own.

When Jesus asks the question in 7:19, "Why do you seek to kill me?" the crowd responds, "You have a demon! Who is seeking to kill you?" The charge of having a demon was an accusation of madness.[24] The character of that madness here seems to be paranoia; for the clear implication of the crowd's question is, "No one wants to kill you." The question in Greek shows them following quite closely in the dialogical dance. Says Jesus, *ti mē zēteite apokteinai.* Says the crowd, *tis se zētei apokteinai.* But is their ignorance real or pretended?

It is possible that the crowd *(ochlos)* asking the question is to be distinguished from the hostile "Jews" who both the reader and the "Jerusalemites" know quite well are seeking to kill Jesus (5:18; 7:1, 25). If such is the case, these interlocutors are innocently unaware of the plottings of their comrades,[25] and the irony plays upon their arrogant, abusive oblivion. It is not altogether clear, however, that we are so neatly to separate *ho ochlos* from *hoi Joudaioi* in this context.

While it is true that the crowd is generally presented more neutrally in this Gospel, and that they are noticeably absent from the trial and crucifixion of Jesus, there are reasons at least to wonder if John presupposes their innocence here: (1) the conversation begins with "the Jews" (vs. 15) and the change of referent in verse 20 shows no intrinsic sign of significance; (2) it is clear from 12:9 that *ochlos* can signify "a crowd of the Jews"; (3) all other accusations of being demon-possessed are from "the Jews"; (4) in 8:48 when "the Jews" tell Jesus he has a demon, their "are we not right in saying" seems to imply they have said so before.[26] The protesting voices of 7:20, then, may belong, at least in part, to the very ones who already have "sought to kill him" (5:18; 7:1). If so, there is here the "Who, me?" verbal irony of the murderer smiling reassuringly while fondling the knife behind his back.

The irony may run still deeper, however. There is in the Fourth Gospel a hint or two that "the Jews" are strangely unaware of their real role in the death of Jesus. In 8:22 they oddly suppose that Jesus may kill himself. In 18:31 they slyly, or uneasily, evade their part in executing him. They constantly want to arrest him (7:30, 32, 44; 8:20; 10:39), take up stones against him (8:59; 10:31; 11:8), and seek to kill him (5:18, 7:1, 25; 8:37, 40; 11:53); but always they are powerless to do it, so much is he in command, so much does his hour alone determine the time and the manner of his death. They are therefore his killers quite in spite of themselves; their involvement in his death is characterized by impotence and ignorance. When the author has them ask, "Who seeks to kill you?" the tone may be not so much sinister as pathetic. Their designs on his death are out of their control. They want him dead, but have grasped neither the meaning of that death, nor their part in it.[27] This is *their* demon—that they are at once so homicidal and so helpless. The one in whom they imagine the demon grimly leaves their poor, protesting question unanswered.

In 8:48 "the Jews" return to the theme that Jesus has a demon. He has issued a blistering attack on their spiritual paternity and tells them in verse 47 that they are "not of God." To this they retort, "Do we not say well that you are a Samaritan and have a demon?" Their language is punctuated with confident, emphatic pronouns: "*We* are the ones who rightly say that *you* are a Samaritan and have a demon." There is a double irony. The first is that Jesus has already made clear that they are themselves dominated by the devil. Like the one who would search out a speck in his brother's eye while a log protrudes from his own, these who charge Jesus with having a demon are the very children of the devil (8:38–45).[28]

A second irony entails their accusation that Jesus is a Samaritan. Some would not call this a separate charge, assuming it is equivalent to the charge of being mad.[29] It seems more likely, however, that *Samaritan* has a nuance of its own. Scholars differ as to whether that slur means Jesus is a heretic,[30] or has a questionable heritage himself,[31] or is a slanderer of God's true people.[32] Perhaps all of these charges are implied. It is important, however, not to overlook this epithet's most basic sense. It is a racial slur, accusing Jesus of metaphorical kinship with an outcast and despised people; and that is sweet irony indeed.

Though there have been excesses in claims of "Samaritan origins" of the Fourth Gospel,[33] there seems to be a general consensus that Samaritan converts early on made some impact on the Johannine community.[34] That Jesus himself was renowned for association with such outcasts, and was despised for it, is abundantly clear. Significantly, in 8:49 Jesus denies only the charge of having a demon. For early readers of the Gospel who were Samaritans, for readers who had learned to call such Samaritans sister and brother, and for Christians of every era weary of elitist and bigoted religion, especially in the church, this intended insult, accepted by Jesus with wonderful silence, elicits the smile of irony. For the sake of the sheep "not of this fold" (10:16) Jesus was and is always a Samaritan.[35]

Four verses later in 52, "the Jews" say again, "Now we know that you have a demon." By now the reader should be aware that anything these *alazōnes* claim to know is ironically suspect. Here their complaint is that Jesus seems to assert superiority over death and therefore over Abraham and the prophets. Their tragi-comic miscalculation of him here has already been noted. The last charge of demon possession comes in 10:20, following Jesus' discourse on the good shepherd who lays down his life. A *schisma* is provoked by these words. "Many of them said, 'He has a demon and is mad; why listen to him?'" By now the refutation may be left to their own associates.

"Others said, 'These are not the sayings of one who has a demon. Can a demon open the eyes of the blind?'" (vs. 21). There is no real irony in this particular exchange; but the cumulative effect of the fourfold charge of a demon, in the face of the works and the words of Jesus cited here, underscores the presence of a demonic blindness in those who accuse.

8:41 *"We were not born of fornication; we have one Father, even God."* This verse is included in a discussion of "accusations" because so many commentators note the possibility of its intent as implied accusation.[36] The possible grammatical clue to irony's presence is the emphatic *hēmeis:* *"We* were not born of *porneia,"* implying, "but *you* were." Such a meaning is by no means certain, for there are other ways to explain the use of *hēmeis* here.[37] It would not be unlike the author, however, to intend such an irony, and the issue of Jesus' parentage was certainly an item of discussion among early opponents of the church.[38] If such is the author's concern here, the subtlety with which the irony works is artful. Jesus has acknowledged their Abrahamic heritage (vs. 37) but makes clear that their actions betray another father, as yet unnamed (vss. 38–40). Their response is to impugn Jesus' heritage while shifting the discussion of their own paternity to the spiritual level: their "one Father, even God" is the nameless one who supercedes Abraham's fatherhood. In making this shift they play directly into Jesus' hands, for their spiritual father is exactly who he wishes to expose. After denying that God is that father, he finally reveals the name: "You are of your father—the devil!" (vs. 44). Jesus' very method of divulging this news—the deliberate withholding of the name, then the devastating disclosure of it—is singularly appropriate for the announcement of illegitimacy.[39] Their remark in verse 41 now appears richly ironic. They are doubly the children of *porneia,* for they have claimed two legitimate fathers, Abraham and God, both of whom turn out to be only nominal fathers, while their secret sire whose telltale features they bear is a murderer and a liar (vs. 44). Furthermore, they have dared contrast their "Father, even God" with shameful implications concerning Jesus' father. In irony's swift and silent reversal, *they* now assume the shame, and Jesus the Sonship.

10:33 "You, being human, make yourself God." The emphatic *su* here underlines their rage. The charge here is blasphemy, as "the Jews" clearly say; and their definition in unexceptionable. There is typical Johannine irony at work, however, in two ways. First, they are quite correct, but to a depth they would never have acknowledged.[40] They are made to say what no disciple can be brought to say of Jesus until a week after his resurrection (20:28). Second, they have at the same time gotten things quite in reverse. The reader will know that, in fact, Jesus is not a human making himself God, but God already made human.[41] In condemning such divinity to death, these mortals with stones in their hands engage in some misguided god-play of their own.

9:16 "This man is not from God, for he does not keep the sabbath." We would not claim heavy irony here. There is, of course, the sadly comic spectacle of legalists in the very presence of God denying his divinity because he fails to meet the religious requirements. There is also the larger misunderstanding that Jesus' activity on the sabbath, rather than negating his oneness with God, is in fact evidence of that oneness; for as he said in defense of another sabbath healing, "My Father is working still, and I am working" (5:17). Jesus *must* work "while it is day" (9:4), until the hour of his death, the true sabbath of God.[42] We focus now, however, on the smaller play in this verse upon keeping and not keeping the law.

Tēreō is a favorite verb in the Fourth Gospel, for Jesus is constantly inviting his hearers to keep his word or commandment. The first such invitation comes just before this chapter (8:51; see 14:15, 21, 23; 15:10). So to begin with, Jesus is not one to watch for what law *he keeps,* but rather one whose very word commands *to be kept.* Furthermore, this Gospel has already been quite clear: Jesus does "keep" the Father's word (again just preceding ch. 9 in 8:55), and his enemies do not (8:42, 55). Specifically they are told in 7:19, "none of you keeps the law." Though in fact Jesus has broken several sabbath technicalities in the healing of the blind man,[43] his gnat-straining detractors only accuse themselves by accusing him. If, as they say, one's relation to God is manifest in what law one keeps, Jesus' origin—as well as theirs—is clear enough. Significantly, some of the Pharisees' fellows help to accuse them, for in the words of the "others"—"How can a man who is a sinner do such signs?" (9:16b) —a crucial truth is underlined. The very deed that some reduce to a sabbath violation is for those with vision nothing less than a sign.[44]

9:24 "Give glory to God; we know this man is a sinner." This text might also be included among those we have called "false claims to knowledge," for part of its irony derives from the overconfident *hēmeis oidamen*. It functions, however, as most of the accusations do, to convict Jesus' opponents of the very charge they level against him. The irony is deliciously heightened by their pious injunction to tell the truth: "Give glory to God!" The phrase is within normal usage as an admonition to honesty (cf. Josh. 7:19; I Esdras 9:8), but it hardly seems possible that the author uses it without a grin.[45] It is comic that venomous inquisitors (then and now) should want to baptize their bitterness in sanctimony. It is tragic that these "Jews" should so piously adjure a man to tell the truth when in the next breath they expose their closed-mindedness to the truth. It is also typical of John's irony that in the expanding profession of faith that follows, the healed man will indeed give glory to God.

The charge that Jesus is a "sinner" is quite serious. "The Jews" have in mind Jesus' flagrant disregard of sabbath law. The implication, however, goes deeper than that he has committed a few infractions; to accuse one of being an *hamartōlos* is to charge that his whole attitude toward the Torah—his very understanding of it—is corrupt. It is to lump Jesus with the *am ha-aretz* and even the Gentiles. In this regard the accusation contains a measure of truth. Jesus has indeed joined himself with those outsiders; and strictly speaking, he lives outside the Jewish legal system.[46] What "the Jews" will not see is that Jesus abrogates sabbath law precisely because he is from God. "Sin" has in fact been redefined. Far from meaning one's failure to adhere strictly to Torah regulations, "sin" now means unbelief in Jesus. He has spoken to them at length about their *hamartia* in the previous chapter (8:21, 24, 34, 46). The last line of the present chapter will reinforce the fact that because of their willful blindness to Jesus, their *hamartia* remains (9:41). In John's thought there is simply no more devastating way to prove one's own sin than to conclude of "this man," "we know he is a sinner."

18:30 *"If this man were not an evildoer, we would not have handed him over."* The author no longer cares to be subtle, and neither do "the Jews." Now they lie outright. In this nonanswer to Pilate's request for an accusation, they can only express themselves negatively and vaguely; and even so, what they blurt out is far from the truth. The dishonesty goes much deeper than the fact that "this one" (contemptuous *houtos*) is no evildoer. More to the point, the enemies of Jesus in John have never been so bothered by his deeds as by his words. We have seen that they would sweep his good works aside to stone him for his words (10:31–33). Now they take the further step and accuse of evil works that never were, and so lie not only against Jesus but against themselves. The author lets them condemn themselves by the second verb he assigns them to speak, *paredōkamen*. They mean it in the rather neutral sense of "handing over"; the readers, however, have already met the verb *paradidōmi* eight times, always in association with the devil Judas, always in the sinister sense of betrayal (6:64, 71; 12:4; 13:2, 11, 21; 18:2, 5). Judas has now vanished into the night, but these stammering accusers who would not defile themselves by entering the praetorium have now assumed both his role and his fate.

The charges leveled against Jesus in the preceding texts are diverse. His detractors say he has a demon, is a Samaritan, is born of fornication, makes himself God, does not keep the sabbath, is a sinner and an evildoer. Yet each of these charges falls under one sweeping accusation: Jesus is a sinner. The author handles this theme of Jesus' relation to sin with consistent irony. The accusers are not only fantastically wrong about Jesus, but are remarkably guilty themselves of the very faults they find in him. Twice there might also be a typically unconscious stumbling onto the threshold of truth about Jesus: that he *is* a Samaritan by association (8:48) and that he is the man speaking as God (10:33).

Suggestions of Belief

In chapters 7 and 9 of John's Gospel several questions are asked concerning various Jewish officials and what they think of Jesus. Each question ostensibly denies their belief in Jesus, but oddly hints at the possibility that they do indeed know who he is. These texts are examined in sequence, for they seem to present something of a progression.

   7:26 "Can it be the authorities really know that this is the Christ?" The Jerusalemites note that though Jesus has been targeted for death no one seems capable of silencing him. The question they ask, whether tongue-in-cheek or simply in passing, is never taken seriously by them. The particle *mēpote* presupposes their doubts; and they immediately go on in verse 27 to explain why Jesus cannot be the Christ. The referent to their question, however, is the group called *hoi archontes,* "the rulers." The reader has only met one *archōn,* Nicodemus; and though his perception was rather dim, it seemed clear that he had more than a passing interest in Jesus as "a teacher come from God." Furthermore, the other two references to human *archontes* in this Gospel will also imply the possibility (7:48) or the fact (12:42) of the rulers' belief in Jesus. The pattern is consistent enough that J. Louis Martyn can plausibly suggest that John's use of *archontes* is a kind of "shorthand" for secretly believing members of the council *(Gerousia)* in the day of the Johannine community.[47] Be that as it may, some of these "rulers" in the Fourth Gospel do indeed believe, and the speakers of verse 27 have typically blundered into an accidental testimony of truth. Though the movement to kill Jesus is gathering momentum, there is in the heart of the synagogue a silent assent to the high claims of Jesus.

   7:47–48 "Have you been led astray also? Have any of the rulers or of the Pharisees believed in him?" It will not be the last time in the Gospel where arresting officers are helpless before Jesus (18:6). These temple police, sent by the Pharisees fifteen verses earlier (7:32), return empty-handed and impressed: "No one ever spoke like this man!" (7:46). The exasperated Pharisees ask the furious question from their own bias. To approve of Jesus is to be "led astray" *(peplanēsthe),* and *surely* this could not befall their own deputies— "not you too!" *(mē kai humeis).* It is too late, however. The officers have already blurted out their high opinion of Jesus. But the Pharisees go on berating the police, this time trying to shame them by citing the exemplary discretion of the officers' employers. "Have any of the rulers believed in him, or any of the Pharisees?" As a matter of fact, a man who is both ruler and Pharisee, though he has not yet openly believed in Jesus, has expressed his private awe before him; and just to make sure we do not forget, the author ushers Nicodemus back onto the stage two verses later to speak a cautious word in Jesus' defense. The result is that 7:45–48 constitute one of the most genuinely comical scenes in the New Testament.

7:52 "Are you from Galilee too?" The Pharisees' incredulous "Not you too!" *(mē kai su)* is now turned upon Nicodemus. They compound the improbability by adding what they suppose to be an unthinkable insult to this their brother: "from Galilee." The question means to ask him if he really wants to be a part of this "accursed" crowd who obviously "do not know the law" (vs. 49); does he really choose to place himself in this ignorant, bastardized stock who tag along with Jesus? They know, of course, that Nicodemus is not a Galilean. Their question is meant to sound ridiculous, and so put the matter to rest. The reader knows, however, what they do not—that though this ruler's interest in Jesus has been tentative and secretive, it is quite possible that he may be a "Galilean" as Jesus is a "Samaritan." It becomes all the clearer that "this crowd who do not know the law" are finding in their number some surprisingly learned, albeit silent, comrades.

9:27 "Do you too want to become his disciples?" For the third time we read, "Not you too!" *(mē kai humeis).* Now the question issues from a man who was formerly blind, and for the first time is aimed at the Pharisees themselves. The man's sense of irony, which grows keener as his sight grows clearer, will be studied more closely in chapter 6. This remark, on the surface at least, is certainly sarcastic.[48] They clearly have no intention of following Jesus. The badgered man's question, as Bultmann says, ironically pretends that they are in earnest, precisely to reveal their insincerity in the endless interrogation.[49]

The question also has its deeply penetrating aspect, for the truth is that these Pharisees are so blind precisely because they willfully do *not* "want to become his disciples." Their predisposition against discipleship is the issue.[50] Is it possible that their predisposition is in some sense *in spite of* what they sense to be the truth about Jesus? Verse 27 represents the fourth time since 7:26 that a question has been raised implying that Jewish leadership has a secret understanding of Jesus; and each of the others has seemed to make an ironic point. Significantly, we have just been informed in verse 16 that there is a division among the Pharisees over Jesus. Though no one is in any doubt about the interrogators' commitment to destroy Jesus, there is a hint at least that when the seeing man asks his sarcastic question, something in his tone leans in and winks and whispers, "We both know who he is, now, don't we?" That their response is to "revile" him is indication that he is probing a sensitive nerve.

The form of these four "suggestions of belief" is consistent. In all, five questions are asked about Jewish officials knowing who Jesus is or believing in him. Each contains the particle *mē* and expects a negative reply. In the last three instances the phrase *mē kai humeis/su* appears as if to punctuate by recurrence the fact that truly "the world has gone after him" (12:19). The progression of these texts is worth noting. At first only bystanders discuss among themselves the possibility of "the rulers'" knowledge (7:26). Then the Pharisees take up the question, first directing it against their own police (7:47), then accidentally implicating their own fraternity and changing the verb from *know* to *believe* (7:48). The Pharisees then ask one of their own if he is one of Jesus' cohorts (7:52). Finally a fledgling convert turns on the Pharisees themselves to ask if they would like to become disciples (9:27). The interrogation thus bears in steadily upon those who oppose the Christ. The author will eventually make clear that some "rulers" did secretly believe (12:42; 19:38–39). That the Pharisees themselves may have understood Jesus better than they let on is never argued outright. The silent probing of irony, however, has planted the seed of that terrible possibility.

Unconscious Prophecy and Testimony

We have seen that the respondents to Jesus can by their false assertions and assumptions point indirectly to the truth. There are several instances, however, in which their unwitting words foretell the import of Jesus' person or work rather directly. In Mark's Gospel it is the demons who scream out the identity of Jesus, and the people remain blind to him (Mark 1:24; 5:7). In John it is the human opponents who blurt out the truth in spite of themselves. These moments comprise some of the most obvious irony in the Gospel. Typically this kind of Johannine irony is found on the lips of Jesus' enemies, but the first two instances are uttered by less hostile voices.

2:10 "Every man serves the good wine first; and when men have drunk freely, then the poor wine; but you have kept the good wine until now." If, as one anthropologist has ventured, the first sign at Cana is presented essentially in the form of a joke,[51] these words by the steward comprise the punch line. They are in fact probably intended by the speaker to be funny, for the implication is that, given a little time at the bar, the guests will not care what they are drinking. On this rather riotous note, however, the author abruptly brings down the curtain on the scene. As Schnackenburg says, "The story breaks off deliberately with the head-waiter's remark, to allow it to echo in the mind of the hearer and to draw attention to its deeper meaning."[52] The next lines belong to the narrator, who tells us this was the first of Jesus' signs, manifesting his glory and inspiring the disciples' belief (vs. 11). This sharp contrast of tone should be sufficient clue that the scene has deeper significance than may have appeared.

We need not detail the symbolism of the story. Wine and wedding feast are common enough images of God's joyous New Age (cf. Amos 9:13–14; Hos. 14:7; Jer. 31:2–6; 1 Enoch 10:19; 2 Bar. 29:5; Matt. 22:1-14; Mark 2:19, 22). Jesus here attends a feast where the wine has given out. (If there is a replacement theme in this story which disparages the resources of Judaism, then Jesus' mother's remark, "They have no wine" [vs. 3] can be seen as ironic.) The miracle Jesus performs to replenish it is done privately. A few of the servants know, but the steward is explicitly said to be ignorant of what has happened (vs. 9)—the very stuff of dramatic irony. His jovial appreciation is called to the bridegroom, whom he believes to be responsible. Readers accustomed to thinking of Jesus as bridegroom (from other traditions or from previous readings of 3:29) will know that though the steward addresses the wrong man, he is quite right to praise the bridegroom. The particular words he speaks are no less ironic. The pronoun *you* is emphatic and in structural opposition to "every man": this bridegroom acts unlike ordinary persons. He brings the good wine *now,* the good wine that will flow freely for the world when Jesus' "hour" finally comes.[53] It should be noted that the steward's remark actually alters the significance of the story, changing the emphasis from water become wine to the wine that is *good,* and thus transforming the account from a mere miracle to a sign.[54] It is also noteworthy that only here in the Fourth Gospel does the author so much depend on a right understanding of *symbols* (wine and bridegroom) for the perception of his irony.

   7:3–4 "Leave here and go to Judea, that your disciples may see the works you are doing. For no one works in secret if he seeks to be known openly. If you do these things, show yourself to the world." There may well be sarcasm in this advice from the brothers of Jesus, for even they do not believe in him (vs. 5). Presumably they have with us just witnessed the mass defection of his disciples in Galilee. Are they taunting him with the suggestion that, given such success in Galilee, he really should move on to Judea so his disciples there can be equally as impressed, so that the whole "world" can take in the spectacle?[55] Whether or not their words are caustic, it is quite clear that in their reference to the world, they indulge in hyperbole.[56] At best they speak metaphorically; at cynical worst they mean that no one will care to watch; or perhaps they really do refer to the cosmopolitan feast-time crowd at Jerusalem. Whatever their intent, they certainly do not mean *literally* that Jesus could be manifest to the world in Judea. But just so, he will be manifest when his "hour" comes for "going up" to another feast. The Pharisees will say in 12:19 that "the world has gone after him" immediately after which some Greeks will seek him and he will say "and I, when I am lifted up from the earth will draw *all* to myself" (12:20–23, 32). The force of the brothers' unconscious prophecy is aptly stated by Dodd:

> We have here a striking instance of the characteristic Johannine irony. On the surface, we are reading about a rustic prophet who leaves the obscurity of the provinces to appeal to the great public of the metropolis.

But the words φανέρωσον σεαυτὸν τῷ κόσμῳ have a weight disproportionate to the ostensible situation. In their deeper meaning they are an appeal to the Messiah to manifest Himself to Israel. But if we go deeper still, they speak of manifestation of the eternal Logos, as life and light, to the world of human kind.[57]

7:35–36 *"Where does this one intend to go that we shall not find him? Does he intend to go to the Dispersion among the Greeks and teach the Greeks? What does he mean by saying, 'You will seek me and you will not find me,' and 'Where I am you cannot come'?"* In verses 33–34 Jesus has spoken the same riddle that in 16:16 sends the disciples into a similar scurry of questions. These Jews, however, not only question and blankly echo Jesus, they stab at a solution: "Does he mean to escape us by fleeing to the Diaspora and teaching Greeks?" What they manage to accomplish by this feeble guess which they themselves doubt is nothing less than a forecast of the Gentile mission of the church.[58] Several of John's regular devices signal this irony: the introductory *mē*, the disparaging *houtos*, the emphatic *hēmeis*, the perplexed repetition of Jesus' words highlighting their ignorance.

The irony here has more than one level. By the time the Fourth Gospel was written, this sneering suggestion had become a reality. The church was largely composed of Gentiles. The community of faith had done precisely as "the Jews" had suggested—gone to the Diaspora synagogues from which they left to evangelize the Greeks, often motivated by a forced "dispersion" of their own.[59] The narrator hardly needs to explain this irony. There is another sense, however, in which the statement carries more meaning. The question had sprung from a misapprehension of Jesus' words about his own death and exaltation. In John's thinking it is precisely that event which took the teaching of Christ to the Greeks (12:20–24). So in one fumbling guess the adversaries of Jesus have uttered a world of truth; and the author, pleased, quietly dims the lights, closing the scene.

8:22 *"Will he kill himself since he says, 'Where I am going you cannot come'?"* The scene is much the same. Jesus has spoken the same riddle about his death, this time adding that his hearers will die in their sin (vs. 21). Again "the Jews" respond by guessing at his meaning; again they ask a question expecting negation *(mēti)*; again they echo some of his words. There is some difference here, however. In their repetition they carefully omit his new phrase, "you will die in your sin," a phrase which Jesus will obligingly repeat in verse 24. Too, their speculation is now even more absurd. From "going away" to "suicide" is quite a leap. Is the author intentionally reflecting their desperate attempt to change the subject, or is he himself stretching imagination to reach for a new irony? Perhaps this is the abruptness of an insult: "He says he's going where we can't follow—maybe he's going to Hell!"[60] In any case, their reference to Jesus' death has inadvertently put them on the right track, for that is what he means by "going away." Further, they are correct in surmising that his death will come voluntarily, for no one takes his life; he will lay it down (10:11, 15). But the irony has one further twist: though he will lay down his life, it will not be as they might think; they themselves are destined to do the killing. Jesus' response is predictably silent about the content of their remark, but points deftly to the reason they cannot see the import of their own words: "You are from below, I am from above."[61]

12:19 "You see that you can do nothing; look, the world has gone after him." We need not linger here. The Pharisees, seeing Jesus' enthusiastic welcome into Jerusalem, resort to the same hyperbole already employed by his brothers (cf. 7:3–4, above; also 11:48, below). They intend a figure of speech but utter a literal truth.[62] The author makes his comment dramatically, choosing that very moment to introduce the Greeks who inquire after Jesus. The irony is signaled in verse 19 with the dramatic *ide,* which as the Passion approaches is used with increasing irony (cf. 16:29; 19:5 [*Idou*], 14). The first clause is difficult, meaning literally, "You see that you benefit nothing." The implication is that as long as they permit Jesus to live, they accomplish nothing.[63] They will shortly succeed in their plans, and accomplish more than they had dreamed.

11:48 "If we let him go on thus, everyone will believe in him, and the Romans will come and destroy both our holy place and our nation." In this verse the reader is privy to an unconscious foreshadowing of what is properly called an *irony of events.* Such irony, it will be remembered, plays upon the occurrence of the unexpected, particularly when "the means we sought to avoid something turn out to be the very means of bringing about what we sought to avoid."[64] The members of the council are clearly in a panic. Their tumbling sentence, using *kai* four times, gives indication that they are in about as much control of their speech as Caiaphas will shortly be of his. They set forth a conditional clause, "If we let Jesus live," followed by three sure unacceptable consequences: everyone will believe, the Romans will destroy the temple, the Romans will destroy the nation. The irony is obvious enough. They choose *not* to let Jesus "go on thus"—and all three consequences come true with a vengeance. The author need say nothing, for not only has the church in his day become cosmopolitan, but the predicted calamities had already come upon Israel; Zion's rubble is comment enough.[65]

Most likely, more than tragic coincidence is intended here. We know the author connects the belief of "all" with the death of Jesus (12:32). It seems probable that he also joined other early interpreters in viewing the subjugation of Israel and the destruction of the temple as direct consequences of Jewish rejection of Jesus (see Luke 19:41–44).[66] Had these patriots heard the double meaning in Jesus' early warning, they might not have fallen victim to their own zeal: "Destroy this temple," he had dared them (2:19). Accordingly, they did. They destroyed the temple of his body to save their own temple. But the temple rejected was in three days built again; and the temple "saved" was destroyed indeed.[67]

11:49–50 "You know nothing at all; you do not understand that it is expedient for you that one person should die for the people, and that the whole nation should not perish." Irony can hardly be richer. Caiaphas, who has waited in the wings these many chapters, now steps on stage to utter his only line. He delivers it with proper conviction and flourish, but cannot hear how he mocks himself, and never perceives that his unseen audience looks on with amusement and pity.

"You know nothing at all," he accuses his colleagues. Indeed they do not, although despite their muddled sense of cause and effect, they have just neatly forecast the future in triplicate. But the ignorance for which the high priest berates them is the very ignorance in which he will excel them. With marvelous alazony he shouts an emphatic *you,* then piles on three negatives and two verbs: by no means do *they* know, nor do they understand. Such swaggering effectively signals the reader that what follows will undo the speaker and exalt his intended victim.

Caiaphas, the realist, thinks it better that one person should die instead of a whole people. Part of John's ironic play is upon the multiple meaning of the preposition *huper*. Caiaphas probably intends the general sense, "instead of"; we are to hear its deeper sense, "for the sake of." There is more at work, however, in his use of the words *laos* and *ethnos, people* and *nation*. For John the words are not merely synonyms. *Laos* is used elsewhere in John only in 18:14, which recapitulates this verse. Wherever the Synoptics use *laos* John is careful to use *ochlos*. As Pancaro convincingly argues, *laos* (like *Israēl*) meant for John what it meant in the LXX: the true people of God.[68] Caiaphas thinks of one *laos;* the author means quite another. Moreover, *ethnos,* for Caiaphas meaning the nation as a political entity, almost universally in the New Testament and the LXX means the *Gentile* nations. So there is a double irony in that word. Like his colleagues, Caiaphas is dead wrong about what will cause his *ethnos* to perish; but unlike them, he gives unconscious testimony that Israel, even as he tries to preserve it, is just another pagan state.[69] To condemn Jesus to death, then, is to condemn the nation to death, a death that descends long before A.D. 70. As of this moment Israel ceases to be a people and becomes an *ethnos.* Meanwhile, a new people—namely, "whoever believes in him"—will "not perish but have eternal life" (3:16).

This ironic testimony to the triumphant work of Jesus and the tragic death of a nation is so strong that the narrator will not risk its being missed. He breaks his usual silence to explain that these words were quite beyond the one who uttered them and that this new people would be cosmopolitan indeed, the "children of God who are scattered abroad," made one family by their exalted Lord (vss. 51–52; cf. 1:12).[70] By this intrusion the author probably weakens the force of the irony. But given the depth of meaning he perceives in these lines, we can hardly blame him for finally bursting out loud with his knowledge of the tragicomic truth.

Further, there is theological significance in his explanation of

Caiaphas' "accidental" testimony by reference to the high priestly office. The issue is larger than the traditional belief that high priests had prophetic powers.[71] The issue is Purpose. All these hints and foreshadowings and testimonies and prophecies we have heard streaming off the lips of everyone who comes up against Jesus are neither accidental nor trivially entertaining. The intrusion in verse 51 helps the reader sense that each unwitting word has been a well-orchestrated note in a divinely directed symphony. The author has broken the silence of his irony to remind us that he himself is not the Ironist.

The testimony of Pilate. Analysis of Pilate's interaction with Jesus and "the Jews" is reserved for the next chapter. It is appropriate to mention here, however, that the governor of Judea shares honors with the high priest of Israel in ironically disclosing who Jesus is. He is more sarcastic than Caiaphas; he knows more. But he could not possibly know all he says. Two such testimonies will be mentioned briefly here. In 19:5 Pilate presents Jesus to "the Jews," scourged, robed in purple, crowned with thorns. His melodramatic words are, "Behold the man!" As we shall later see, there is extended ironic play upon the word *anthrōpos* in John's Gospel. This is its climax. No one in Jerusalem sees what the author sees: that Jesus is more than man, that in particular he is heavenly Man, Son of man, at the hour of exaltation and judgment (5:27).[72]

Pilate's other testimony, one that is given an almost unbearable irony, is that Jesus is "King of the Jews" (18:33, 39; 19:3, 19–22). It is a theme found in the Synoptic Passion narratives as well, but never with such fiercely underscored irony as John's account renders. Pilate means the title as a jibe at "the Jews," but is even more correct than he knows. He is more prophet than he knows as well; for when he posts the *titulus* in irrevocable Greek, Latin, and Hebrew, he proclaims to all that this "man" will be named King of a far greater realm than anyone there—including a provincial governor—would be comfortable knowing.

Nine instances of irony by unconscious prophecy or testimony have been considered, seven spoken by Jesus' adversaries, one by his own brothers, one by an unsuspecting head waiter. The techniques are by now familiar: repetitions, unanswered questions, negative expectations, contemptuous pronouns, hyperbole, overconfidence. A new signaling device is the overt authorial intrusion of 11:51–52. Another device which both enhances the ironic effect and marks the gravity of these sayings is that no less than four of them are "curtain lines." The ironic words are no sooner uttered than the curtain quickly falls, leaving us to ponder their hidden significance (2:10; 7:35; 12:19; 11:49–50).

When we inquire about the themes of these ironies, a remarkably clear pattern emerges once again. Every instance is concerned with the purpose or result of Jesus' death and exaltation. In his death he freely lays down his life (8:22), he manifests himself to the world and the Greeks (7:4, 35), and the world is drawn to him (11:48; 12:19). By his death he is exalted as Son of man (19:5) and "King of the Jews" (19:19–22). By his death also Israel is destroyed (11:48–50). The testimony of 2:10, a text different from the others in a number of respects, is less immediately concerned with Jesus' death. Nevertheless the story is full of overtones of the Passion. The fullness of the wine this bridegroom has "kept . . . until now" will be most evident in "the hour" to which Jesus refers; and the "glory" somehow manifest in that sign is a foretaste of his cruciform exaltation. Taken together, these nine testimonies comprise a strange but compelling witness to the irresistible power of Jesus' saving work.

Conclusion

This examination of local ironies has brought to the surface several tendencies in John's ironic style. The author quite often gets at his irony by way of *questions*. No less than twenty of the texts considered contain questions, five of them intentionally ironic by Jesus (3:10; 7:23; 10:32; 13:38; 16:31), fifteen of them unintentionally ironic by others (1:46; 4:12; 6:42; 7:15, 26, 35–36, 41b–42, 47, 48, 52a; 8:22, 53, 58; 9:27; 16:17–18). As is irony's way, these questions tend to be left *unanswered*. Only five of the twenty questions receive direct reply (7:15; 8:58; 9:27; 10:32; 16:17–18). Furthermore, of the ironic remarks made in declarative form, eleven (of nineteen) receive no specific response (2:10; 7:20, 28, 52b; 8:48, 52; 11:16, 48; 12:19;

16:29; 18:30). Like all ironists the author of the Fourth Gospel creates his power out of the silence. In the hush that follows the ironic word is the invitation to ponder and leap to new dimensions of meaning. Such is especially the case in the six texts where the ironic word is used as the curtain line (2:10; 7:35–36, 52b; 11:16, 49–50; 12:19). The necessary information enabling the reader to see the irony is most often given previously in the text, frequently in the Prologue, which has established the origin and identity of Jesus. Sometimes, however, the necessary knowledge is extra-textual, for example the destruction of Jerusalem or the worldwide scope of the church (11:48). In one case the narrator intrudes to signal the irony overtly (11:51–52).[73]

We may recall other indicators of John's irony. *Repetition,* a favorite Johannine stylistic feature, often functions ironically (3:10; 6:42; 7:20, 28, 35–36; 8:22, 58; 11:16; 13:38; 16:17–18, 29–30). The *emphatic personal pronoun* can underline irony (3:10; 4:12; 6:42; 7:47, 52a; 8:41, 48, 53; 9:24, 27, 29; 10:33; 11:49), as can the *derogatory demonstrative* (6:42; 7:15, 26, 27, 35, 36; 9:16, 24; 18:30). Signs of swaggering are clues to irony, as when speakers wrongly boast, *"we know"* (6:42; 7:27; 8:48, 52; 9:24, 29; 16:30), or when their predisposition prefaces a question with the negative particle *mē* (4:12; 7:26, 35–36, 41b, 47, 48, 52a; 8:22, 53), or when they attempt the cutting irony of *sarcasm* (1:46; 4:12; 7:3–4, 35[?]; 8:22, 53; 9:27; 11:16; 12:19). These instances of sarcasm are usually intended by the speakers as ironic *overstatement* (see also 11:48), but are transformed by the perceptive reader into literal truth or understatement. The irony may also play upon the typical Johannine device of *double meaning* (e.g., 3:10; 7:52; 8:48; 9:24; 11:49–50; 18:30). We have so far seen one instance in which the irony depends upon the right reading of symbols (2:10).

Again, not all examples of what could be called "local irony" have been included here. Our choice to divide the study between local and extended ironies has necessitated two unfortunate results. First, to avoid repetition some ironies properly "local" have been reserved for the next chapter because in configuration with other texts they are also "extended." Second, by separately examining the texts in this chapter as we have done, some of the sustained ironic artistry of John has inevitably been slighted. (For example, 7:25–8:59 is a sweeping combination of many punctual ironies, the total effect of which merits a unified analysis.) Our method, however, has been fruitful in at least one important regard. The grouping of John's isolated ironies according to their various speakers and types has yielded the discovery that in Johannine irony, *form follows theme.*

Of course, the fact that the different speakers deliver a different type or degree of irony is no surprise. It is inevitable that Jesus will speak a different kind of irony than anyone else, and that the Johannine disciples will be made lesser victims than the antagonists. Further, it is not terribly surprising that every instance of disciple irony but one is concerned with their failure to deal with his death. That Jesus' friends were scandalized by his suffering and death is attested in all traditions. In John, of course, it is not his suffering and shame that are at issue, for he suffers no shame. There is still, however, the scandal of his *absence* and the persistent fact that his death was not with his disciples but for them. There is also the clear note that some disciples will later suffer for him. John's ironizing of the disciples, then, has affinities with a broader tradition. Given the fact that many early congregations were tempted by crossless theologies (the incipient docetism of the Johannine church being one example—see 1 John 4:2), it was imperative that the tradition, with its direct and indirect reproofs of easy discipleship, be maintained.[74]

What is fascinating about our findings is the frequent correlation between form and christological theme in the remarks of the respondents treated in this chapter. When the irony plays upon false claims to knowledge, the theme is Jesus' origin. When false assumptions are put forth in the form of negative questions, the subject is the sovereignty of Jesus extending into the past, particularly his superiority over the patriarchs. When unwitting testimonies or prophecies are uttered, the theme is the meaning of Jesus' death. To be sure, these boundaries are not rigid. Elements of form often cross categories (e.g., 7:35 and 8:22 express their prophecies in the negative-expecting questions typical of the "false assumptions") and the theme of some texts ranges beyond the primary theme of the category (e.g., 11:48–50 go beyond the general theme of Jesus' death to the related theme of Israel's simultaneous self-destruction).

Nonetheless, the categories and themes are remarkably consistent. What can we conclude from such patterns?

One obvious suggestion is simply that the Johannine community, as it developed its own theology and its own "loves and hates," developed also its own patterns of expression, including not only a particular vocabulary and a particular love for meditative discourse, but a special affinity for certain forms of ironic expression. As we saw in chapter 2, a shared sense of irony is often the result of a community of minds. This is an issue to which we must return in chapter 7. For now we simply raise the question: is it possible that through years of reflection and preaching, a community such as the Johannine church might have come to cluster certain types of ironic expression around certain themes of their christology?

The polemical character of much of this irony is obvious enough. Those forms we have designated "accusation" and "suggestions of belief" make bitter sport of "the Jews" who opposed Jesus. They are guilty of the very charges they pressed against him; and they are preeminently guilty of having the clear evidence before them, of even inwardly knowing he is Light, yet willfully shutting their eyes to him. In the other ironic forms they are depicted as hopelessly arrogant, abusive, and dishonest, and as having achieved by their rejection of Jesus nothing less than the forfeit of their place as God's people. If irony is a weapon, John's Gospel is a bristling arsenal; and the regular victims of its onslaughts are the people of Israel who rejected Jesus.

This fact seems consistent with the christological themes we have isolated. The Fourth Gospel occasionally addresses nonchristological themes (e.g., pneumatology, eschatology, ecclesiology) and does so without irony. Furthermore, it makes some of its claims about Jesus without irony (e.g., that he was a worker of miracles and his relation to John the Baptist). The themes presented ironically are again the origin of Jesus (in relation to scriptural and popular expectations of the Messiah's or the Prophet's origin), the preeminence of Jesus in the past (especially his relation to the patriarchs), and the meaning and effect of his death (particularly Israel's forfeiture of its status to the Greeks and the world). These are themes of peculiarly Jewish interest, crucial issues of early dialogue and debate between church and synagogue. Is it possible that as a result of the synagogue's regular questions, doubts, or accusations, the Johannine community developed and refined rather "stock" ironic responses? The repetition of some of the ironies is so exact (cf. 4:12/8:53; 7:33–35/8:21–22) as to suggest "stock responses" indeed. These reflections are certainly not to suggest that the Fourth Gospel was written for Jews. We only note that whatever other functions John's ironies might have, they bear the marks of former conversation and combat; and their regularity of form suggests the wear of repeated use.

To say more about possible origins or functions of the ironies discussed here would be premature. These issues are held for more deliberate consideration in chapter 7. For now it is sufficient to have noted the patterns, to have raised the questions, and to move on to the larger ironies of this Gospel.

5

EXTENDED IRONY

Wayne Booth has applied to irony the prosaic but fruitful metaphor of reconstruction—the tearing down of one habitation and building of another on higher ground overlooking the rejected site.[1] If this metaphor may be extended, it might be said that the previous chapter made a series of concentrated explorations of the "higher house" in John's Gospel, one room at a time. By inspecting numerous units of John's local irony we have noted various recurring features. We have gazed out many windows, observing the author's rejected world from many angles, and we have discovered (bleary-eyed and footsore perhaps) that in this Gospel's house are many rooms—with a view. Now the tour takes a different turn. In the present chapter we propose a more sweeping excursion: to take in whole corridors of rooms together; to trace the long beams and boards which cut through and connect the rooms; to step outside and survey the whole house; to climb onto the roof and take in the whole view at once.

In this chapter we will survey various types of ongoing situational irony which weave in and out of episodes and perhaps undergird the Gospel's whole structure. Our focus is here upon characterization, upon motifs and images whose extended treatment in the Gospel is ironic, and upon the Gospel as a whole. We begin with the narrowest of these situational ironies and gradually widen the circle until the whole Gospel is included.

Ironic Characterization

Some characters in John's Gospel are never ironized: Jesus, the Beloved Disciple, Lazarus, John the Baptist, and the *basilikos* of

4:46–54, to name a few. We have just seen how many characters are victimized by their unwitting words. Here we focus on how characterization itself—the extended portrayal of a person by attribute, action, thought, and word—may be presented ironically. Two characters whose portrayal seems consistently ironic are Simon Peter and Judas Iscariot.

Simon Peter. Simon Peter is the impulsive disciple whose overeagerness stems from a failure to understand the death of Jesus. The irony of his character is twofold: he who is so anxious to follow Jesus *now* is forestalled by his own unreadiness to follow; and the aspect of Jesus he cannot grasp, the laying down of life, is precisely that aspect of discipleship he will most fully embrace. These motifs are intertwined.

It is well known that Peter is presented in the Fourth Gospel in some tension with the Beloved Disciple. Peter is not denigrated, nor is his leadership denied; but his centrality has shifted, and it is clear that the idealized "disciple whom Jesus loved" commands an authority which is equal if not superior. The issue of the relation between these two centers of authority, of passionate interest to the Johannine community, concerns us little as such. The diminution of Peter, however, quite apart from the place of that other disciple, has bearing upon his characterization. Peter emerges as an incomplete disciple. The confession that Jesus is the Christ is not made by Simon but by his brother, who brings him to Jesus (1:41). When he makes his confession (6:68–69) it is genuinely moving but vaguer than its Synoptic equivalent (Mark 8:29 par.), equally ignorant of the dimension of suffering, and firmly situated in a context of desertion (6:66–67) and betrayal (6:70–71).

With the coming of the Passion, Peter's misunderstanding of the necessity and efficacy of Jesus' death emerges. When Jesus washes the disciples' feet, an act symbolizing his death for them,[2] Peter does not understand. He first forbids the act (13:8; cf. Matt. 16:22) then implies it is insufficient (13:9). Later when Jesus announces he is going where the disciples cannot come (13:33), Peter, unaware that the immediate destination is death, asks, "Lord, where are you going?" (13:36). Jesus' cryptic promise is in the classic style of intentional dramatic irony: "Where I am going you cannot follow now, but you will follow afterward." For Peter following means tagging along; for Jesus it means death. Jesus' veiled language, understood by the reader, will not be grasped by Peter until much later. He now responds, undaunted, "Lord, why cannot I follow you now? I will lay down my life for you" (13:37). Whether or not he now senses that to follow is to die, Peter in a fit of loyalty swears he is prepared to go that far; and asks, given such resolve, "Why cannot I follow you *now?*" That question focuses the character of Simon Peter. What he asks for now he neither understands nor wants, as his denial will soon show; but what he asks for is precisely what he will eventually receive, a discipleship unto death. That is the irony of Jesus' response. The question, "Will you lay down your life for me?" (see pages 49–50) on one level promises failure to an overeager disciple. In its more probing aspect, however, it points to the distant day when Peter will fulfill his pledge.

Before a glimpse of that day can be granted there must be stark exposition of Peter's present unreadiness. In the garden comes the incident with the sword (18:10–11). The story differs from the Synoptic versions not only in identifying the swordsman as Simon Peter but also in setting the incident in ridiculous contrast to the situation. Jesus is so in command of the arrest that helpless soldiers litter the ground. All are powerless before him. How remarkably inappropriate then—*after* Jesus has concluded his own arrest and dismissed his disciples—that Peter should suddenly draw his sword and wreak havoc on the right ear of poor Malchus. The enemies of Jesus have fallen before him as he strides triumphantly toward his chosen death; and there stands Peter swinging a sword to defend him. John's artful appropriation of this bit of tradition could hardly illustrate better both Simon's impetuosity and his pathetic failure to understand Jesus' death.

Next comes Simon's actual attempt to "follow" (vs. 15) and the subsequent denial. Now the sword-slinging defender melts before the word of a servant girl. Is it significant that while in the Synoptics Peter denies being "with Jesus" or being "one of them," in John he denies being a *disciple* (18:17, 25)?[3] Ironically, too, his denials frame a segment of Jesus' trial before the high priest in which Jesus is questioned about his disciples. As Culpepper states it, "While Annas is concerned that Jesus' disciples may pose a threat, Peter is busy denying Jesus."[4] The author withholds any mention of Peter's remorse. More the ironist, he simply lets the cock crow (18:27) and grimly closes the scene.

If chapter 21 is a later addition, it stands as a fitting complement—even a necessary one—to the total portrayal of Simon Peter. As before, he takes his cues from the Beloved Disciple, but still rushes into the water to reach Jesus first (cf. 20:3–6). The conversation after breakfast is an obviously ironic play upon Simon's threefold denial by another charcoal fire (*anthrakia*, cf. 18:18; 21:9). Jesus' three probing questions offer gentle and excrutiating reproach. Simon, no longer the *alazōn*, endures the shame and answers with appropriate humility. Jesus' threefold response assigns to him the task of a shepherd. In Johannine thought that role is not merely pastoral, it portends voluntary death, for "the good shepherd lays down his life for the sheep" (10:11). Peter has already unwittingly anticipated this vocation by claiming in 13:37 that he would lay down life for Jesus. In 21:18–19 Jesus confirms this martyrdom by cryptically alluding to Simon's own crucifixion. Only after this solemn revelation does Jesus say to Simon with great gravity, "Follow me" (vss. 19, 22).

Peter had wanted to know at the Supper why he could not follow *now*. Here at breakfast, after the dark night of his own denial and the death of Jesus, he knows at last why following had been impossible; and, perhaps to his amazement, it is precisely at this point that he hears the call: *"Follow."* Overeagerness melts before such a call. Jesus tells him that when the final following comes, this hitherto impulsive disciple will not wish to go (vs. 18). But go he will, no longer the *alazōn*, but the disciple of the Shepherd who lays down his life.

So persistently is Simon's genuine discipleship postponed in this Gospel, that Jesus' use of the future tense when they meet—"You shall be called Cephas" (cf. "You are Peter," Matt. 10:2)—seems remarkably apropos, if not intentional.[5] In his pre-Easter inadequacy Peter is not alone but acts as representative of the Twelve.[6] In a unique way, however, his character brings into focus the demands of martyrdom. This is not the only path of discipleship (cf. the Beloved Disciple), but in the character of Simon Peter the author dramatically presents the necessity of martyrdom for some.[7] Ironically, it is the one who rushes to shout his early commitment first, the one who understands death least, who will come to himself only by miserable failure and will come to Jesus by freely chosen death.

Judas Iscariot. Judas is a flatter, more static character than Simon Peter. He does not change; unlike the Synoptic Judas, he comes to no self-awareness in the end. Consequently the irony of his character is not as developed as Peter's, but there are some aspects of that irony worth noting briefly. The most obvious is the emphasis that he was one of Jesus' own. John shares the practice of the Synoptic authors in never mentioning Judas without reminding us that the betrayer was a disciple. The first mention is indicative: "He spoke of Judas the son of Simon Iscariot, for he, one of the twelve, was to betray him" (6:71). Again in 12:4, "And said Judas Iscariot, one of his disciples, he who was to betray him . . . ."[8]

John uniquely heightens this incongruity in two ways. First he deepens Judas' depravity, making it absolute. No silver pieces tinge the betrayal in John's Gospel; the deed is done purely because in diametric contrast to true disciples into whom the Spirit of Christ enters (14:20, 23), Judas is entered by Satan (13:2, 27; cf. Luke 22:3).[9] The chosen one is himself a devil (6:70). Second, this incongruity is dramatized by the events of the Last Supper. The Synoptics make the point that the betrayer was not only present at the intimate meal, but used the same dish as did Jesus (Matt. 26:20–25; Mark 14:18–21; Luke 22:21–23). Only John, however, ties the betrayal so closely to the receiving of food from the hand of Jesus. In 13:18 Jesus predicts treachery by recalling Psalm 41:9, "He who ate my bread has lifted his heel against me." After Jesus gives Judas the morsel, the narrator says, "Then after the morsel, Satan entered him" (vs. 27); and again, "So, after receiving the morsel, he immediately went out; and it was night" (vs. 30). Judas betrays Jesus on freshly washed feet and with the taste of sacrament still on his tongue. Precisely at the moment of greatest grace from Jesus he wrenches himself from intimacy with the Light and plunges into outer darkness. Participation in this incongruity is shared, of course, not only by Judas and Satan, but by Jesus himself, who knew his betrayer, we are told, "from the beginning" (6:64).

Judas, like everyone else who plots against Jesus, is only an instrument of the divine will. Jesus knows him and chooses him. When Jesus tells him, "What you are going to do, do quickly," he can only obey (13:27–30).[10] The author may even intend a subtle reference to the great service inadvertently rendered to the world by this demonic disciple. Earlier he had pretended to plead for the poor (12:4–6). When he leaves the Supper the disciples wonder if perhaps Jesus has sent him "that he should give something to the poor" (13:29). Culpepper suggests, "From another vantage point one can see that he gave more to the poor than he realized."[11]

Like Simon Peter, Judas has a representative role in the Fourth Gospel. As suggested by the remarkable parallels in 1 John to "the children of the devil" (3:10) who "went out from us, but they were not of us" (2:18–19; 4:1), Judas represents those who have been part of the community of faith and have defected.[12] From this point of view it makes all the more sense that there is no suicide for Judas in John's Gospel. It is death enough that "he immediately went out; and it was night." It is condemnation enough that when Jesus faces the powers of darkness with his awesome "I AM," the narrator gives us one last glimpse of Judas: "And there stood Judas, who betrayed him, with them" (18:5).[13] His fate in the Synoptics is infinitely more kind.

Irony of Identity

An oft-used device of situational irony, particularly of ancient dramatic irony, is the situation of unknown or mistaken identity. One character or group of characters fails to recognize the true identity of another—a loved one, an enemy, a god—and consequently acts or speaks in ways either grossly inappropriate or accidentally appropriate. Countless examples follow this pattern: Joseph's brothers do not know him, Tobit does not know the stranger is Raphael, the suitors do not recognize Odysseus, Oedipus is ignorant of the identity of his father and mother, and in the plays of Euripides many pairs of loved ones—Electra and Orestes, Ion and Creusa, Helen and Menelaeus, Agave and Pentheus, Admetus and Alcestis—fail in some ironic way to recognize each other. Inasmuch as the Fourth Gospel is eminently concerned with the identity of the Revealer from God, through whom the world was made, "yet the world knew him not" (1:10), such irony is inevitable. Here we focus on two episodes where the theme of unknown or mistaken identity is dramatically developed and examine one motif of the irony of identity that spans this Gospel.

The Woman at the Well. A first-century reader steeped in the stories of the Hebrew faith would recognize the ironic situation of John 4 more quickly than do modern readers. The situation is precisely that of some Old Testament stories in which a man meets a woman at a well (Gen. 24:10–61; 29:1–20; Exod. 2:15b–21).[14] The common theme of these stories is betrothal. The common structure is striking: (1) a man is traveling in a foreign land; (2) he goes to a well; (3) he meets there a maiden; (4) water is given; (5) the woman hurriedly runs home to tell; (6) the man is invited to stay; (7) a betrothal is concluded. There are naturally variations upon this pattern consistent with major themes of plot and characterization,[15] but these variations are meaningful precisely because the structure itself was so set in the consciousness of the people. When Jesus therefore ventures into foreign territory and meets a woman at a well, the properly conditioned reader will immediately assume some context or overtone of courtship and impending marriage. Such an assumption is rewarded here, for not only do narrative and dialogue keep well within the structure outlined above, but the author has placed this account closely following a story in which *water* transformed into wedding wine is attributed to the *bridegroom* (2:1–11), and almost immediately after John the Baptist has talked about hearing *the Bridegroom's voice* (3:29). Such a context enriches the irony of the woman's ignorance of Jesus' identity. The reader knows that Jesus is not only the Christ, the Logos of God, but that he is the Bridegroom who will shortly win this woman to himself. Her initial resistance, her questions, evasions, and gradually unfolding faith in him become occasions for the rich laughter of irony.

The scene begins typically. Jesus greets the woman with a request for water (cf. Gen. 24:17), an irony in itself in view of who will eventually give water to whom. The woman's resistance is atypical of these stories, though the motif of opposition itself is not. The issue for her is the difference between Jesus, the Jewish male, and herself, a Samaritan female (4:9). Robert Alter notes of the Old Testament betrothal stories that the foreign land archetypally signifies not only "sheer female otherness," but "the hero's emergence from the immediate family circle."[16] Jesus has so burst the bounds of his people's circle that the woman herself is astonished. Jesus does not answer her objections, however, suggesting instead that she has perceived neither the gift of God nor the identity of the one speaking with her, else she would have asked and he would have given her living water (vs. 10). This emphasis on her ignorance of who he is serves both to increase dramatically the sense of otherness already expressed and at the same time to show the Stranger moving deftly toward her. True to Johannine style, the woman misconstrues *hudōr to zōn* to mean spring water, and reminds him he has no equipment to get it. Significantly, she addresses him as *kurie*—meaning for her now, *sir,* but for Christian readers and progressively for herself, *Lord.*[17] Interestingly, *kurie* may also mean "husband" (Gen. 18:12 LXX; 1 Peter 3:6).[18] The irony of verse 12 has already been discussed (p. 70). The woman suggests a negative comparison of the Stranger with her father Jacob and his bountiful gift of water. When Jesus replies that his gift relieves thirst forever, the woman responds, still confused but more impressed, "*kurie,* give me this water, that I may not thirst, nor come here to draw" (vs. 15). The element of the gift of water in the betrothal type-scene has been elaborated to an eight-verse exchange, by means of double meaning and misunderstanding. Such expansion functions not only to underline the symbolic significance of water, but also to mark the gradual and inexorable movement of the two characters toward each other. In the betrothal type-scenes the drawing of water is "the act that emblematically establishes a bond—male-female, host-guest, benefactor-benefited."[19] In elaborating Jesus' offering of water and the woman's dawning (though misdirected) desire for it, the author dramatizes how Jesus draws her to himself.

The next exchange now has new interest. Jesus asks her to go get her husband, and she replies that she has none. A woman with no husband is precisely what we expect in such a type-scene, for that is the role to be filled by the traveler. What is surprising is Jesus' sudden revelation that contrary to both the reader's expectation and the woman's implication, her unmarried status is not because she is a maiden but because she is a five-time loser and currently committed to an illicit affair. This is situational irony par excellence. The Old

Testament well scenes invariably feature a *naarah,* a girl whose virginity is assumed and sometimes made explicit (Gen. 24:16). When the heavenly Bridegroom Jesus plays this scene, however, his opposite turns out to be a tramp. He weds himself not to innocence but to wounded guilt and estrangement.

The woman, amazed, calls him *kurie* once more and "prophet." She promptly changes the subject, however, to differences of worship between Samaritans and Jews, thus trying desperately again to put distance between herself and Jesus. His reply quickly closes the gap by shifting from mountains and temples to spirit and truth. Further, he now addresses her as *gunai,* which, while not necessarily significant (e.g., 2:4), can mean "wife," as it does in other Greek literature when a stranger ironically addresses his unsuspecting wife.[20] Whether or not such irony is intended (I do not argue that it is), the words *pisteue moi, gunai* do serve to obliterate any distance between the woman and Jesus. Her response in verse 25 accords with this "irony of identity," for now she speaks in third person about Messiah, though her hearer is Messiah himself.[21] Upon his revelation that he is Messiah, the disciples arrive and the woman quickly leaves to tell her village. Even now she is ironically unsure that the stranger is the Christ (note vs. 29b, *mēti*), but her proclamation inspires the villagers to come out and invite him to remain (the regular enthusiastic response of a maiden's kinsmen— Gen. 24:31–32; 29:13–14; Exod. 2:20–21). Shortly they come to embrace Jesus as "Savior of the world" (vs. 42).

The foregoing analysis is not offered as an alternative to other exegeses, but as a supplement. To see that this narrative closely follows the structure of Old Testament betrothal scenes does not deny that such an encounter really transpired; nor do we claim that the author consciously kept the betrothal imagery at the forefront of his mind. We do contend, however, that the author's account of the story reflects that he has drawn from the deep reservoir of these associations, and relates the event with echoes and overtones of a divine courtship. The reader attuned to this underlying music hears a deep and delightful irony. An unlikely daughter of God and her outcast people are gently but irresistibly wooed and won by the Stranger who will "remain" far longer than two days, and who will finally even take their name (8:48).

Mary Magdalene at the Tomb. Readers of John's Gospel know that Jesus has risen from the dead before Mary does. We are told of the resurrection as early as 2:22 and as late as 20:9, the penultimate verse preceding her scene with the risen Christ. The author relates the account in a way which maximizes the difference between what we know and what Mary knows. Clue after clue is laid before her which she does not grasp; and, as the evidence mounts, so does our gleeful suspense: when will she know? why can't she see? how much longer before the light breaks through her tears? The result is a deeply satisfying narrative that bit by bit builds the joy of Easter.

Verse 11 finds Mary outside the empty tomb, weeping because someone has taken the body—an irony in itself, for had she found the corpse for which she was weeping the outcome would be joyless indeed. Her weeping is mentioned four times in five verses; her grief is proportionate to her imminent gladness. When she stoops to peer into the grave she sees the first clue: "two angels in white," says the narrator, but Mary sees no significance. Their question to her in verse 13 is a subtle and delightful irony: "Woman, why are you weeping?" Mary in her grief hears it only as a natural inquiry into the cause of her crying, but, especially in view of the question's repetition by Jesus, we are probably to hear the undertone: what is there indeed to weep about? After explaining again, "they have taken my Lord, and I do not know where they have laid him," she turns and is startled by the ultimate clue, Jesus himself. Yet still she does not see, so he speaks. He reiterates the question of the angels and adds, "Whom"—not what—"do you seek?" (vs. 15).[22]

Now the irony of identity blossoms full. She weeps for a dead Jesus, and when the living Jesus stands before her asking, "Why weep?" and inviting her to speak his name, she thinks he is the gardener.[23] She then asks him the whereabouts of his own corpse![24] She calls him *kurie,* sir.[25] She has twice before spoken of how "they have taken the *kurios* out of the tomb" (20:2, 13). Now as she complains the third time, she speaks of the corpse as "him" and unwittingly transfers *kurie* to the gardener. The Greek repetition of the pronouns seems to underline Jesus' alleged absence: *Kurie ei su ebastasas auton eipe moi pou ethēkas auton kagō auton arō* (vs. 15).

The last clause is especially rich. He stands there resplendently alive on his way to the Father and she wants to take her dead Jesus away.

Now the ironic tension could hardly be higher. So Jesus whispers the one word that will break the spell. It is still no direct announcement of who he is, it is rather an appeal to who she is. He calls her name, and her whirling recognition is proof of his earlier promise: "his sheep hear his voice as he calls by name those who belong to him.// I know my own and my own know me" (10:3, 14). The rest of the scene is heavy with significance and even continues an ironic motif already raised: Mary wishes to possess the risen Jesus (vs. 17). The act of recognition itself, however, is the denouement of the irony, so our analysis ends here.

The point has been to demonstrate how the author deliberately shows us what Mary cannot see and plays our knowledge against her ignorance. This is not done at her expense, for she is portrayed sympathetically; nor is it done to make the story merely thrilling. On the contrary, we note at least two far-reaching effects upon the reader. First, we are made in a vivid way to walk through the Easter event. It is one thing to read an angel's announcement, "He has risen, he is not here,"—to be *told* about resurrection. But to watch tear-blinded Mary stumbling over angels and oblivious to the nearness of the one she mourns until she hears her name on his lips—that is to be *shown* resurrection, to savor it, and somehow to experience it.[26]

More importantly, by granting the reader better vision than Mary, by elaborating her oblivion to a degree the reader finds incredible, John puts us in a position where faith itself is now more credible than before. The same thing happens in reading of the Samaritan woman. In our *literary* experience, the failure of these two characters to perceive the identity of the character Jesus only intensified our conviction about his identity (as a character). That conviction, furthermore, was the satisfying center of the reading experience. Does not this experience increase the likelihood that such a conviction will transfer to the reader's own story? Far more forcefully than any outright declaration of the identity of Jesus, the subtle indirection of irony invites and confirms the insight of faith.

Jesus, "the Man." R. Alan Culpepper has noted that in John's

Gospel "when Jesus is called simply 'a man,' the implied author winks at the reader."[27] John does seem to use *anthrōpos* for Jesus in a doubly ironic sense. On the one hand, those who refer to him as "the man," whether innocently (4:29; 9:11) or contemptuously (5:12; 9:16, 24; 10:33; 11:47, 50; 18:17, 29), are guilty of gross understatement. Of particular interest are two verses already cited as ironic. The syntax of 9:16 is peculiar, emphatically disparaging Jesus' humanity. Some Pharisees say, *Ouk estin houtos para theou ho anthrōpos*—"He is not from God—this man."[28] In 10:33 their complaint against Jesus is precisely that he, a mere human, makes himself God. On the other hand, there are occasional hints that such references point us to Jesus' real identity as *the* Man, or Son of man.

Some texts seem to contrast Jesus with *anthrōpoi*. In 2:10 the practice of Jesus is contrasted with the practice of *pas anthrōpos*. In 5:7 the sick man complains that he has no person to help him; but, of course, he has Jesus.[29] Especially intriguing is 7:46, though a textual difficulty complicates the issue. The better reading seems to be *oudepote elalēsen houtōs anthrōpos*—"Never has there spoken like this a human being."[30] The emphasis is on *anthrōpos;* the police officers find Jesus unlike any person they have heard. If the longer reading is adopted the irony is even more forceful: "No person ever spoke like this person," emphasizing *anthrōpos* all the more while stressing that an *anthrōpos* is precisely what Jesus is (compare also the contrasts in 2:25; 5:34, 41).

Of crucial concern is the last designation of Jesus as *ho anthrōpos,* Pilate's "Behold the man!" (19:5). There is more at work here than Pilate's intended sarcasm or appeal for pity: the author permits Pilate to say more than he knows. Such a conclusion seems obvious in view of the heavily ironic context of the trial, the statement's parallel structure and proximity to 18:39 ("King of the Jews"), and its parallel to 19:14 ("Behold your King!").[31] As we will see, the whole trial might be viewed as an ironic enactment of a king's enthronement.[32] In this scheme of things, the proclamation, "Behold the man!" becomes "a title, a throne-name given to the 'King of the Jews.'"[33] "The man" may itself function as a messianic title,[34] but given the context, a connection with "Son of man," the judge (5:27) also seems implicit.[35]

In John's Gospel the Son of man is truly an awesome figure, most of all because he is no longer a figure yet to come, but one who already invades the world with his terrible judgment.[36] "Behold"—he is *here!*—"the man!" Ostensibly, a freshly flogged human being— manifestly mortal—stands mocked and condemned. We are to see that precisely by that condemnation the divine Son of man executes judgment and receives the glory of one who is "lifted up."

Clearly, Pilate's *Ecce homo* is a richly evocative phrase.[37] On one level the abject humanity of the Word made flesh is starkly affirmed. Whether Pilate intends to evoke pity or scorn, he is profoundly correct in presenting Jesus as the epitome of *anthrōpos*. By the same word, however, Jesus is exalted far above the world of ordinary humanity. Pilate, the Gentile, cannot be made to say *Son of man* outright, for that would not only be historically implausible but violate the sanctity of that title as Jesus' own.[38] Pilate can, however, be permitted to say with plausibility and great sarcasm, "Behold the *man!*"—not only a majestic title itself, but one that evokes for perceptive readers a vision of "heaven opened, and the angels of God ascending and descending upon the Son of man" (1:51). Thus, in three devastating words the author has crystallized a great depth of ironic truth which no direct utterance could convey. With great artistry the evangelist has unfolded the identity of this human being who, thoroughly human, is infinitely more than human—and so offers "the true light that enlightens every human being" (1:9).

Ironic Imagery

The Fourth Gospel is rich in symbolic imagery. A symbolic image itself, of course, need not be ironic. When, for example, Mary comes to the tomb "while it was still dark" (20:1), we need not speak of that imagery as ironic.[39] Though by now Jesus has risen, the text has not yet said so. For the moment, Mary is in the night of unrelenting grief and she knows it. The symbol fits the facts and her feelings, however briefly. Truer to the nature of irony is imagery painfully or comically incongruous with what a character perceives the situation to be or with what the reader knows the situation to be. Ironic imagery is the author's implied commentary whispering to the reader: all is not as it appears.

John's constant play with light and darkness provides some instances of ironic imagery. An early example is 3:1-2.[40] The irony stems from the contrast to Nicodemus' credentials in 3:1. He is a Pharisee and a ruler of the Jews. Furthermore, he comes professing to know Jesus is "a teacher come from God." The author, however, literally casts a shadow over the credentials and the confession by enshrouding them in night. Nicodemus is in the darkness of fear and ignorance. The fear is not self-evident here, but is the reason for his secrecy later with Joseph of Arimathea, and is a historically plausible motivation for a nocturnal meeting.[41]

More evident in the context, however, is the darkness of his ignorance. It is the ignorance of a mind impressed with surface signs (the connection between the threefold negative reference to sign-believing *anthrōpoi* in 2:25 and the immediate reference to an *anthrōpos* of the Pharisees in 3:1 is obvious), yet unable to grasp the most elementary of spiritual truths (3:4, 9). It is in a way a necessary night, for his coming to Jesus is a movement from night to light (cf. 3:21); or to put it more consistently with the theme of the dialogue, Nicodemus speaks from the darkness of the womb.[42] The author, however, seems to find it amusing that the eminently respected sage of Israel is presently so lost in the dark. The imagery of night intends to pose the same question raised by Jesus, "Are you the teacher of Israel and do not understand this?" (3:10).

A more tragic use of this image occurs in 13:30, where Judas "went out; and it was night." *Night* stands in incongruous contrast with the sacred meal just shared, the morsel from the hand of Jesus, the positive expectation of the disciples, and the sobering fact that Judas' journey into darkness is launched from the very presence of the light of the world. Unlike Nicodemus, who moves from night toward the light, Judas is chosen by the light, lives with the light, yet even in that brilliance can be possessed of Satan and "immediately" be plunged into night. But he is not the only disciple vulnerable to darkness. While Jesus stands trial in the high priest's house, Simon Peter stands outside in the cold, where a charcoal fire is tragic substitute for the light he is denying (18:18). It will be different when day finally breaks and Jesus himself makes a charcoal fire (21:9) by which Simon will be fed and called to feed.

A rich mix of ironic images decorates John's account of the arrest of Jesus in 18:1–8. Judas comes to the garden with a *speira,* or cohort, of soldiers. At the very least, the word refers to a *maniple* of two hundred men, but it normally indicates six hundred men. The word used in verse 12 for their captain, *chiliarchos,* means the leader of a thousand men. These figures generally provoke commentators to discuss historical plausibilities, but we do better simply to let the text speak.

The scene is almost apocalyptic. "The ruler of this world" has come (14:30) to seize one man, and absurdly he marshals hundreds of soldiers to help—plus the temple police and Pharisees. The obvious "overkill" is ironic testimony to the enemy's fear of Jesus, which will soon be graphically demonstrated. These hundreds of henchmen come prepared "with lanterns and torches and weapons." Raymond Brown notes this "ironical touch" and explains: "Judas has preferred darkness rather than the light which has come into the world (3:19); when he left Jesus it was truly night (13:30), and now he needs artificial light."[43]

Verse 4 says both that Jesus had full knowledge of what was to happen and that he "came forward" to ask them whom they sought; he is clearly in command. When they answer, "Jesus of Nazareth," and he responds, *Egō eimi,* the narrator reports with great irony: "they drew back and fell to the ground." Hundreds of Caesar's well-armed troops join the zealous defenders of Israel's temple to converge on one man in a garden; and when he breathes two words they all collapse like corpses. As Brown notes, while in the Synoptics Jesus prays prostrate in the dust of Gethsemane, the only ones prostrate in the dust here are the arresting officers.[44] They are so speechless that Jesus must ask them again whom they seek. When they have answered, he reiterates who he is and tells them to let his disciples go. Following the pathetic incident between Peter and Malchus, Jesus is bound and led away. A summary of the actions of the arresters is instructive. They have answered two questions of Jesus, fallen to the ground, and—at *his* command—have released the disciples and taken Jesus away. The scene is therefore a comic enactment of the impotence of "the ruler of this world" to take the life of Jesus (14:30; 10:18). When an army of the ruler's minions comes hoping to seize Jesus, he must do their work for them and conduct his own arrest.[45]

A final instance of the Fourth Gospel's ironic imagery occurs in 19:38–42, the account of the burial of Jesus. There are perhaps some ironies of reversal here. Two men who had never dared to profess public allegiance to Jesus while he lived now seek to honor him in his death. Perhaps we are to notice, too, that in contrast to these newly courageous fledgling disciples, the Twelve are still scattered. In particular, we may observe with Loisy, "Judas had been scandalized at the use of one pound of perfume for the living Jesus (12:3–5) and here are one hundred pounds brought to his corpse."[46] It is an immense offering of spices, the equivalent of nearly eight gallons liquid or seventy-five pounds dry measure. Such extravagance could intend to image for us the majestic interment of a king, a motif dominating the Passion story and consistent with the remark that the garden tomb had never before been used.[47]

Some interpreters wonder, however, if the author does not also conceal a quiet smile here. We know Jesus will be raised; Nicodemus clearly does not. Wayne Meeks says the "ludicrous one hundred pounds of embalming spices indicate clearly enough that he has not understood the 'lifting up' of the Son of Man."[48] The image evoked is of two remorseful half-disciples sadly piling a mountain of embalming materials onto a body they obviously think is going nowhere. The sound reader, alerted by hyperbolizing imagery (as in 18:3–6), is prompted to leap once more to the post-Easter vantage point of the author. From that height is foreseen a tomb wherein certain lavishly anointed linen cloths lie alone eloquently unnecessary.

Although other instances of ironic imagery may be found,[49] sufficient examples have been discussed. Most of these instances occur in the latter chapters of the Gospel which is only to be expected. For not only do the closing chapters seek to convey the Gospel's deepest truths in narrative form, but the imagery John employs cannot be used with fullest force until the early chapters have done the necessary work of developing symbols and clarifying perspectives.

The ironic imagery is possible because the author has done a masterful job of conditioning us to "judge not by appearances, but judge with right judgment" (7:24).

Irony of the Gospel

Here we wish to survey the broadest movements of irony in John. It has been said that "in the Fourth Gospel theology *is* irony."[50] As we will see in chapter 7, this fundamental ironic vision stems largely from the profound dualism at work in this Gospel. Two worlds have collided in the coming of Jesus, and the inevitable result is the clash of opposition called irony. Human ignorance clashes with divine omniscience, religious institutions clash with "spirit and truth," surface meaning clashes with hidden meaning, appearance clashes with reality. Fundamentally, then, there is irony in John's most basic assertion that "the Word became flesh and dwelt among us" (1:14). That, of course, is the irony of all Christian proclamation; but John's keen eye for incongruity draws it large. In the remainder of this chapter we summarize the larger incongruities which the author has woven together to create the consistently ironic fabric of his proclamation.

Perhaps the most obvious of John's ironic incongruities is summarized in 1:11, "He came to his own and his own received him not."[51] The people of God are visited by the Logos of God and they spurn him. This tragic irony fans the fiery polemic against "the Jews" which burns throughout this Gospel with progressive intensity. In the beginning they are only baffled by Jesus or suspicious of him (cf. 1:19–28; 2:18–20; 3:1ff.); but by 5:16–18 they are persecuting Jesus for his sabbath healing, and seeking to kill him because he is "making himself equal with God."[52] Their hostility intensifies from that point and their blindness deepens until their sole desire is to be rid of him, at devastating cost to themselves (19:15).

Jesus' rejection by his own is not confined to Israel itself, however. More broadly, the *world* was made through him yet does not know him (1:10). More narrowly, Jesus' own brothers do not believe in him (7:5); and his disciples defect (6:66) or deny their discipleship (18:17, 25, 27), or satanically turn on him (13:2). So at more than one tragic level his own do not receive him. Yet there is an accompanying comedy, for if his own reject him, some surprising outsiders come forward to receive him (an irony amply noted in the Synoptics). "The Jews" who have spurned their Christ and consequently their heritage are quickly replaced by a willing company of Samaritans, Galileans, and Greeks—many of them women. Jesus loses many of "his own," but their rejection of him ironically opens wide the door for the world to go after him (12:19–23). The gathered councils of Israel condemn their one hope to death (11:47–53), and in lifting him up to die, draw the scattered children of God to receive him indeed (1:12; 12:32).

With two ironic motifs John elaborates the failure of Jesus' own to receive him. The first could be stated as follows: that which clearly bears witness to Jesus is taken up as evidence against him. This is constantly the case with Scripture. Early on we read that both Moses and the prophets bear witness to Jesus (1:45; 2:22; 5:39, 46). "The Jews" use these very Scriptures, however, as proof against him (5:39–40; 7:42, 52); they claim discipleship to Moses against a discipleship to Jesus (9:28); and when they finally plead with Pilate to kill him, they insist it is their law that demands his death (19:7).

The same is true of Jesus' signs and works. "These very works which I am doing," says Jesus, "bear me witness that the Father has sent me" (5:36; cf. 10:37–38). Accordingly, Jesus' signs are regularly said to evoke belief (2:11; 4:53; 6:69; 9:38; 11:45), as well as inadequate faith too riveted to the signs (2:23–25; 3:2–3; 4:48). Those who oppose Jesus, however, sweep the signs aside and even use them against him. Their blindness to the signs is illustrated in 6:30, where following the multiplication of loaves they ask, "Then what sign do you do, that we may see and believe you? What work do you perform?"[53] They take signs and twist them into reason to persecute him (5:16) or evidence that he is not "from God" but a "sinner" (9:16, 24).

It is supremely ironic that immediately after the Lazarus sign—performed "that they may believe" and resulting in the belief of many—the chief priests and Pharisees plot Jesus' death precisely on these grounds: "For this man performs many signs" (11:47). They even say as they betray him to Pilate, "If this man were not an evildoer, we would not have handed him over" (18:30). Theologically, we may infer that the signs are essentially ambiguous, or as Dodd said, "a σημεῖον is not, in essence, a miraculous act, but a significant act, one which, for the seeing eye and the understanding mind, symbolizes eternal realities."[54] For the author, however, the ones who should have had seeing eyes for the realities behind the signs and the Scriptures are precisely those who blinded themselves (9:41).

A second elaboration of the failure of "the Jews" is more bitterly ironic. By their killing of Jesus they think they save the life of their nation and their temple. In the author's view it is precisely in killing Jesus that they achieve the death of their nation and their temple. In a tragic irony of events, they die the death they intend for Jesus. This theme has already been noted in 2:19–20 and 11:48–50. The death of the nation will be dramatically enacted in the trial scene, discussion of which is reserved for the next chapter.

The destiny of Jesus himself is the subject of some of the Gospel's undergirding ironies. John is not noted for stressing the incongruity of Jesus' death, but that motif does not entirely escape him. We glimpse that incongruity only once, late in the narrative, but it takes its shape from the Gospel's earlier episodes. In 2:1–11 Jesus makes excellent wine. In 4:7–15 he proposes to give a Samaritan woman the water which banishes thirst. In 19:28, however, he cries from the cross, "I thirst," and is given sour wine (oxos). To be sure, he cries not in desperation but "to fulfill the scripture." Jesus must remain sovereign. Having assured us of that, however, the author can make his point that the King who lays down his life does so utterly. He who called all the thirsty to himself for water (7:37–38) will for their sakes embrace thirst. He who inaugurated his work with the excellent new wine of joy must in the hour when that work is "finished" receive the bitter wine of death.

The dominant irony concerning Jesus' destiny is that his death is in fact an exaltation. Other early Christians may have been concerned to preach starkly the incongruous scandal of Jesus' humiliation. The path chosen by John is to reinterpret that humiliation as nothing less than glorification. Ingeniously he chooses the word hupsoō, already common in Christian parlance as an expression for God's exaltation of Jesus (Acts 2:33; 5:31; Phil. 2:9), and three times uses it in reference to crucifixion (3:14; 8:28; 12:32). These three texts, however, comprise only the verbal overture to the grandly dramatized coronation that is John's passion narrative. In the arrest, the trial, and the crucifixion itself Jesus seizes his death in kingly command over all who pretend to capture him and judge him. Rather than cry out for a God who has forsaken, the crucified Jesus in John is already on his way to the Father. Thus the scandalous irony of history is itself ironized. George W. MacRae is correct in saying of the Fourth Evangelist, "His interpretation of the death of Jesus as exaltation and return to the Father, the 'lifting up of the Son,' is his unique and crowning irony."[55]

Two major movements of John's irony have emerged: the downward plunge of those who will not receive Jesus; and the upward sweep of Jesus' exaltation, with the associated triumph of those unlikely people who believe in his name. One is a movement toward tragedy. The other is a movement toward high and holy comedy. Both have their passage through the two-way door of irony.[56]

Conclusion

It is more difficult to draw conclusions about the techniques of John's extended irony than of his local irony. Extended irony may be more amorphous; and, as has been freely confessed, one cannot always be certain that one's own perception of irony is the same as the author's. Nonetheless, there is reasonable certainty about most of the instances cited here, and there have emerged some patterns of technique that are noteworthy.

The extended irony in John is often no more than a creative combination of the local ironies already discussed, and these techniques need not be detailed again. Two of these, however, are occasionally given distinctive shape in the texts discussed here. While several instances of ironic dialogue cited in chapters 3 and 4 contained overstatement, it has been seen in this chapter that John also signals irony with hyperbolizing imagery (18:3; 19:39). More importantly, the Johannine technique of repetition also finds an expanded usage in the sustained ironies. For example, the author may signal an ironic contrast by repeating a word he has associated with a character, but the second time with a different significance ("the poor"—12:5; 13:29; and "charcoal fire"—18:18; 21:9); or he may repeat the same word many times throughout his Gospel, playing different nuances against each other ironically (e.g., "follow," "man," "thirst"). In addition to such lexical repetition, in the following chapter we will observe semantic repetition in particular narratives in which the irony is heightened by the use of subtly associated words (chapter 9 uses *oida* and *phaneroō* as well as *phōs, tuphlos, blepō, oraō*) or images (the trial narrative's *Königsepiphanie* sequence, the judgment seat, the garb, and the *titulus*).

There also has surfaced a rather regular pattern of "irony of identity" in which (1) a character not knowing Jesus' identity addresses him as *kurie*, (2) makes reference to Messiah/Son of man/Jesus, thought to be absent, after which (3) Jesus immediately discloses himself (4:19–26; 9:35–37; 20:14–16; cf. 5:7–8). Finally there is also the recurrence of the simultaneous upward and downward movements already elaborated.

The themes of these ironies, though not as narrowly associated with particular forms, are within the same realm as those of the local ironies. Discipleship is occasionally ironized with characterization. More fundamentally, the issue of Jesus' identity is constantly treated with irony, as is the progressive destruction of those who reject him.

6

SUSTAINED
NARRATIVE IRONY:
Two Case Studies

We have studied John's ironic technique at numerous points in his Gospel and have surveyed the larger ironic images, motifs, and themes which appear throughout the work. There are two episodes, however, in which the author so skillfully employs the full range of his ironic art that the Johannine irony cannot be fully appreciated until they have been carefully considered. These two narratives, the story of the man born blind (ch. 9) and the trial of Jesus (18:28—19:16), bear some striking similarities in form and theme. More importantly, they combine many of the techniques already discussed and present the ironic structure of this entire Gospel in miniature.

The Man Born Blind

John's prologue says, "The true light that enlightens every person was coming into the world." This light was not received by "his own," but to those who did receive him "he gave power to become children of God" (1:9–12). These verses, summarizing the Gospel's central irony, are brought to vigorous life in the drama of chapter 9,[1] where the author's art is at its consummate best. Brown rightly observes, "no other story in the Gospel is so closely knit. We have here Johannine dramatic skill at its best."[2]

Since the work of J. Louis Martyn, it has been widely recognized that this chapter represents a "two-level drama" in which the time of Jesus and the time of the Johannine community are viewed in "stereoptic vision." The triumphs and conflicts of past and present are so overlaid they become appropriately indistinguishable.[3] Since our concern is with the narrative as a literary unit we will not dwell here upon the historical levels on which it works except to note that for those first readers whose world was one of the stages on which this drama was played, the taste of the irony was all the richer.

As has been frequently observed, chapter 9 is presented in seven scenes. According to the ancient rule of drama that "no more than two active characters shall normally appear on stage at one time, and that scenes are often divided by adherence to this rule,"[4] John has made each scene an exchange between two primary characters or character-groups. George MacRae has noted a symmetrical arrangement of these scenes which enriches interpretation and irony at several points. The following is MacRae's list of the scenes, with one alteration.[5]

A .   1–7   Jesus and the blind man
B .   8–12   The blind man and his neighbors
C .   13–17   The blind man and the Pharisees
D .   18–23   The Pharisees and the parents
C'.   24–34   The blind man and the Pharisees
B'.   35–38   The blind man and Jesus
A'.   39–41   Jesus and the Pharisees

Our analysis will be by scene, not attempting complete exegesis, but tracing the ironic movements of the narrative. They are the same simultaneous upward and downward movements we have already observed in the Gospel as a whole. The man born blind is the one who sees with increasing clarity; the ones who claim sight plunge into progressively thickening night.[6]

Scene One: verses 1–7. Scholars differ on the original extent of the healing story, an indication that the author integrated it well. Notable for its total effect on the narrative is the very general way in which the blind man is introduced. He is not even called *tis anthrōpos,* but simply *anthrōpos,* thus de-emphasizing his particularity and hinting that for John all humankind is born blind. The disciples are present only as foils. Their line in verse 2 is a red-herring remark in its immediate context but serves both to clarify the purpose of Jesus' signs and to initiate the recurring motif of *hamartia* in this chapter.[7] Jesus' explanation—that the blindness is "that the works of God might be made manifest in him"—has a parallel in 11:4 where Lazarus' illness is "for the glory of God." The choice of *phanerōthē* in 9:3, however, is peculiarly appropriate to the theme of blindness and sight (see 3:21). All available vocabulary is summoned to carry the image of Light. Most significant is the simple fact of Jesus' gift—not restoration—of sight. He takes all the initiative; the blind man's only part is obedience—"he went and washed and came back seeing." Of this fact we will constantly be reminded: he can *see*. Significantly, no mention is made of Jesus when the man returns. Verses 8–34 comprise the longest absence of Jesus in John's Gospel.

Scene Two: verses 8–12. The neighbors now discuss the fact and the method of this miracle and the whereabouts of the one who performed it. First they must establish the fact: "Is not this the man who used to sit and beg?" Ironically, both answers given are correct: "It is he"; and then again, "No, but he is like him."[8] The man's brief "*Egō eimi*" affirms all. Having established the miracle, the neighbors ask *how*—a seemingly inconsequential question which will be asked four times in this chapter. The reply is to the point and contains the healed man's first innocently suggestive reference to Jesus:[9] "The *anthrōpos*, the one called Jesus, made clay and anointed . . . and said. . . ." The particularity of Jesus is stressed, as is his initiating activity; and the designation *anthrōpos,* as we have seen, is both the least that can be said of Jesus and also much more than the healed man can now comprehend. Understandably, the crowd asks of Jesus' whereabouts, to which the man must confess, *Ouk oida,* "I do not know." It is worth noting that in chapter 9 the prominent motif of *knowledge* is always expressed by *oida,* rather than *ginōskō.* Conceptually, the word *oida* belongs to the realm of *seeing,* as its early relationship to *eidon* (both are derived from $\digamma \iota \delta$-, root of *vision* and *wisdom*) makes clear.[10] The newly-sighted man, like the one in Mark 8:24 who at first saw people as moving trees, confesses what he does not yet perceive.

Scene Three: verses 13–17. The man is now brought to the Pharisees, perhaps because, as we are now told, the healing has transpired on the sabbath. They ask their first *how* and the man's response is now the sixth reference to the fact of his sight (vss. 7, 10,

11, 13, 14, 15). Ironically, some of the Pharisees instantly conclude that Jesus cannot be from God since he has broken the sabbath. The man is not sure where Jesus is, but the Pharisees are very sure where he is not from.

Implied in the accusation is the charge that Jesus is a "sinner," which others of the Pharisees promptly question: "How can a man who is a sinner do such signs?" A *schisma* ensues between those who have seen the sign and those who have seen the sinner. As a result they venture a personal question of the healed man, "What do you say about him, since he has opened your eyes?" The man is thus nudged by Jesus' enemies into taking a step of faith in Jesus: "He is a prophet." It is the man's second, more developed ascription to Jesus, another faltering step on the way to perfect sight. The Pharisees do not argue, but their discomfort is evident in the abrupt close of scene and their immediate change of tactic in what follows.[11]

Scene Four: verses 18–23. No longer is there a faction of Pharisees speaking for Jesus. They leave the stage as quietly as did Jesus and the neighbors, and as the parents will shortly. The cast is dramatically narrowing in preparation for the focused dualism of one fledgling believer against the hardened opposition of disbelief. "The Jews" (a term withheld until sympathetic Pharisees have left) are altering their point of attack. Since the charge of sabbath violation has failed, their only hope of escape is to deny that the miracle has happened. The neighbors' question in verse 8 is now pursued again, but with a crucial change.

Instead of "Is this the man who was born blind?" they accuse: "Was this man ever blind?" The man can clearly see—*how* do the parents propose to explain his vision, unless someone has lied about his past? The parents are not especially courageous, but they will not misrepresent the central fact. "We know [*oidamen*] that this is our son, and that he was born blind." As for the *how* and the *who* ("the Jews" had not asked "who" but John would have no one forget), the parents defer, saying, "Ask him. He is of age, he will speak for himself." There is irony here, of course, for the parents' stammering fear has boxed in "the Jews" once more. The Pharisees have *already* questioned the son, and he has already spoken for himself—quite clearly. Their uneasiness with his version is precisely what had led them to this new tactic—which has failed. As Bultmann says, the noncommittal answer of the parents "mercilessly leaves the authorities with the responsibility for their own judgment."[12]

Most importantly, there is now no denying the miracle. As verse 18 makes clear, even "the Jews" now recognize that the man had been blind and received his sight. The subsequent interrogation and persecution must be done *in spite of* the established miracle of opened eyes. This crucial point, along with the revelation here of the terrible cost for Jews who confess Jesus in a later day, explains the centrality of this scene in the structure of chapter 9.[13] Here we are told that belief in Jesus will result in expulsion from a cherished community, and that disbelief in him will require deliberate blindness to the undeniable works of God.

Scene Five: verses 24–34. If chapter 9 dramatizes the rising of a believer and the falling of those who will not believe, scene five presents the critical point at which their paths intersect and their eyes briefly meet. Left with no alternative, the hostile authorities call the man a second time. Again their tactic has changed; now they employ categorical assertions and pure intimidation. The multiple irony of "Give glory to God; we know this man is a sinner" has already been noted.[14] "The Jews" invoke the name of God to deny the work of God; they command the man to speak the truth, and in the next breath prove they are closed to the truth; emphatically they shout what they *know* and prove their utter ignorance.

Unlike them, the man is willing to admit (again) what he does not know, though we may suspect he is beginning to indulge in understatement. Like his parents, he confronts "the Jews" only with the incontrovertible fact of his sight. Their retort reflects total frustration, for they revert a third time to the question of how the miracle was done. They even ask twice, the first instance perhaps inadvertently hinting at the larger change in the man: "What did he do to you?" Weary of this pointless repetition, the man born blind accuses them of being deaf: "I told you and you didn't hear!" Then he smiles the sly smile of irony and with wonderfully feigned innocence asks, "Why do you want to hear it again? Do you too want to become his disciples?" (See pp. 81–82.)

The man's verbal dagger apparently finds its mark, for they now "revile him." Their response is an interesting achievement. They juxtapose their discipleship to Moses with the man's discipleship to Jesus. Significantly, nothing has yet been said about the man's discipleship—his real belief is still to come. So, as in verse 17 where they led him to profess Jesus as prophet, they now prod him toward discipleship. Verse 29, another verse already discussed, (pp. 68–69) contains their third confident claim to knowledge—now about Moses—and their first admission of ignorance.

They do not mean it as an admission, of course; they intend *we do not know where he comes from* to be a slur of Jesus' origins. But as usual they say more than they know. Now the healed man's mockery of them takes wings. "Why this is a marvel! You do not know where he comes from, and yet he opened my eyes." He underlines their ignorance with the pronoun—*humeis ouk oidate: "You* of all people do not perceive!" The remark bears resemblance to Jesus' verbal irony in 3:10, "Are you the teacher of Israel and do not understand this?"

The healed man is as fully an *eirōn* as his healer. Also, like Jesus' repetition of Nicodemus' *we know* in 3:11, the healed man now didactically matches the *oidamen* of "the Jews" (vs. 31). He no longer mocks them, however, but genuinely advances an argument. Expertly, he begins with the ideas agreed upon by all—that God does not listen to sinners but to those who do his will. Reminding them that such gift of sight as he had received was unheard of, the newly sighted man concludes: God did this thing; therefore Jesus is no sinner, but is from God (vss. 31–33). Given the mutually accepted presuppositions and the undeniable evidence, the argument is irrefutable, decisively settling the schism of verse 16. On no reasonable grounds may Jesus now be rejected. As the author has constructed the trial, one may now only embrace the facts—or shut one's eyes to them.

"The Jews" leap to the latter darkness. The only response left them is vilification: "*You* were born in utter sin, and would *you* teach *us*?" In this wonderful line the author has his fun. The emphatic pronouns are present to underline their alazony. The answer is, of course, yes. He of all people *has* taught them, and done so with savvy as well as insight. It should be recalled that in their earlier interview with him they had ventured to ask his opinion of Jesus. Now they have gotten what they asked for in full.[15]

Their remark about his being "born in utter sin" is both cruel and ludicrous. It takes up the long-discarded view of the disciples in verse 2 that blindness was punishment for sin, which is particularly ridiculous in view of the fact that the man can now see.[16] Of course, "the Jews'" capacity to identify "sinners" is already in serious question; and to the man's credit, he is now honored with the same charge they have laid against Jesus. Perhaps the most telling aspect of their remark is that it is an admission of their knowledge that this sighted man had indeed been born blind. So they must be rid of him. The narrator's next line closes the scene on a sobering note that abruptly ends all laughter: "And they cast him out."

Scene Six: verses 35–38. No sooner is the man cast out than Jesus is at his side; again, "the Jews" have done the man an accidental favor. As before, Jesus is active and initiating: he hears, finds, and says, "Do you believe in the Son of man?" The man's reply, "And who is he, sir, that I may believe in him?" is exactly like the other two instances of "irony of identity" we have observed (4:19–26; 20:14–16). In all three cases, a character, not knowing who Jesus is, addresses him as *kurie* and makes reference to Messiah/Son of man/Jesus—thought to be absent. In all three Jesus then quickly reveals his identity in the most appropriate way.

To the woman at the well who is given to misunderstandings he speaks directly, "I am he, the one speaking to you" (4:26). With his dear friend at the tomb, he need only call her name (20:16). Now to the man born blind Jesus beams and says, *"You have seen him* and he is the one speaking to you" (vs. 37). *Oraō,* in contrast to *blepō* used elsewhere in this story, probably hints that this sight is now more than merely physical; the use of the perfect tense points to its permanence.[17] Verse 38, missing from p[75] and ℵ*, is probably a very early liturgical interpolation; but it adds a fitting conclusion to the scene. His fully-aware *kurie* provides a pinnacle for the man's progressive faith (cf. vss. 11, 17, 33, 36).

Two aspects of this scene can be compared with its parallel scene, verses 8–12. There the neighbors ask the man where Jesus is, and he responds, "I do not know." This exchange serves little function in its context. It may now be seen as an important exchange, however, for the man finally gets his answer: Jesus is outside the synagogue, at the side of those who are cast out. His presence is the embodiment of 6:37: "All that the Father gives me will come to me; and the one who comes to me I will not cast out." The *how* question of the neighbors has been answered, "The *anthrōpos,* the one called Jesus. . . ." Now when Jesus appears he is Son of man. Scholars often note that "Son of man" in verse 35 is a bit surprising; we expect "Son of God."[18] Quite possibly, the title is used here because the theme is one of judgment. In view of the man's remark in verse 11, however, and the Pharisees' contemptuous use of *man* for Jesus in verses 16 and 24, "Son of man" in verse 35 serves a crucial ironic function, fulfilling and expanding the healed man's word and mocking the contempt of his accusers.

Scene Seven: verses 39–41. The irony of chapter 9 is epitomized by Jesus' saying of verse 39, "For judgment I came into this world, that those who do not see may see, and that those who see may become blind." As Jesus speaks, the healed man fades from view and a spotlight falls on a group of Pharisees.[19] Their sneering question, "Are we also blind?" is the kind we have come to expect. The particle *mē* signals negative expectation, so we are certain that Jesus will tell them they *are* blind, or better still, the author will answer them with awful silence. To our surprise—and surely theirs—the tactic is changed. Jesus *agrees* with them. They are not blind. "If you were blind, you would have no sin. But now that you say, 'We see,' your sin remains."

The irony is ruthless and has all the more power because the author alters his established technique. The blindness Jesus means is the kind of blindness a person *knows* as blindness. It is a blindness that knows to beg and to obey (vss. 7–8). Of this infirmity the Pharisees unfortunately have none. Their disease, quite different, is an illusion of sight, which has led them to a far deeper darkness than they know.

They have been raging about the blind man's sin and the sin of Jesus. Their claim to *see* such sin is precisely what traps them in their own. Given the hallowed tone with which the Johannine community used the word *menein,* to say of anyone that "sin remains" is a particularly horrible judgment. John thus ends the chapter with a dark parallel to its beginning; Jesus now consigns those who "see" to a terrible darkness.

The simultaneous upward and downward movement of which we have spoken is carefully crafted by the author and indeed has been noted by commentators before. The man's rise to belief is marked by his progressive evaluations of Jesus (the man, a prophet, from God, Lord), and his increasing boldness and skill as ironist and defender of Jesus. (Is it significant that this man, the clearest representative of Johannine apologists in conversation with the synagogue, is depicted as a quick-witted *eirōn?*) Ironically enough, his progress upward seems at least partially assisted by the downward plunging Pharisees, who give him opportunity to reflect on Jesus' identity (vs. 17), think of the man's discipleship before he does (vs. 28), and then cast him into the very presence of Jesus (vs. 34). Their fall is even more clearly marked than his triumph.

They begin by seeming to accept the fact of healing (vs. 15); some of their number are positive about Jesus (vs. 16); and they are willing to ask the healed man's opinion (vs. 17). By scene four, however, they are trying to discredit the healing. Having run up against undeniable evidence for it, they lose all interest in the truth and try to trap the man (vss. 24ff.), hurl accusations at him and at Jesus, and finally "cast him out." In the end they are judged to be hopelessly in the darkness of sin. Their alazony is in stark opposition to the simple openness of the man. In contrast to his threefold confession of ignorance (twice *ouk oida,* I do not know/perceive/see, vss. 12, 25; followed by his irony of identity, vs. 36), they make three confident statements of what they know (twice *hēmeis oidamen, we* know/perceive/see, vss. 24, 29; see also vs. 16).[20]

The irony is intensified by the author's juxtaposition of parallel scenes. We have tried to demonstrate this technique in the analysis, but can summarize in the following figure:

Jesus and blind man	1–7	39–41	Jesus and Pharisees
"blindness" given sight	7	41	"seeing" made blind
blind man and neighbors	8–12	35–38	blind man and Jesus
where is Jesus?	12	35	Jesus outside synagogue
the man Jesus	11	35	Jesus, Son of man
blind man and Pharisees	13–17	24–34	blind man and Pharisees
this man not from God	16	33	this man is from God
what do you say?	17	34	would you teach us?

18–23	Pharisees and parents
18–20	the miracle is irrefutable
22	confessing Jesus means expulsion

The theme is clearly trial and judgment. The Pharisees begin by trying Jesus *in absentia*. When the evidence upholds him, and their star witness defends him, they quickly pronounce Jesus guilty and put the man on trial, whom they also find guilty and condemn to exile. Jesus' appearance then vindicates the man and reveals dramatically that it is the Pharisees who have been on trial—and their guilt remains.

With artful restraint the author withholds the word *judgment (krima)* until the last scene, a brilliant correspondence to the sudden turning of the tables, though that process, like the *krima,* has been silently at work from the beginning. Perhaps we thought at first that this giving of light would be a purely positive manifestation of the works of God (vs. 3). Now we recall the grimmer aspect of what Jesus had said about the light. The light is not only the life of humankind (1:4), it is "the judgment" (3:19)—the dreaded brilliance which exposes the deeds of those who fear it (3:20), and so drives them into the deepest darkness of all, the willing refusal to see.

The Trial of Jesus: 18:28—19:16, 19–22

The Johannine trial before Pilate is presented in 18:28—19:16. These verses contain their own structural unity and comprise a thematic whole. We include 19:19–22 in the discussion, however, for though these verses are part of a new episode and structure, they both continue the theme of the trial and conclude the adversarial relationship between Pilate and "the Jews" concerning Jesus. They comprise Pilate's final verdict and so provide an ironic epilogue to the trial.

Like the drama of the man born blind, the trial narrative is presented in seven scenes.[21] The organizing principle, in fact, is the shifting of scenes from outside the praetorium to the inside and back again. The author is quite deliberate in repeating that Pilate "went out to the Jews" (18:29, 38; 19:4, 13) and "entered the praetorium" to converse with Jesus (18:33; 19:9). The result is what Dodd has called "two stages . . . a front stage and a back."[22]

In Pilate's shuttling back and forth the author portrays the human predicament in which one must choose between Jesus and the world. Pilate unfortunately believes he can escape responsibility by not choosing. John's irony in part entails the fall of Pilate who sinks deeper and deeper into complicity in Jesus' execution as his protestations of Jesus' innocence intensify.[23] More terrible yet is the downward movement of "the Jews," who now reach the point of complete self-destruction.

Over against this double downward movement is the ironic elevation of Jesus to the office of King, Judge, and Son of God. So again there is a trial motif in which the apparent judge and accusers are in fact judged and condemned by the One thought to be on trial. Blank is quite right in saying that the best title for this narrative is "Pilate and the Jews before Jesus."[24]

Scene One: 18:28–32. The scene opens when "it was early." Is this allusion another instance of John's silent commentary by way of ironic imagery? Bultmann, recalling the night of 13:30, says of 18:28, "the day of the victory of Jesus over the world is breaking."[25] While such an intention cannot be categorically denied, the mention of only *prōi*, without any reference to darkness or light lessens the likelihood of the term's symbolic significance.

Without doubt, however, a weighty irony is intended in the next line: "They themselves did not enter the praetorium, so that they might not be defiled, but might eat the Passover." Ingeniously, John presents a motive for "the Jews" to hang back which both makes possible his double staging and is itself supremely ironic. These soon-to-be murderers are at pains to maintain their purity. They are quite eager to enlist a pagan in the disposition of their crime, but they will not dream of entering his house. Further, their concern is Passover, a compound irony that Brown expresses well: "they fear that ritual impurity will prevent their eating the Passover lamb, but unwittingly they are delivering up to death him who is the Lamb of God (1:29) and thus are making possible the true Passover."[26]

When Pilate asks what Jesus has done, they reply, "If this man were not an evildoer, we would not have handed him over to you." Some interpreters stress a tone of insolence here,[27] but as already indicated (p. 79), we find in this rather vague untruth a desperate and embarrassed evasion of Pilate's question. One of the several progressions in the trial narrative is the degree of fearless specificity with which "the Jews" falsely accuse Jesus.

They get off to a stammering start but will warm up to their treachery as they go along. The fact that treachery is the issue is revealed in their word *paredōkamen,* a verb meaning in this Gospel not simply "hand over" but "betray." Pilate's response to them throughout the trial seems to be motivated both by a desire to avoid dealing with Jesus and a desire to humiliate them. Both motives are at work when he says, "Take him yourselves and judge him by your own law," but the dominant tone, if not for Pilate then certainly for the author, is sarcasm. The truth is, since chapter 5 "the Jews" have been trying furiously to judge Jesus by their own law, with embarrassing results. The law of Moses simply will not condemn him. So Pilate's words mock their impotence to kill Jesus; and they themselves are more correct than they know in confessing they have no legal ground for the deed.

"The Jews'" conscious reason for not disposing of Jesus themselves is presumably that he undergo the shame of Roman crucifixion. The narrator's comment in verse 32, however, makes mockery of their designs. Their carefully plotted plan to put Jesus on a Roman cross is only in fulfillment of what Jesus himself has already chosen. The phrase "signifying what death he was to die" is repeated verbatim from 12:33, where Jesus had spoken of being lifted up and drawing all unto himself. By pointing to this previous prediction, the author indirectly presents the larger irony of his Gospel. "The Jews" have him shamefully crucified to prevent the world from going after him, when in fact he long ago had chosen just such a way to gather the world unto himself.[28]

Scene Two: 18:33–38a. Pilate now goes into the praetorium and faces Jesus. He asks rather bluntly, "Are you the King of the Jews?"[29] Ironically, the representative of Caesar addresses the One through whom the world was made about a provincial dominion he is sure the prisoner does not possess. We have not been told that pretending to kingship was the charge made against Jesus, and he himself will raise the question of where Pilate got the phrase in verse 34. In any case, the charge is firmly in the tradition, for Pilate begins with this question in all four Gospels. Only John, however, makes so much of it, for Jesus is called king no less than eleven times in the Johannine Passion account.

Jesus responds, "Do you say this of your own accord, or did others say it to you about me?" While some interpreters take the question to be seeking out necessary information,[30] it is better to hear Jesus—who "knew what was in man" (2:25)—speaking ironically. Not unlike the blind man who asked "the Jews" if they too wanted to become disciples (9:27), Jesus deftly turns the trial on Pilate from the outset. The issue for Pilate cannot be what the world thinks of Jesus but what *he* thinks. In our judgment, Jesus hears Pilate repeating a charge made by others, and with the feigned innocence of his own question confronts the governor with the necessity of making his own decision. In any case, Jesus has now taken up the interrogation; it is clear who is judging whom.

Pilate's response is fittingly about himself: "Am I a Jew?" These words are a shrug, denying his knowledge of Jewish religious issues or perhaps denying personal interest in Jesus. The question is prefaced, however, with one of those negative particles *(mēti)* out of which the author has fashioned so much of his irony. Here it stands as a clue for us to ask: *Is* Pilate a Jew? Insofar as "the Jews" represent the world's rejection of Jesus, Pilate is already in the process, even while despising them, of joining them. His constant movement toward them in the trial is an enactment of that ironic alliance.[31] It can also be said that, given Pilate's designation of Jesus as "King of the Jews," the question "Am I a Jew?" hints at the deeper question, "Are you my king?"

From this unwitting mockery of himself, Pilate quickly moves to unwitting mockery of "the Jews." "Your own nation and the chief priests have handed you over to me." In this remark (cf. 1:11) Pilate slurs his adversaries more than he knows. To the reader an *ethnos* is a pagan state, the chief priests represent a temple doomed, and the word for *handed over* here means "betrayed." Given such rejection, Pilate wants to know, "What have you done?" This is a crucial question indeed, the answer to which establishes not the guilt of Jesus but the guilt of "the Jews" also. What he has done is "many good works from the Father," (10:32); and "these very works which I am doing bear me witness that the Father has sent me" (5:36).

Jesus does not answer Pilate's question, but enters into a brief discourse explaining that his kingship is "not of this world" (vs. 36). Pilate seizes on this statement as an admission of kingship: "So, then, you are a king?"[32] The personal pronoun at the end of the sentence stresses the incongruity of such a claim for such an unlikely person.[33] Jesus answers as he does in the Synoptics *(Su legeis):* "You say that I am a king." Scholars argue whether this remark is affirmative, adversative, or qualifying.[34] What must be seen, however, is the profound rightness of this reply in a Gospel in which strangers and enemies have borne constant witness to the identity of Jesus. The author would have us reflect on the fact that indeed Pilate has said it, just as Caiaphas has said it in his way, and others have said it in theirs: this Jesus whom they will neither recognize nor receive is by their own unconscious admission who he claims to be.

The rest of Jesus' answer is a summary statement of his function in the world: "to bear witness to the truth." His final remark opens the door again for Pilate to engage himself in the real issue: *"Everyone who is of the truth hears my voice* (vs. 38). But Pilate resists. The tone of his "What is truth?" is impossible to decipher. It may be scornful or cynical, it may reflect the beginnings of interest or the blank incomprehension of one who has no idea what Jesus means.[35] The dramatic irony of the question lies in our knowledge that the one to whom the question about truth is asked is himself the Truth (14:6).

The fact that the scene ends on that question provoked Bacon long ago to pen that marvelous line: "'What is truth?' said jesting Pilate, and would not stay for an answer."[36] It is just as possible that the unanswered question concludes the scene because the Johannine ironist invites us to reflect upon what—and who—the Answer is.

Scene Three: 18:38b–40. Pilate leaves Jesus and returns outside to "the Jews." Though the author has not disclosed to us the procurator's mind, we now see that Pilate is impressed enough, or disturbed enough, to announce, "I find no crime in him," the first of three protestations of Jesus' innocence (18:38; 19:4, 6). The narrative has reached a critical point.[37] As in the drama of the man born blind, the essential fact of the case is settled early on. The trial will proceed with the judge knowing full well the innocence of the defendant. The whole issue now becomes: what will Pilate do with what he knows?[38]

The answer is immediately clear. Instead of acting on his conviction, he forfeits the decision to the world outside. He tells "the Jews" he will release one prisoner for them and asks if they want "the King of the Jews." It is difficult to say why he uses that phrase for Jesus here, reported also in Mark 15:9. If he is taunting "the Jews" with it, he is also lessening the chance of Jesus' release, revealing an ambivalence about dealing with him justly. Dramatically, the phrase does force "the Jews" to make their choice about Jesus with the sound of his rightful title over them ringing in their ears. They do not pause, however. Though no other candidate has been offered for release (cf. Matt. 27:17) they quickly cry out, "Not this fellow but Barabbas!" The narrator intrudes to whisper the irony: "Now Barabbas was a robber."

The word *lēstēs* has already been used to signify a false alternative to the Good Shepherd (10:1, 8). Meeks puts the matter well: "the Jews reject their king and choose instead a *lēstēs;* unable to hear the voice of the Good Shepherd, they follow one of the 'robbers' who comes before him."[39] Ironically, too, "the Jews" have presumably brought Jesus to Pilate claiming the "King of the Jews" poses a political threat; but when offered a choice, the one for whom they plead is a political criminal.[40]

Scene Four: 19:1–3. In this, the central scene of the trial, Jesus is scourged and mocked as King of the Jews. According to Matthew and Mark, the scourging took place following the sentencing, just prior to the crucifixion; and indeed normal procedure in such matters would substantiate their report.[41] John moves the scourging to make it part of Pilate's strange way of trying to help Jesus (cf. Luke 23:16, 22). The irony here is macabre. Pilate pronounces Jesus innocent both before and after the episode; he is apparently trying to win sympathy and release for him. Yet in the process he is half-killing the one he would so discretely defend. Pilate's sense of justice is steadily warping.[42]

Unlike the other Gospels, John does not call the soldiers' gaming with Jesus "mockery," but simply lets us see and hear and reflect. They crown him with thorns, robe him in royal purple, and hail him King of the Jews. They speak better than they know and perhaps prefigure the coming days when Gentiles would call him king. The dramatic position of this event is crucial. While Matthew and Mark place it at the end, John makes it the trial's centerpiece. Unlike the Synoptics, there will be no indication of removal of the royal garb (cf. Matt. 27:31; Mark 15:20); Jesus will stride toward his cross in kingly attire. As Meeks says, "In John the scene is not the satirical aftermath of Jesus' condemnation, but the prelude to his paradoxical exaltation."[43]

The hypothesis of Josef Blank is appealing. He maintains that John presents the trial in the form of "an ironic and bizarre distortion" of a "King's Epiphany."[44] The presentation of a king to his people should include first a proclamation of kingship, as has been provided by Pilate, and then the enthroning and investiture, which the soldiers brutally conduct. Two other elements, the king's grand appearance before his people and their unified acclamation of his sovereignty, are given lurid portrayals in what follows.

Scene Five: 19:4–8. Pilate goes out to "the Jews" for the third time and again proclaims Jesus' innocence. Jesus *came out*—was not "led out"—and he is *wearing* the crown and robe—not "clothed" in them.[45] He still commands his coronation.

The rich irony of Pilate's ascription, "Behold the man!" has been probed already (pp. 106–107). He means either to provoke sympathy or ridicule; the reader knows he points to Jesus' dignity as Messiah, Son of man, and the ultimate human being. The chief priests and officers, however, can only cry out, "Crucify, crucify!" Does "cried out" recall the Hosannas "cried out" earlier to the "King of Israel"?[46] Pilate is outraged and tells them "with wrathful irony"[47] to crucify Jesus themselves, for (for the third and last time) "I find no crime in him." Pilate knows they cannot crucify, and he mocks their helplessness. Strangely, however, even while maintaining his refusal to condemn Jesus, he will not choose to set him free.

"The Jews" respond with another self-indictment: "We have a law, and by that law he must die, because he has made himself the Son of God." The reader knows by now that their law has an entirely different word to say about Jesus. Still, they are, as usual, more correct than they know. Their law does indeed bear witness to the necessity that this Son of God should die.[48]

It is interesting that now at the end they should finally refer to Jesus as "Son of God." Brown has noted, in fact, that in this denied ascription is completed a mock reversal of the titles given to Jesus at the close of chapter 1.[49] There, in a "crescendo of belief," Jesus is called Son of God (1:49), King of Israel (1:49), and Son of man (1:51). Here he is mockingly or incredulously called King of the Jews (19:3), the man (19:5), and Son of God (19:7). The last word rattles Pilate. Like the hundreds of Caesar's soldiers who fell terrified before Jesus' "I AM," Caesar's governor is now terror-stricken to hear that Jesus claims to be Son of God, and anxiously rushes back into his presence.

Scene Six: 19:8–11. Pilate's desperate question is "Where are you from?" It is an even more pertinent question than his earlier "What have you done?" Indeed the whole Gospel has been answering the question of Jesus' origin; and accordingly, Jesus himself now offers only a weighty silence. Pilate, in panicked exasperation, continues, "You will not speak to *me*? Do you not know that I have power to release you and power to crucify you?" Ironically, he boasts of his power to release, when it is clear that before the pressures of the world outside he has no such power. Soon he will explicitly try to release Jesus and will miserably fail (vs. 12).

Jesus defuses his pathetic threat. What power Pilate has is his only by higher authority. Even Pilate could not fail to fathom this *double entendre:* Jesus speaks less of the Caesar above Pilate than the God above both Caesar and Pilate. Since Jesus is "Son of God" and his *pothen* (vs. 9) is the very *anōthen* from which Pilate's little power is granted, it is clear again that the defendant is the judge; the prisoner has authority over the one who boasts authority.[50]

Further, Jesus' next remark makes the outcome clear: "therefore he who betrayed me to you has the greater sin." If on one level this cryptic saying extends to Pilate a measure of grace, it also signifies the governor's impotence. No matter what Pilate claims about a power to release, he is now destined to play a part in killing Jesus; and for all his blustering about his importance in this affair, the little governor will not even rate the larger share of guilt. His "power to release" is now non-existent; his "power to crucify" shrinks to the dubious role of minor accomplice.

Scene Seven: 19:12–16. Pilate now proves Jesus' point. Genuinely frightened, he is determined to release Jesus and at last makes an overt attempt. He is much too late. "The Jews" know their game with him and are prepared to play their ace. "If you release this man you are not Caesar's friend; every one who makes himself a king sets himself against Caesar." Their mention of the Son of God has set them back, so they return to the lie about Jesus' political kingship—with the inadvertent truth that Jesus *is* in a way set against Caesar.[51] C. F. Evans notes that with this outcry, "The roles are now reversed. In place of the Roman governor offering the Jewish people the choice, 'Which will you have, Jesus or Barabbas?' the Jewish people offer the governor the choice, 'Which will you have, Christ or Caesar?'"[52]

From this point on, Pilate knows Jesus will die. He has sought cooperation from Jesus inside and a bargain with the world outside. Beaten by both, his final recourse is to belittle them. He brings Jesus out for the second time, and what he does next scholars will forever debate. He either sits upon the judgment seat or sits Jesus upon it.[53] Grammatically, either is possible, but the better case can be made for Pilate taking the seat, for *kathizein* is most often intransitive (see 12:14).

Theologically and stylistically, one can argue that John envisioned Jesus on the *bēma*. It is not impossible that the author is deliberately ambiguous, honoring both the historical probability that Pilate sat and the suggestive possibility for perceptive readers that Jesus sat. There is no doubt, however, that even if only the intransitive sense is intended, we are still to see Pilate's presence on the *bēma* as ironic. No matter who holds the bench, Jesus is the judge (5:27).

Obviously this scene is crucial, for the author pauses to locate its geographical and temporal coordinates. The time is of particular significance, given as it is in reference to Passover. Though the scholars may be correct who say that John deliberately identifies the hour of Jesus' condemnation with the hour that slaughter of the paschal lambs began, in our judgment the real irony does not lie in any sacrificial imagery. "The Jews" are about to renounce their covenant with God. How terribly ironic that the chief priests will abandon Israel's faith at the very moment when they are to begin preparations for the celebration of God's faithfulness to them![54]

Pilate now sneers at them: "Behold your king!" There is no ambiguity here as there was in "Behold the man!" Now he presents only the taunting truth and he knows it. Their response, as before, is "an ironic and bizarre distortion" of a people's acclamation of their king:[55] "Away, away—crucify him!" They have utterly rejected Jesus; but in the author's view this is not enough. They must be made to confess the full implication of their choice. Pilate with wicked irony invites them into the final noose: "Shall I crucify your king?" Ironically enough, while "the Jews" have just urged Pilate to be true to his king, this pagan now invites them to consider their own. Will they forfeit the Messiah, and so cease to be the messianic people of God?

They will, with gusto. "We have no king but Caesar!" is the unspeakable answer spoken by the chief priests of Israel. It is a sacrilege no Jew could utter without forfeit of faith. Israel has but one King (Judg. 8:23; 1 Sam. 8:7; Isa. 26:13). In the Passover Haggadah soon to be rehearsed, the concluding hymn of the Greater Hallel, the *Nismat,* would read:

> From everlasting to everlasting thou art God;
> Beside thee we have no king, redeemer, or savior,
> No liberator, deliverer, provider.
> None who takes pity in every time of distress and trouble.
> We have no king but thee.[56]

The death of the nation, so dreaded by the chief priest (11:47–50), is now wrought by their own hand. To reject Jesus they renounce God, and so reveal after all that Jesus and the Father are one. Lindars remarks, "So with splendid irony John makes the Jews utter the ultimate blasphemy in the same breath as their final rejection of Jesus."[57] Heinrich Schlier marks a wider circle of victims:

> How reigns the irony of God! The Jews win a worldly triumph over Jesus, and indeed over Pilate, and thereby surrender that for which they wanted to triumph: their own Messiah and their own hope. Pilate wins a worldly triumph over the Jews, who now have bound themselves to Caesar, and over Jesus—and thereby surrenders what is given him by his Caesar: the authority and the justice of his political-judicial office.[58]

Mindful of irony's varying moods, Culpepper writes, "The implied author does not wink or smile. Is that grim satisfaction or tears in his eyes?"[59]

The tragedy can go no deeper. Verse 16 concludes the trial and condemns both Pilate and "the Jews." The governor "hands over" Jesus, that is, *betrays* him to them, the chief priests, to crucify him. The fact that the soldiers actually crucified Jesus (vs. 23) does not alter the author's point. "The Jews" have confessed that their law forbids them to kill, but the law is forsaken along with their faith. The chief priests of Israel, charged with purity of person and fidelity to the law, befoul themselves completely by nailing their King to a tree.

Epilogue: 19:19–22. When the King has been enthroned Pilate takes his last revenge on "the Jews" and pays his last twisted homage to Jesus. The *titulus* is mentioned in every Gospel, but in none is it elaborated so much as in John. It summarizes the irony of Jesus' relationship with Israel. "King of the Jews" is ironic because he is obviously not their king, and again because obviously he is. It is ironic because he himself has in life fled the people's desire to crown him (6:15). It is supremely ironic because it is precisely "the Jews"—the name reserved for those who hate him and have demanded his death—over whom he has triumphed and, quite unknown to them, reigns.[60] Pilate writes the *titulus* in Hebrew, Latin, and Greek, thus making his testimony a proclamation to the world, extending Christ's kingship far beyond "the Jews," and fulfilling Jesus' prophecy that when he is lifted up he will draw all people to himself. Significantly, "the Jews" are disturbed by this placard,[61] but Pilate refuses to reduce the title to a claim of Jesus and leaves it his own testimony. Just as Jesus has pointed out following the governor's first unwitting acclamation of kingship, "You say . . . ," so now Pilate affirms of this final ascription, "I have written." The irrevocability of the testimony provides a far-reaching conclusion to this drama of trial and enthronement.

Like the drama of the man born blind, this narrative in seven scenes has a chiastic structure. We do not reproduce it here because other writers have done so.[62] Its pertinent features for irony have been noted in the analysis. We can only add that the account of the *titulus,* designated here as an epilogue to the trial, provides a fitting counterpart for the trial's central scene in which Jesus is explicitly hailed as "King of the Jews." We have witnessed in this narrative two downward movements and one exaltation. Pilate, while being progressively impressed by Jesus inside, is at the same time progressively abusive of him, and enslaved by the disbelieving world outside. "The Jews" move from an intent to kill Jesus, through a repudiation of their God, into the murder of their King. Jesus, accused, threatened, and mocked, processes royally through the trial, interrogating his own judge, wearing well his robe and crown, and moving in stately silence through the rubble of his people's forsaken covenant to his own throne—uplifted, inscribed, and spanning the world.

7

IRONY AND
THE JOHANNINE CONTEXT

Robert Browning's poem, "A Death in the Desert," portrays the aged author of John's Gospel in the final minutes of life. True to form, the old man is meditative, repetitious, simple, difficult, profound—and smiling: "For certain smiles began about his mouth." Chapters 3 through 6 have confirmed the Johannine smile—and the tears that sometimes frame it. Irony has emerged as a persistent technique and prevailing mood in the Fourth Gospel. The time now comes to note the significance of our literary findings in terms of the Gospel's setting, its history, thought, intent, and effect. Given the data in chapter 2 concerning irony's presuppositions and functions, the relationship between the author and the readers, do our findings in the Gospel itself shed any light on the context and the purpose of this book?

Irony and the Johannine Milieu

Johannine irony undeniably gives witness to a religious setting shaped by Judaism and a cultural setting influenced by Hellenism. The issue of this Gospel's religious and cultural background is a long-standing one which need not be detailed here.[1] The trend in recent years has been to locate the Fourth Gospel's religious thought primarily in a Jewish setting,[2] and with this we concur. At the same time many scholars maintain that this Gospel has affinities with a much broader intellectual base. This feature may stem from a deliberate syncretism designed to reach a diverse audience,[3] or from the indisputable fact that Judaism itself, even in Palestine, was in many ways "Hellenized" in the first century. The irony of John's Gospel

139

takes its place among many other features pointing to a Jewish/Hellenistic milieu; it represents *primarily Hellenistic technique* employed to treat *themes of primarily Jewish concern.*

To say that John's irony reflects "primarily Hellenistic technique" is not a concession to those who would call irony "a Greek thing."[4] As has been demonstrated here and elsewhere, irony's art was well known to ancient Israel, and seems in fact to be a universal phenomenon. Johannine irony, however, is in some ways different from the irony in the Old Testament and even from the rest of the irony in the New Testament. Ironies of reversal, of course, the upward and downward movements which we explored earlier, are thoroughly consistent with Hebrew thought. Likewise there is nothing distinctively Greek about "ironies of simple incongruity" (e.g., 10:32) or "irony of events" (e.g., Jesus' death effecting the opposite of his enemies' desire), or even "general dramatic irony" (when readers know what characters do not). There is, however, an element foreign to typical biblical irony—in John's persistent focusing and underlining of irony by the unwitting speeches of his characters. In this "*specific dramatic irony,*" unsuspected *double entendre* abounds, so that the reader may savor to the utmost the truth which the characters cannot or will not see. As we have already seen, Hebrew irony rarely indulged in this kind of elaboration; those Jewish writings engaging in such irony tend to come later (e.g., Esther, Tobit), well after the famous works of the fifth-century Greek tragedians.

The ironic techniques of the Fourth Gospel are far more akin to the techniques of Greek drama. The most fruitful sources of parallels to the ironic speeches and situations in John's Gospel are the tragedies of Sophocles and Euripides and the presaging epic narratives of Homer. It is a commonplace that the Fourth Gospel is presented in dramatic form,[5] but it would be worthwhile to note here just how much like drama—and especially Greek drama—it is.

There is first an *omniscient prologue* in which the essential information about Jesus' origin, identity, and destiny is disclosed to the audience, thus elevating us to a "godlike" perspective, granting knowledge that the groping characters below cannot have, and making us heirs of irony.[6] Once this perspective is bestowed, the narrative and dialogue unfold with subtleties visible only "from above." Scenes are arranged to provide a climactic progression toward the assured outcome. Anticipation and suspense heighten the story's movement.[7] Individual scenes come to climactic conclusions, with endings as suggestive as they are abrupt.[8] Reflections on what has transpired are sometimes offered, much in the style of the chorus in a Greek play.[9] The tale told has no surprises, but is drawn out with marvelous detail of subtlety and suggestion, maximizing the meaning for the reader.[10]

So similar is the dramatic style of John to the classic drama of the Greeks, and so unlike the restrained economy of other biblical writers, that the author's acquaintance with the tradition of classical Greek drama in some form must be postulated. It would be ridiculous, of course, to suppose the author intended to write anything like a play,[11] nor is such acquaintance itself any ground for postulating a birthplace for this Gospel near some cultural center such as Ephesus where Greek theater was in vogue. It is sufficient to say that the Fourth Gospel reflects a cultural milieu in which the ironic style of Homer and the Greek tragedians had made its imprint; and in the late first century few locations would have precluded such an influence. The point is that John's Gospel clearly *reflects* such a milieu more than do other New Testament writings.[12] Explanation of this phenomenon is presently beyond our grasp, but this stylistic feature of the Fourth Gospel is another mark of Johannine eclecticism that students of *Religionsgeschichte* might well pursue.[13]

If the technique is primarily Greek, however, the subject matter of John's irony is largely of Jewish concern. As we observed in chapter 3 John's local irony not only does a great deal of polemicizing specifically against Jews who rejected Jesus, it takes up themes of particular relevance to church/synagogue discussion: the origin of Jesus in relation to scriptural and popular expectations of the Messiah or Prophet; the preeminence of Jesus over the patriarchs; and the meaning and effect of Jesus' death, particularly the coincidence of his rejection and the death of the nation.

Not only is the subject matter of Jewish concern but the effect of the irony sometimes *depends* upon some knowledge of the Old Testament or Jewish tradition. One thinks, for example, of 7:52, where the Pharisees say, "Search and you will see that the prophet is not to rise from Galilee." The irony depends partially upon either the fact that Scripture says nothing of the origin of the Prophet or the fact that several biblical prophets arose from Galilee. Pilate's "Behold the Man!" is a far richer irony if one recalls Zechariah 6:12.[14] The irony in Jesus' encounter with the Samaritan woman at the well is enriched if the Old Testament bethrothal scenes are deeply ingrained. The Old Testament, however, is not the only Jewish presupposition of Johannine irony. Some irony even depends upon a knowledge of the extrabiblical apocalyptic expectation of the Messiah's unknown origin (see 7:27; 9:29; 19:9).

To be sure, not all the Johannine irony requires a Jewish context. The issue of Israel's forfeit of faith is obviously of concern to Gentile Christians, and John's ironic imagery and characterization are universally meaningful. No irony in the Fourth Gospel, however, is better understood outside a Jewish milieu; and most of the ironies are of markedly Jewish interest. We conclude, therefore, that while the techniques employed in John's irony are those of a Hellenistic world, the themes, the targets, and the frequent presuppositions of John's irony all point to a setting very much shaped by relations with Judaism.[15]

Irony and Johannine Duality

We intentionally speak here of the Fourth Gospel's duality rather than its dualism *per se*. That Johannine thought is dualistic is well known and a perennial source of discussion regarding its intellectual heritage. Our concern here, however, ranges beyond John's theology and worldview to explore how consistently the Gospel itself as a literary expression *functions* dualistically, employing a number of devices which invite the reader from one level of meaning to another. Such devices include metaphor, double meaning, misunderstanding, and irony. The word *duality* here refers to the thoroughgoing bilevel literary vision created by the convergence of these devices. There is no question, of course, that the literary techniques grow out of and lead back into the philosophical/theological dualism at the heart of the Gospel's thought. These are no mere "devices." Yet by focusing on them as such, by distinguishing their functions and demonstrating their essential relationship, light may be shed upon the larger dualism which they serve. Our purpose here is not to offer detailed analysis of these devices but to describe them briefly in relation to one another, and particularly to illuminate irony's place among them.

Metaphor

The discourses of the Johannine Jesus are richly metaphorical. One thinks immediately of the "I AM" sayings in which Jesus applies such metaphors as "bread," "light," "the door," "the good shepherd," "the way," and "the vine" to himself. To some of these images are attached extended metaphorical elaborations, and in some cases such elaboration occurs apart from an "I AM" saying (e.g., the discourses on "living water," 4:10–15; 7:37–38). In addition, there are narrower metaphorical references such as 3:8; 5:35; 8:34–35; and 12:24.

A fundamental definition of metaphor is offered by Norman Friedman: "it is a device which speaks of one thing (tenor) in terms which are appropriate to another (vehicle), with the vehicle serving as the source of traits to be transferred to the tenor."[16] In the case of John's Gospel, this means that earthly images are presented as vehicles richly suggestive of the higher reality of who Jesus is. Metaphor is integrally related to symbol.

A symbol is by nature stable and repeatable, characteristics not necessarily held by a metaphor,[17] and symbol need not reveal to the reader the precise tenor to which it refers, as metaphor usually does.[18] A recurring metaphor, however, easily takes on such stability and by expanding its suggestiveness becomes a symbol. This is usually the case with metaphors in the Fourth Gospel.[19] In both metaphor and symbol the relationship between tenor and vehicle is intimate and complex. The two realities are not merely compared; they infuse and transform each other. As Wheelwright says, "What really matters in a metaphor is the psychic depth at which the things of the world, whether actual or fancied, are transmuted in the cool heat of the imagination."[20]

In John's Gospel such earthly realities as "bread," "water," and "light" are continually stretched and filled by the Son of God to whom they constantly point and by whom they are irrevocably transformed. The effect upon the reader is a conditioning to the fact that earthly things have more significance than may appear, and in particular, that the earthly flesh called Jesus is far more than he appears. We are taught by metaphor to look beyond surface significance into deeper identifications. It may even be said that metaphor and symbol invite the reader into a whole new world of meaning, for by their suggestive economy they signify, as one writer has said, "an area which can be glimpsed, never surveyed."[21]

Metaphor is like irony in that it says one thing and means another, presenting two levels of meaning which the reader must entertain at once. In metaphor, however, the two levels are deeply identified; in irony they are in opposition. Irony demands a negative judgment of some kind; it demands that the reader discern and decide. Metaphor's discernment, on the other hand, invites extension, connection, and exploration; it is addition or multiplication rather than subtraction. Both devices presuppose duality. Irony says the world of reality is *other* than the world of appearance. Metaphor says the world of reality is *more* than the world of appearance. As distinct from each other as they are, it is obvious that these two devices may function harmoniously to invite the reader *beyond* the world of appearance.

Double Meaning

The Johannine device of double meaning is much like that of metaphor, and, in fact, the two are often confused. Yet the distinction can be made that while metaphor unites two conceptions, with one reality used figuratively to illumine another, double meaning presents two concrete meanings at once, both of which are true and crucially related—yet still distinct.[22] Thus Jesus' usage of "living water" is not actually an instance of double meaning but of metaphor,[23] since Jesus unites a figurative reality with a higher one, rather than intending two meanings at once. More properly such Johannine expressions as *anabainein* (7:8); *anōthen* (3:3, 7); *apothnēskein huper* (11:50–51; 18:14); *ethnos* (11:50; 18:35); *katalambanein* (1:5); *tetelestai* (19:30); and *hupsoun* (3:14; 8:28; 12:32, 34) constitute double meanings, for they convey a deliberate ambiguity allowing two meanings at once and thereby encouraging the reader to explore dual possibilities. The effect is related to metaphor and irony. The reader may feel satisfaction to have grasped a double significance which other readers might not catch and which some characters manifestly miss (3:4; 11:50); or the reader may be caught off guard by one of these expressions and in the process of deciding which meaning the author intended—or whether he intended both—be forced to realize again that in this Gospel we are beckoned beyond the surface of things. The reader is thus taught to read deeply, to "not judge by appearances but judge with right judgment" (7:24), and to trust the narrator as a reliable guide through the expanding possibilities of meaning.

Like metaphor, double meaning differs from irony in that it *extends* meaning rather than negates one level of meaning. At the same time, double meaning provides a kind of opposition, for the reader must reject the first sense as insufficient by itself. Thus double meaning stands between metaphor and irony; it is used ironically when the two meanings stand in opposition to each other (e.g., *hupsoun)* or when a character who ought to know better can grasp only one dimension of the meaning (3:4; 11:50).

Misunderstanding

The Johannine technique of misunderstanding has received more numerous and varied explanation in recent years than have the other devices discussed here.[24] Definitions and criteria differ: Leroy isolates eleven instances of a narrowly defined form while Carson claims no less than sixty-three Johannine misunderstandings. Culpepper takes a middle ground, not including every instance of failed perception in the Gospel but helpfully delineating a pattern of misunderstanding related to Jesus' words. In this pattern (1) Jesus utters some ambiguity, (2) his interlocutor reveals confusion, and (3) usually either Jesus or the narrator explains.[25] Dialogue partners can misunderstand metaphors (2:19–21; 4:10–15, 31–34; 6:32–35, 51–53; 11:11–15), double meanings (3:3–5; 12:32–34) or other kinds of cryptic or ambiguous expression (7:33–36; 8:21–22, 31–35, 51–53, 56–58; 11:23–25; 13:36–38; 14:4–6, 7–9; 16:16–19).

Like the other techniques discussed here, misunderstanding is far more than a matter of style. As Luise Schottroff says, "misunderstanding is for John not only a literary device but a component of his theological perception."[26] Culpepper isolates three effects of the misunderstandings upon the reader of John's Gospel.[27] First, they widen and clarify the perceived gap between "insiders" and "outsiders." The reader is made to feel superior to the hopelessly slow characters who cannot or will not grasp Jesus' meaning. The information given us draws us into a circle of enlightenment that inevitably casts judgmental shadows upon those who misunderstand Jesus. Second, this device provides the author with opportunity to clarify or elaborate his theological point. Ironically, misunderstanding becomes a means of furthering the reader's understanding. Third, says Culpepper, the misunderstandings "teach readers how to read the gospel." They underline the bilevel nature of Johannine language, orienting us to the necessity of reading rightly and warning us that failure to do so identifies us with a nearsighted circle of characters.

The relationship between misunderstanding, metaphor, and double meaning can therefore be stated as follows: misunderstandings result from characters failing to perceive metaphors or double meanings (or other ambiguous expressions); they have the effect of conditioning us to read all metaphors and double meanings (and other ambiguous expressions, including irony) with appropriate sensitivity. The relationship of misunderstanding to irony is more complex. Some misunderstandings are presented ironically, as when the guessed-at meaning unwittingly portends the truth (7:33–36; 8:21–22), or when the misguided interlocutor gives an overconfident reply (8:56–58; 13:36–38). Many of the misunderstandings, however, function without irony, yet with an effect similar to irony. Both devices drive a sharp wedge between "insiders" and "outsiders," have their own didactic agendas, and teach readers to be sensitive to hidden levels of significance. The misunderstandings do this in a rather heavy-handed way which even novice readers can grasp. Irony's subtle whisperings are more perceptible because of the forerunning cries of the misunderstandings, and carry us deeper into the mysteries toward which this Gospel so persistently beckons.

In summary, irony is one of several members of the Johannine literary family, all of which point the same direction. The direction is *beyond*. It is mystery, height, depth—hidden significance in need of crucial illumination. All of these "devices" are, in other words, elements of an invitation to abide "above," in the presence of him who is the revealing and penetrating light of the world.

Irony and the Johannine Community

In recent decades there has been a virtual consensus among writers on John that a unique community or communities of faith gave rise to the Fourth Gospel and its associated epistles.[28] While it is beyond the purview of our study to summarize the evidence on this issue, it is quite appropriate to lay what we have learned of Johannine irony alongside this community-hypothesis to see if any corroborating light can be shed. As has already been intimated, there may be a conceivable correlation between the persistence of Johannine irony and the existence of a Johannine community.

Irony is both an invitation to kindred minds and a sign that such kinship is present.[29] Irony is a remarkably indirect mode of communication, and as such it presupposes or demands a relationship of shared knowledge, values, and expression between writer and reader. Such a relationship can be established within a literary work itself, of course; and the narrator of John's Gospel does precisely this in his early disclosure of vital information, his persistent conveyance of reliability,[30] and his ongoing concern to teach us how to read. At the same time, however, the regularity of the Johannine irony—its thoroughgoing presence as an attitude and its regular repetition of form—is not the type of discourse we would expect of a solitary author appealing to an entirely unknown audience. The numerous ironic silences of the Gospel and its rich suggestiveness of language seem to presuppose an audience at least partially conditioned to this mode of expression.

Some scholars have suggested that the "self-referring" language of John marks it as an "in-house" document, not meant to be particularly intelligible to the uninitiated.[31] While there is an unjustifiable excessiveness especially in the latter part of such a claim, there is a germ of truth as well. Though by no means indecipherable to outsiders, the language of John's Gospel and particularly its irony is infinitely richer and more evocative for those who not only agree that "Jesus is the Christ, the Son of God," but who are already immersed in the Johannine mode of thought and expression. Irony has its greater power with those who share its presuppositions; and when its mode of expression falls into recurring patterns of implied speech, we may suspect a degree of previous intimacy between the author and at least a portion of the audience.[32] All this is not to claim that the existence of a Johannine community can be posited on the basis of the Johannine irony. We are only saying that the character and regularity of John's irony accord quite well with what many scholars have come to believe about such a community.

Irony tends not only to corroborate the hypothesis of a Johannine community but to reinforce what some scholars have said about the character of that community—that it was particularly shaped by *writing.* The Johannine community has been characterized as a school, in which teaching, learning, studying the Scriptures, and writing were regular, important activities.[33] One author even suggests on the basis of 21:25 that the Johannine community's conception of the world resembled a book.[34]

While we might question the accuracy of that particular assessment, there seems no doubt that behind the Fourth Gospel is a strong, corporate literary consciousness, evidenced by the very character of this Gospel in comparison with the Synoptics. John's writing follows long spiraling paths with constant allusions to words already spoken or words yet to come. The movement of this Gospel reflects a carefully sustained crafting of language and thought. The Synoptic style of weaving together short, memorable sayings or stories—even though their oral forms and purposes are creatively transformed by the evangelists into the new medium of textuality[35]— nonetheless reflects a mindset far more conditioned by an oral culture. While the Fourth Gospel is by no means free of such a mindset, it reflects far more than do the Synoptics a way of thinking that has been chirographically conditioned.[36]

The significance of this observation for our study is manifest. While irony does exist in oral settings, it is only in a milieu conditioned by the controlled distance of writing that irony can take on the kind of sustained subtlety that it does in the Fourth Gospel.[37] The Johannine perspective is one in which the reader is removed from the world and with the author views at a distance the goings-on of characters below. This kind of distancing is only conceivable in a setting where reading and writing have shaped consciousness by externalizing and objectifying the word and the world. The Johannine irony is thus a consequence at least in part of a community of minds immersed in the book.

Presumably John's irony also springs from the particular purposes of the Fourth Gospel. The community had its reasons for writing. The Johannine irony reflects two major intents which we now examine both in their possible historical context and in their ongoing effectiveness.

Irony and the Johannine Polemic

Irony's function as a weapon was demonstrated in chapter 2. "Irony is criticism," says Good.[38] An early ironologist once remarked, "[Irony] is a weapon properly belonging to the armoury of controversy and not fitted to any peaceable occasion."[39] Recent studies of John have argued that in fact the Johannine community had little peace—that this Gospel reflects a severe controversy with the synagogue of its day.[40] We have already observed the sharp polemical edge of much of John's irony. The object of that irony, strictly speaking, is not the synagogue but unbelief in Jesus. Unbelief in all its forms constitutes *hamartia* in John (16:8–9); unbelief is the greater antagonist of the drama of this Gospel and so the primary object of its irony.

The *victims* of the irony, however, are most often "the Jews." This is the case not only because they are the dramatic representation of the world's unbelief, but because in John's view the nation of Israel was singularly culpable in rejecting Christ. "The Jews" are victims of irony because they of all people—"his own"—should have received Jesus yet did not. They are victims by virtue of the alazony the author ascribes to them.

The *alazōn*, irony's perennial victim, is one who pretends to more knowledge, more power, or more privilege than he really has. Pilate is an *alazōn* when he claims power over Jesus (19:10). Peter, who by all accounts was historically a bona fide *alazōn,* is portrayed as such by

John, though never brutally so. The persistent occupants of this role, however, are "the Jews," who constantly shout their certainty that Jesus is a sinner (9:24), who piously appeal to the law they reject (19:7) and the spiritual heritage they have betrayed (8:39), and who, in order to silence the one they accuse of blasphemy, will exalt Caesar above God (19:15). Their victimization is not without its comic touches. The height of John's mockery of them is that they constantly bear unwitting witness to Jesus' dignity and are themselves instrumental in his exaltation and the consequent belief of many. In all this "the Jews" are spared a great deal of direct attack, but by way of irony's indirection, they are condemned to the crueller fate of accusing themselves.

So scathing is the tone of John's irony against "the Jews" that it almost certainly reflects a period when the Johannine community had broken its ties and its active witness to the synagogue. Though some scholars still maintain that the Fourth Gospel is a missionary tract to diaspora Jews,[41] the evidence of the irony concurs with the majority opinion that the final form of the Gospel was written when relationships had become mutually hostile, and no new converts from Judaism were being actively sought.[42]

Many scholars reasonably contend that an earlier form of the Gospel, including the signs material and a passion account, was indeed used as a missionary tract to the Jews.[43] Significantly, however, Robert Fortna's much respected reconstruction of such a source contains almost none of the material treated here as ironic (only 1:46; 2:10; and a few ironic aspects of the trial). The irony is a later development. Its sharpness signals a point at which dialogue has ended and mockery has begun. So insistent is the scornful silence of John's irony, in fact, that if a hostile Jew of the first century were to read this Gospel, he would not only miss some of the irony, but he might quite easily misunderstand it as victimizing Jesus![44] In this sense, then, Kierkegaard was right about irony: "it reinforces vanity in its vanity and renders madness more mad."[45] The Johannine irony functions analogously, then, to the presence of the Johannine Jesus in the world. Those who will not receive him are made all the more blind.

Irony and the Johannine Witness

The light that blinds may also give sight. John's irony is witness as well as weapon, and the positive function outstrips the negative. Wayne Booth's evaluation of irony's effect, cited earlier, should now be recalled:

> . . . the building of amiable communities is often far more important than the exclusion of naïve victims. Often the predominant emotion when reading stable ironies is that of joining, of finding and communing with kindred spirits. . . . every irony inevitably builds a community of believers even as it excludes.[46]

Where there is any previous inclination to agree with the ironist's position, where there is the least degree of sympathy with his cause, irony has an enormous potential for quietly drawing the reader more deeply into whole-hearted assent. It might even be said that the power of irony upon readers is in direct proportion to their willingness to assume the author's point of view. Where the Gospel of John is read with openness to the claims of Jesus, therefore, the irony is an attractive element which by its indirect witness may lure the reader closer to faith. More certainly, however, where the reader already assents to Jesus' claims, the ironies are more fully perceived and exercise more power in confirming and deepening belief. Some ways in which this process works, even on contemporary readers of the Gospel, will be mentioned presently. It would be well, however, to ask what significance this aspect of irony might have in an evaluation of the Johannine community.

One obvious implication already alluded to is that Johannine irony is largely an in-house affair. Its mockery of "the Jews" would provide some satisfaction to synagogue outcasts and confirm them in the rightness of breaking their former ties. The irony's constant silent invitations to recognize Jesus in his fullness would lend literary-devotional pleasure, offer the sense of belonging to a perceptive community of minds, and solidify confidence in the Christ and his people. As problematic as 20:31 is textually and contextually,[47] its most likely and immediate sense is that the Gospel is written to confirm and strengthen faith, to inspire ongoing fidelity, and—in Vouga's phrase—"to persuade believers to become Christians."[48]

Might such a purpose have ranged beyond the established community itself? Such would be the case if there were a group of prospective readers inclined to sympathize with Jesus but not yet committed wholeheartedly to his claims or to his community. As it happens, just such a group has been inferred from the Gospel by a number of scholars. Several references are made in the Gospel to Jews who believed in Jesus, yet in some obviously inadequate way (cf. 2:23; 8:31; 12:42). In particular, there are numerous mentions of belief that is hesitant to declare itself openly because of "fear of the Jews" (7:13; 19:38; 20:19), and especially a fear of being put out of the synagogue (9:22; 12:42). The characters of Joseph of Arimathea, Nicodemus, and, to some degree, Pilate seem to represent a response to Jesus that is privately favorable but publicly intimidated. For these reasons it has been suggested that the Fourth Gospel is addressed not only to its own community of faith but to a group of "crypto-Christians"—secret believers or half believers—impressed with Jesus but not sufficiently so to face synagogue expulsion and fully embrace the faith-community of Christ.[49]

Some of the qualities attributed to such a group seem relevant to what has been learned of John's irony. Brown infers that these crypto-Christians probably did not hold as high a christology as the Johannine Christians did, seeing no need, for example, to exalt Jesus over Moses.[50] It will be recalled that virtually all the local irony in John is christological. The major themes are the origin of Jesus, his preeminence over the patriarchs, and the far-reaching effects of his death. These brief, pointed ironies have a regularity of form, as we have seen, that suggests repeated use. Were they employed in part to offer subtle appeal to those not sure enough of Jesus? Likewise, the polemic against "the Jews" might have been intended to sway believers still at home in the synagogue. If fear of expulsion was the barrier, John's irony whispers repeatedly that synagogue and temple are now bankrupt and ought to be deserted.[51]

Martyn finds hints that such a group of Jewish semi-believers would have wanted the community to provide midrashic proofs for the validity of Jesus' claims. Though some Christian writers had taken up this exegetical gauntlet (e.g., Matthew, Justin, and to a degree the author of the Signs Gospel), the Johannine community, according to

Martyn, rejected it, subverting the plea for rational argument and confronting their interlocutors with "decision dualism."[52] The Fourth Gospel explodes the ordered rule of midrash and brings the inquirer face to face with Jesus, where a choice must be made. Martyn does not mention irony in this connection, of course, but John's use of it accords well with such an understanding. Irony is precisely the appropriate instrument when reasoned argument has been set aside. It demands of its audience a choice, but its method is to win from *behind*—to launch an assault whose power is indirection, whose argument is a whisper.

Again, no leap from literary analysis to historical claim is being ventured here. On the basis of the irony, all that can be said is that *if* the Johannine community was in any dialogue with such a group of secret believers in the synagogue, much of this Gospel's irony would have made a remarkably appropriate appeal to them. Given their predisposition toward Jesus, the irony will have found an open door through which to beckon them away from fear and into the fullness of faith. Such a hypothesis must be balanced by the fact that at the same time, John reveals a real contempt for fearful believers who "loved the praise of men more than the praise of God" (12:43), and actually portrays "the Jews who had believed in him" as hostile sons of the devil who are murderers and liars (8:31–47).[53]

Furthermore, even if an implicit invitation was still being made to such people, we cannot limit the "missionary activity" of John's irony to these alone. Pilate is present as a Gentile representative, as one whose cloistered sympathy for Jesus is overwhelmed by the hostility of the world. Though much of the Gospel's irony has a peculiarly Jewish cast, most of it can function quite well outside of strictly Jewish circles. Any first-century reader with some predisposition toward Jesus, particularly one whose cultivation toward the Christ had included an introduction to the Old Testament witness, would have been a candidate for this irony's lure.

How can such a lure be described as it functioned among John's first readers and as it functions centuries later among those who take up this Gospel? The process is in some ways inexpressible; and, in a way, our whole analysis up to now has been an attempt to illumine this complex system of indirect appeal. But perhaps the beckoning powers of Johannine irony can be summarized under three headings.

The transfer of delight. There is an ironic sonnet by Shakespeare called "My Mistress' Eyes," which, while appearing to degrade the author's beloved, is quite indirectly offering her high praise. When Wayne Booth discusses this poem he elaborates upon the reader's necessary and enjoyable task of rejecting surface meanings and ascending to the higher, unspoken meaning. He concludes: "all the intellectual energy required by the climb, and all the resulting pleasure in making the secret journey successfully, are at the end transferred to the mistress' glory."[54] Shakespeare, in other words, presents his readers not only with content about his mistress, but with a literary technique that gives pleasure in itself; and the thrill experienced by the readers does not remain focused on the technique but somehow accrues to the mistress as well.

John's irony functions similarly. Technically it is well executed and makes for reading that is deeply satisfying. In particular, the ironic technique consists in continually offering us a subtle literary choice—for the surface level of meaning or for an alternate level—and our successful reading experience depends upon risking negation of the surface meaning, leaping to the alternative, and finding it sound. It so happens that the sound literary alternative is always a higher estimation of Jesus than appears on the surface (just as the sound alternative in Shakespeare's sonnet is a higher estimation of his mistress). The reader in other words is repeatedly rewarded for choosing Jesus in the literary experience. The result is a tendency to associate that sense of *rightness* with the theological point of view offered in this literary adventure. We have rehearsed leaping to Jesus many times, and found it good. We think well of the author and his work, but more of this Character that consumes him. Now it is far easier to leap once more, quite beyond the printed page, toward the promise that He is, after all, the Truth.

The experience of community. This crucial aspect of irony has already been elaborated and it need only be summarized here. Irony establishes a bond between reader and author, instilling a sense of belonging to an elite fellowship of understanding. The author has quietly pointed to the presence of a magnificent reality standing almost obscured behind a great screen of apparent contradiction.

There are characters below who can see nothing but the screen; and presumably there are spectators who are likewise deceived. But *we* see the truth—we, and the author who has confided in us. Irony offers the privilege of election. We are granted the secret, initiated into the company of those who see, and are invited to remain. We may choose to leave, but to do so demands a denial of the knowledge already given, the abandonment of a gracious host, and an identification with those characters already shown to be blind. It is easier to remain.[55]

The engagement of choice. A third aspect of irony's appeal, while related to the first two, is worthy of separate focus. Although irony chooses us, so to speak, it also demands our active involvement. Irony is indirect communication; it whispers a clue or grants a glimpse, but resolutely refuses to spell out for us all that is implied. (Indeed what irony often implies is that beyond the clues and glimpses is a reality incapable of being spelled out.) It is left to the reader to discern the realm to which the author points and to decide whether or not that realm is worthy of his or her own commitment.

Part of the power of the Johannine irony, then, is that it so forcefully engages us in what we read. Instead of setting out propositional arguments, it jolts us with incongruity or nudges us with possibilities—then grows suddenly silent, leaving us to choose a meaning or a value or a commitment. Having set our minds in a whirl with the grace of a fleeting glimpse, irony awaits our decision. In this regard irony is much like parable, and indeed like the Incarnation itself.[56] It gifts us, compels us to choose, yet leaves us enormously free. Such demanding gentleness and generosity seem precisely the invitation to which "the scattered children of God" (whether in the first century or the twentieth) are inclined to respond.

Conclusion

This study has found in John's Gospel a quality and persistence of irony that seem unique in early Christian expression. If our overriding question has been how to account for such a phenomenon, this last chapter has, among other things, touched upon several contributing factors: (1) A community setting in which repeated patterns of thought and expression rendered indirect modes of communication possible; (2) a communal consciousness shaped by writing, which instilled the externalizing perspective necessary for ironic vision; (3) a dualistic system of thought which accentuated the distinction between appearance and reality; (4) a breakdown of relationship with the synagogue in which dialogue with the opposition gave way to mockery; (5) a desire to draw people of marginal faith, including perhaps "secret believers" in the synagogue, into the full circle of faith; (6) a desire to confirm and deepen the commitment of those already in the community of faith. The first three factors indicate how ironical discourse might have become possible for the Johannine community; the last three show why it may have become desirable. No two of these factors are mutually exclusive.

One factor remains which must not be set aside. The Fourth Gospel is testimony to a unique vision of the Christ-event, the vision of one community of faith and of its evangelist-author(s), and perhaps even of the Beloved Disciple himself. It is a vision that has perceived in the Christ-event itself something fundamentally ironic. All other explanations of the Johannine irony must finally be secondary to this one: the life and death in history of Jesus of Nazareth made its deep impression on one group of his followers as an event which was ironic to its very core.

They had beheld a man—and now, "Behold the man!" They had beheld flesh—and he was the Word; in him what they had beheld was glory. He came graciously to a world he had made—and was unrecognized. He visited his own chosen people—and was spurned. They lifted him up to shame—and he was lifted up indeed. He was beheld there by the outcast and accursed—and he made them his friends and the children of God. So crucial is this irony to the Johannine message that it may fairly be said, if we do not grasp the Irony we do not grasp the Gospel. Yet it is precisely here that it must be recalled, irony is by its very nature beyond grasp. John employs irony not only to whisper to us by name that the resplendent Christ is among us, but to remind us that he is beyond holding (cf. 20:16–17)—and that is the greatest Gospel of all.

If John punctuates his witness to Jesus with an occasional wink or grin or tear, if he now and then falls into awesome silence, it is ultimately because there is no better way to tell this story.

NOTES

INTRODUCTION

[1]Søren Kierkegaard, *The Concept of Irony,* trans. Lee M. Capel (New York: Harper and Row, 1965), 265. It will become clear as we proceed that what Kierkegaard meant by irony is not precisely the meaning of irony considered here. Nevertheless, many of his insights are appropriate to irony's full range of meaning.

[2]The earliest application of the word *irony* to the Gospel of John was apparently made by George Salmon in the nineteenth century. See his *A Historical Introduction to the Study of the Books of the New Testament* (London: John Murray, 1885), 346–349, esp. 347, n., where he refers to an earlier paper of his on the subject.

[3]R. Alan Culpepper, *Anatomy of the Fourth Gospel* (Philadelphia: Fortress Press, 1983), 165–180.

[4]Previous essays on Johannine irony include the following: Henri Clavier, "L'ironie dans le quatrième Evangile," *Studia Evangelica,* I (Berlin: Akademie-Verlag, 1959): 261–276; George W. MacRae, "Theology and Irony in the Fourth Gospel," *The Word and the World,* ed. Richard J. Clifford and George W. MacRae (Cambridge, Mass.: Weston College Press, 1973), 83–96; David W. Wead, *The Literary Devices in John's Gospel,* Theologischen Dissertationen, IV, ed. Bo Reicke (Basel: Friedrich Reinhardt Kommissionverlagen, 1970), 47–68, and "Johannine Irony as a Key to the Author-Audience Relationship in John's Gospel," *American Academy of Religion Biblical Literature: 1974,* comp. Fred O. Francis, 33–50.

[5]D. A. Carson, "Understanding Misunderstanding in the Fourth Gospel," *Tyndale Bulletin,* 33 (1982), 59–60. Carson's objection to calling misunderstanding a literary device is primarily in reaction to the work of Herbert Leroy, *Rätsel und Missverständnis* (Bonn: Peter Hanstein Verlag, 1968).

[6]By "author" I do not mean to deny the real possibility that some kind of multiple authorship produced the Fourth Gospel. It is helpful, however, to speak of "author" rather than "authors," not only for the

sake of convenience, but because even in a work of multiple authorship the image of a single, unified author, the "implied author," is presented to the reader. This point is made by Seymour Chatman, *Story and Discourse* (Ithaca: Cornell University Press, 1978), 149. The helpful distinction between "real" author and "implied" author was established by Wayne C. Booth, *The Rhetoric of Fiction* (Chicago: University of Chicago Press, 1961), esp. 71–76.

[7]On these lines Wayne Booth gives a well-put word: "But it would be a serious mistake to see it [irony] only in the service of the spirit of eternal denial. Though the devil is a great ironist, so is the Lord; the great prophets have used irony as freely as the great sinners." *A Rhetoric of Irony* (Chicago: University of Chicago Press, 1974), 30.

CHAPTER 1. The Meaning of Irony

[1]Edwyn Clement Hoskyns, *The Fourth Gospel,* ed. Francis Noel Davey, 2d ed. (London: Faber and Faber, 1947), 20.

[2]D. C. Muecke, *The Compass of Irony* (London: Methuen, 1969), 3.

[3]Walter J. Ong, *Interfaces of the Word* (Ithaca: Cornell University Press, 1977), 287.

[4]G. G. Sedgewick, *Of Irony, Especially in The Drama* (Toronto: University of Toronto Press, 1935), 7.

[5]The first extant usage is in Aristophanes, *The Clouds* (423 B.C.), 449, in a list of words imputing every sort of cunning deception.

[6]Quintilian, *The Institutio Oratio of Quintilian,* trans. H. E. Butler, The Loeb Classical Library, (Cambridge, Mass.: Harvard University Press, 1953), IX, ii, 46.

[7]This passage, according to Sedgewick, *Of Irony,* 11, contains the first extant use of the "fully grown nominative" *eirōneia.*

[8]Francis MacDonald Cornford, *The Origin of Attic Comedy,* ed. Theodor H. Gaster (Gloucester, Mass.: Peter Smith, 1968), 181–184.

[9]Audiences have been laughing at essentially the same conflict for centuries. Recent popular characterizations of the *alazōn* have included Oliver Hardy, Barney Fife, and Donald Duck. The *eirōn* has been manifest in Charley Chaplin, Stanley Laurel, and the unlikely detective Columbo.

[10]Aristotle, *The Nicomachean Ethics,* trans. H. Rackham, The Loeb Classical Library (Cambridge, Mass.: Harvard University Press, 1926), IV, vii, 14, 16; see also IV, iii, 28.

[11]Cicero, *On Oratory,* trans. E. W. Sutton, The Loeb Classical Library (Cambridge, Mass.: Harvard University Press, 1942), II, 270–271.

[12]The translation is Sedgewick's, *Of Irony,* 60. Five of Euripides' extant plays conclude with these lines: *The Bacchae, Helen, Medea, Andromache,* and *Alcestis.*

[13]J. A. K. Thomson, *Irony: An Historical Introduction* (London: George Allen and Unwin, 1926), 2.

[14]See Erich Auerbach, *Mimesis,* trans. Willard R. Trask (Princeton: Princeton University Press, 1953), 6–11. Auerbach does not make reference to irony, but his insights as to the "uniform illumination" of the Greek style versus the reticence of the biblical style is helpful for understanding the comparative extravagance of Greek irony.

[15]M. H. Abrams, *A Glossary of Literary Terms,* 3d ed. (New York: Holt, Rinehart and Winston, 1971), 80.

[16]Bishop Connop Thirlwall, "On the Irony of Sophocles," *The Philological Museum,* 2 vols. (Cambridge, Mass.: Deightons, 1833), 2, 483.

[17]Booth, *A Rhetoric of Irony,* ix. Booth gives a good theoretical analysis of Romantic and Cosmic Irony, especially on 232–277. The best historical analysis is probably that of Muecke, *Compass,* 119–215.

[18]See Cleanth Brooks, "Irony as a Principle of Structure," *Literary Opinion in America,* ed. Morton D. Zabel, rev. ed. (New York: Harper and Brothers, 1951), 729–741; "Irony and 'Ironic' Poetry," *College English* 9 (1948), 231–237; and *The Well Wrought Urn* (New York: Regnal and Hitchcock, 1947).

[19]Muecke, *Compass,* 14.

[20]Ibid., 19–20.

[21]A. E. Dyson, *The Crazy Fabric* (New York: St. Martin's Press, 1965), x.

[22]Haakon Chevalier, *The Ironic Temper* (New York: Oxford University Press, 1932), 42.

[23]Kierkegaard, *The Concept of Irony,* 278.

[24]Ibid., 279. Kierkegaard found this to be the role of Socrates, who (in his view) achieved by his constant, empty questioning the destruction of Hellenism, while offering nothing to replace it. Interestingly, Kierkegaard found a New Testament counterpart in an unlikely ironist, John the Baptist. "He was not the one who should come, did not have a knowledge of what should come, and yet he destroyed Judaism," *The Concept of Irony,* 279–282.

[25]David James Amante, "Ironic Speech Acts: A Stylistic Analysis of a Rhetorical Ploy," (Ph.D. dissertation, University of Michigan, 1975), 69–73.

[26]Muecke, *Compass,* 35.

[27]E.g., Eleanor N. Hutchens, "The Identification of Irony," *ELH* 27 (1960), 353; Chevalier, *The Ironic Temper,* 42.

[28]Alan Reynolds Thompson, *The Dry Mock* (Berkeley: University of California Press, 1948), 11, 15.

[29]Northrop Frye, *Anatomy of Criticism* (Princeton: Princeton University Press, 1957), 285. See also 161–162.

[30]Muecke, in his shorter book, *Irony* (London: Methuen, 1970), includes both the comic element and the element of detachment in his description of irony.

[31]Booth, *A Rhetoric of Irony,* 5–6.

[32]W. K. Wimsatt, Jr. and Monroe C. Beardsley, "The Intentional Fallacy," *The Verbal Icon* (Lexington, Ky.: University of Kentucky Press, 1954), 3.

[33]A fact persistently denied by biblical interpreters with mechanistic understandings of inspiration. See Walter C. Kaiser, Jr., *Toward An Exegetical Theology* (Grand Rapids: Baker Book House, 1981), passim.

[34]Booth, *A Rhetoric of Irony,* 5. It should be mentioned here that Muecke operates with a slightly different, less restrictive understanding of overt irony. For him, overt irony is irony that is immediately perceived, but not necessarily announced, for example, sarcasm and "heavy irony."

[35]Ibid., 206.

[36]Ibid., 6.

[37]Kierkegaard, *The Concept of Irony,* 278.

[38]Muecke, *Compass,* 119–121. General irony, he says, is "the irony of the 'open ideology,'" 129.

[39]Abrams, *Glossary,* 80.

[40]Gilbert Highet, *The Anatomy of Satire* (Princeton: Princeton University Press, 1962), 57, defines sarcasm as "irony whose meaning is both so obvious it cannot be misunderstood and so wounding that it cannot be dismissed with a smile."

[41]"Already you are filled! Already you have become rich! Without us you have become kings! And would that you did reign, so that we might share the rule with you" (1 Cor. 4:8). "For you gladly bear with fools, being wise yourselves!" (2 Cor. 11:19). In 2 Corinthians 12:13 he reminds them that he never sponged from them and then says, "Forgive me this wrong!" For an analysis of Paul's irony in 2 Corinthians 11—12, see Aida Besançon Spencer, "The Wise Fool (and the Foolish Wise). A Study of Irony in Paul," *Novum Testamentum* 23 (1981), 349–360.

[42]*Medea,* 1081–1089. The translation is by Philip Vellacott, *Ironic Drama* (Cambridge: Cambridge University Press, 1975), 51. Though it is possible that these lines reflect real modesty rather than irony, the fact that they occur in a play in which the heroine has far more intelligence than her male counterpart makes irony probable. Vellacott demonstrates Euripides' persistent protest against the subordination of women, 17, 82–126.

[43]A brief discussion of biblical overstatement, litotes, and irony is given by G. B. Caird, *The Language and Imagery of the Bible* (Philadelphia: The Westminster Press, 1980), 133–134.

[44]These and other methods of verbal irony are given by Booth in his list of techniques for "impersonal irony," *A Rhetoric of Irony,* 67–82.

[45]D. A. Raeburn in an unpublished paper, cited by Vellacott, *Ironic Drama,* 23.

[46]Chevalier, *The Ironic Temper,* 41.

[47]Philip Whaley Harsh, *A Handbook of Classical Drama* (Stanford University: Stanford University Press, 1944), 316. A classic example is the prologue of Euripides' *Ion.* The play, full of dramatic irony, relates the story of a separated mother and son who do not know each other and very nearly kill each other. To insure that none of the irony is lost, the author begins the play with an explanation by Hermes, who discloses the identity and the ignorance of everyone, and then clearly foreshadows that the end of it all will be good fortune. This kind of

"omniscient prologue" was particularly used by Euripides, and was copied from him by Aristophanes and certain writers of the "New Comedy." See also A. W. Pickard-Cambridge, *Dithyramb* (Oxford: The Clarendon Press, 1927), 311.

[48]Sedgewick, *Of Irony*, 50. Harsh, *Handbook*, 29, makes the same point when he remarks, "Irony and surprise, of course, tend to be mutually exclusive; for irony depends on knowledge, surprise on ignorance of the true situation or its outcome."

[49]Abrams, *Glossary*, 80.

[50]Sedgewick, *Of Irony*, 49.

[51]Herodotus, I, 53; cited by David Worcester, *The Art of Satire* (Cambridge, Mass.: Harvard University Press, 1940), 115.

CHAPTER 2. The Functions of Irony

[1]On reliable and unreliable narrators see Booth, *The Rhetoric of Fiction*, 169–240. On the importance of a reliable narrator for most dramatic irony, see 175.

[2]Booth, *A Rhetoric of Irony*, 206.

[3]Ibid.

[4]On irony as "implicit commentary" see Ross Chambers, "Commentary in Literary Texts," *Critical Inquiry* 5 (1978), 327–328. A fascinating image of irony's silent communication is offered by Kierkegaard, *The Concept of Irony*, 56–57. Though his eye is primarily on the philosophical "nothingness" of irony, his analogy applies beautifully to the hushed technique of any subtle ironist. "There is an engraving that portrays the grave of Napoleon. Two large trees overshadow the grave. Between these two trees is an empty space, and as the eye traces out its contour Napoleon himself suddenly appears; and now it is impossible to make him disappear. The eye that has once seen him now always sees him with anxious necessity. It is the same with Socrates' replies. As one sees the trees, so one hears his discourse; as the trees are trees, so his words mean exactly what they sound like. There is not a single syllable to give any hint of another interpretation, just as there is not a single brush stroke to suggest Napoleon. Yet it is this empty space, this nothingness, that conceals what is most important."

[5]Muecke, *Compass*, 61–63.

[6]Norman Knox, "On the Classification of Ironies," *Modern Philology* 70 (1972), 55–56.

[7]Walter Ong makes this point in *Interfaces*, 288. He elsewhere suggests that this is the reason that irony first comes to its full fruit in Greek drama, which was the ancient world's most tightly controlled chirographic—not oral—genre, its first pure literature, even though it was ultimately intended to be heard rather than read; "Irony Dead and Alive," (unpublished paper, 1980), 2; see also *Interfaces*, 89, 212.

[8]Quintilian, *Institutio*, VIII, vi, 54.

[9]Both Booth, *A Rhetoric of Irony*, 49–52, and Muecke, *Compass*, 57, recognize that Quintilian might better have said that any *two* of these three together will signal irony.

[10]Booth, *A Rhetoric of Irony*, 53–76; Muecke gives another set of criteria which includes the same material, generally, as Booth's categories.

[11]Amante, "Ironic Speech Acts," 155.

[12]Frye, *Anatomy of Criticism*, 61, says of the definite article that it may be "linked with the implicit sense of an initiated group aware of real meaning behind an ironically baffling exterior."

[13]See Booth, *A Rhetoric of Irony*, esp. 33–44 and 10–12.

[14]Ibid., 12.

[15]Ibid., 99–100; quotation from 3.

[16]Muecke, *Compass*, 232–233.

[17]Cited by Muecke, *Compass*, 217.

[18]Anatole France, *Oeuvres Complètes*, VII, 43, cited by Thompson, *The Dry Mock*, 1.

[19]Chatman, *Story and Discourse*, 229.

[20]Perhaps correlative to this process is Robert Boies Sharpe's theory, *Irony in the Drama* (Chapel Hill: The University of North Carolina Press, 1959), 82–103, that ironic drama produces in the audience a kind of cathartic shock, out of which emerges a sense of purgation.

[21]Worcester, *The Art of Satire*, 128.

[22]Booth, *A Rhetoric of Irony*, 29.

[23]Kierkegaard, *The Concept of Irony*, 85–86. Kierkegaard is speaking in reference to the power of Socrates, a power which to his

mind is dangerous. He is right, of course, though such danger is rarely as insidious as he suggests.

[24]Booth, A Rhetoric of Irony, 28.

[25]Booth, A Rhetoric of Irony, 13–14, relates the testimony of Edith Wharton, who wrote of her growing friendship with Henry James: "The real marriage of true minds is for any two people to possess a sense of humor or irony pitched in exactly the same key, so that their joint glances at any subject cross like interarching search-lights." Booth concludes that such irony can be "the key to the tightest bonds of friendship" and that "Real intimacy" may be "impossible without it!"

[26]Muecke, Compass, 30.

[27]Muecke, Irony, 28.

[28]Kierkegaard, The Concept of Irony, 273–274. It is remarkable how Kierkegaard's polemic against the nihilistic philosophical irony of his own day has such applicability to irony as a literary device.

[29]Booth, A Rhetoric of Irony, 44.

[30]Cited by Chevalier, The Ironic Temper, 3.

CHAPTER 3. Local Irony: The Socratic Christ and His Little Children

[1]Edwin M. Good, Irony in the Old Testament (Philadelphia: The Westminster Press, 1965), 81–82, similarly speaks of punctual irony, expressions of irony at more or less isolated points; episodic irony, an entire episode with ironic intent; and thematic irony, the conjunction of a number of episodes all pointing to an ironic theme or motif. My use of the word local approximates Good's punctual. Extended irony is a term embracing both episodic and thematic irony.

[2]See Amos N. Wilder, The Language of the Gospel (New York: Harper & Row, 1964), 32–33.

[3]A similar instance, though less forcefully ironic, is found in Plato's Protagoras, in which Socrates once addresses his Sophist opponent with these words: su de allōn pollōn empeiros ōn tautēs apeiros einai phainei—"But you, as learned as you are in many things, appear to know nothing of this," 341 A.

[4]Raymond E. Brown, The Gospel According to John, Anchor

Bible Series, 29 (Garden City, N. Y.: Doubleday, 1966), I, 115, following Lagrange, offers this reading as possible but uncertain; he does admit relationship between verses 2 and 10. Even more is made of the parallels between verse 2 and verses 10ff. by I. de la Potterie, "Jesus et Nicodemus: de necessitate generationis ex Spiritu (John 3, 1–10)," *Verbum Domini* 47 (1969), 195; and "Naître de l'eau et naître de l'Esprit," *Sciences Ecclésiastiques* 14 (1962), 428-430. There he writes, "Likewise the title διδάσκαλος, which Nicodemus offered Jesus in verse 2 with politeness and a nuance of flattery, is returned to him by Jesus in verse 10, not without a nimble irony," 428.

[5]The significance of the article for highlighting the position and/or representative character of Nicodemus is discussed by several commentators. See J. H. Bernard, *A Critical and Exegetical Commentary on the Gospel According to St. John,* International Critical Commentary (New York: Charles Scribner's Sons, 1929), 108–109; Rudolf Bultmann, *The Gospel of John,* trans. and ed. George R. Beasley-Murray (Philadelphia: The Westminster Press, 1971), 144, n. 2; C. K. Barrett, *The Gospel According to St. John* 2d ed. (Philadelphia: The Westminster Press, 1978), 211 (hereafter referred to as *John*); Barnabas Lindars, *The Gospel of John,* New Century Bible (Grand Rapids: William B. Eerdmans, 1972), 154.

[6]François Vouga, *Le cadre historique et l'intention théologique de Jean* (Paris: Éditions Beauchesne, 1977), 20, maintains that the *oidamen* of verse 11 is a more pointed ironic allusion to the *oidamen* of Nicodemus. Repetition is a form of overstatement. It intensifies, not only doubling a word semantically but doubling the noise with which it is said, and so creating and underlining irony. In John 3:10 Jesus employs both "lexical repetition" *(didaskalos, tauta)* and "semantic repetition" *(ginōskeis).* See Dwight Bolinger, *Degree Words,* Janua Linguarum, Series Maior, 53 (The Hague: Mouton and Co., 1972), 288, cited and supplemented by David James Amante, "Ironic Speech Acts," 157–160.

[7]This is persuasively demonstrated by Severino Pancaro, "'People of God' in St. John's Gospel," *New Testament Studies* 16 (1969), 114–129. Pancaro notes the irony of 3:10 on 125. That the word *Israel* underlines the irony is also observed by J. N. Sanders and B. A. Mastin, *A Commentary on the Gospel According to St. John,*

Harper's New Testament Commentaries (New York: Harper & Row, 1968), 126.

[8]*Kala* clearly intends to recall the image of the good *(ho kalos)* shepherd, a phrase used three times in this chapter (vss. 11a, 11b, 14).

[9]Again, the irony is not unlike that of Socrates. In the *Apology,* after being condemned by the court, he speaks to the issue of the penalty: "And so he proposes death as the penalty. And what shall I propose on my part, O men of Athens? Clearly that which is my due. And what is my due? What return shall be made to the man who . . . has been careless of what the many care for—wealth, and family interests, and military offices . . . and plots, and parties. . . . I did not go where I could do no good to you or to myself; but where I could do the greatest good privately to everyone of you, there I went. . . . What should be done to such a one?" 36, b, c, d.

[10]B. F. Westcott, *The Gospel According to St. John,* reprint (Grand Rapids: William B. Eerdmans, 1978), 159, sees the irony working in the opposite direction. "The irony of the speech becomes the expression of stern indignation. The miracles of Christ had in fact called out the bitterest hostility of the Jews." It must be stressed, however, that in John all hostility toward Jesus' miracles is ancillary to the outrage against his words. In my judgment the often valuable work of José Porfirio Miranda, *Being and the Messiah,* trans. John Eagleson (Maryknoll, N. Y.: Orbis Books, 1977), 108, is exegetically marred at this point. Ignoring the irony of 10:32 (and a good deal of evidence from the Gospel), he uses it with a handful of other texts (1:13; 3:18–21; 7:6–8) to claim, "the relationship between Jesus' 'good works' and his death is the thematic mainspring of John's narrative." The irony of 10:32 is noted by G. H. C. MacGreggor, *The Gospel of John,* The Moffatt New Testament Commentary (London: Hodder and Stoughton, [n. d.]), 240; Jakob Jónsson, *Humour and Irony in the New Testament* (Reykjavik, Iceland: Bókaútgáfa Menningarsjóts, 1965), 203; and Sanders and Mastin, *John,* 258.

[11]Brown, *John,* I, 311, translates 7:28 as a question, as does MacGreggor, *John,* 202, and RSV.

[12]Bultmann, *John,* 297, n. 5.

[13]Ibid., 297–298.

¹⁴Brown, *John,* II, 726. Bernard, *John,* II, 522, disagrees, seeing here only a confirmation of the disciples' faith in verse 27.

¹⁵Bultmann, *John,* 591, n. 6, makes the appealing suggestion that *nun* implies "now at last" and *arti* implies "now already." The tone of the irony favors such shading, but John's use of the two words elsewhere renders no such pattern (cf. 13:36–37). G. Stählin, *"νῦν (ἄρτι)" Theological Dictionary of the New Testament,* ed. Gerhard Kittel, trans. and ed. Geoffrey W. Bromiley (Grand Rapids: William B. Eerdmans, 1967), IV, 1107, n. 8, observes that in the Fourth Gospel as in the rest of the New Testament, these two words "are almost completely interchangeable." If there is any difference at all between the two in John it may be, as Bernard, *John,* II, 522, suggests, that while *nun* is rather vague, ἄρτι tends to emphasize "at this moment."

¹⁶While Mark 14:27 and Matthew 26:31 present the same prediction, citing the same text from Zechariah to which John alludes in 16:32, there is in the Synoptic version no irony, save the fact that the prediction immediately follows the Supper. There is a rough parallel, however, in another Synoptic passage, Mark 10:38 par. There in response to James' and John's request for future privilege, Jesus asks, "Are you able . . . ?" The Johannine repetition is absent, but the effect is roughly the same.

¹⁷These two texts are not only related to each other formally, but have a fascinating relationship with the Synoptic texts mentioned in n. 16 above. Mark 14:27–31 par. contains the same prediction of scattering as does 16:29–32. Interestingly, that Markan text also contains the prediction of Peter's denial and his pledge of loyalty, which is found in John 13:29–33 separate from the prediction of scattering. In other words, while the sayings of John 13:37–38 and 16:32 are found coupled in the Synoptics, they have a parallel structure in John *not* found in the Synoptics. Further, Mark 10:38, which has already been noted to have some formal similarity with John 16:31, has *another* formal connection with John 13:36. In the Synoptic passage Jesus assures his overeager disciples that they will indeed drink his cup and undergo his baptism, as they have blithely assured him they can. In John 13:36 he informs the eager-to-follow Simon that he will indeed follow one day. Both passages cryptically

promise future suffering to disciples now intoxicated with superficial faith. There is dramatic irony in both, though the later allusion to Simon's death in John 21:19 and the ongoing Johannine association of that disciple with martyrdom make the Johannine irony more overt.

[18]Bultmann, *John*, 125, cites Amos 4:4 and Isaiah 8:9. The position is also argued by Wead, *Literary Devices*, 65. It makes only a minor difference if we follow some interpreters in calling the clause not a simple imperative but a conditional or concessive imperative. Cf. *A Greek Grammar of the New Testament*, ed. F. Blass, A. Debrunner, and R. W. Funk (hereafter referred to as *BDF*) (Chicago: Chicago University Press, 1961), 387, n. 2; also C. H. Dodd, *The Interpretation of the Fourth Gospel* (Cambridge: Cambridge University Press, 1953), 302, n. 1; and *Historical Tradition in the Fourth Gospel* (Cambridge: Cambridge University Press, 1963), 90, n. 1.

[19]Wead, *Literary Devices*, 65, maintains that verse 21 does not turn us completely from a reference to the literal temple. Xavier Léon-Dufour likewise insists that the scene is not credible unless the evangelist intends us to think of the destruction of both temples; see "For a Symbolic Reading of the Fourth Gospel," *New Testament Studies* 27 (1981), 447. It seems to me, however, that when "the Jews" misunderstanding of Jesus is located so emphatically in the fact that they thought of their temple while he meant another, the narrator effectively shifts the literal temple from the reader's consciousness.

[20]Against Jerry H. Gill, "Jesus, Irony and the New Quest," *Encounter* 41 (1980), 142; and Henri Clavier, "L'ironie dans le quatrième Evangile," 270.

[21]See Charles H. Giblin, "Suggestion, Negative Response, and Positive Action in St. John's Portrayal of Jesus (John 2:1–11; 4:46–54; 7:2–14; 11:1–44)," *New Testament Studies* 26 (1980), 197–211.

[22]Against Clavier, "L'ironie dans le quatrième Evangile," 272. It is possible, however, to see in Jesus' wordplay with his brothers a deception consistent with dramatic irony. When he says, "I will not go up to this feast," the verb is *anabainō* widely used elsewhere of his ascension (cf. 20:17). If, as many believe, Jesus secretly means, "I will

not ascend to the Father at this feast," he is certainly playing the *eirōn*. Cf. Brown, *John,* I, 308.

²³Vouga, *Le cadre historique,* 22, 31. Bruce Vawter, "The Gospel According to John," *Jerome Biblical Commentary,* ed. Raymond E. Brown, et al. (Englewood Cliffs, N. J.: Prentice Hall, 1968), II, 419, also blurs the distinction between irony and double meaning, and so mistakenly refers to such expressions as "living water" as ironic.

²⁴There are instances in the Fourth Gospel, of course, in which Jesus asks unanswered questions that are not ironic (cf. 2:4; 5:47; 6:67). 6:67 merits some inquiry, perhaps. I have read no scholar who treats it as ironic, but there are aspects which might tempt one to wonder. Jesus asks the Twelve, "Will you also go away?" The whole context is that of disciple-desertion. This first mention of the Twelve pictures them less as chosen ones than as a remnant, and only three verses later we are told that even one of these is a devil who will betray him. (These insights are from R. Alan Culpepper, *Anatomy,* 117.) Jesus later assures the remaining eleven that they will scatter and leave him alone (16:32), and in fact when the arrest comes, Jesus tells the soldiers to let his disciples *"go away" (hupagein,* 18:8, as in 6:67, but see 15:16). "Will you also go away?"—Yes, they also will go away. Militating against an *intentional* irony here, however, is the fact that the question begins with the negative particle *mē,* which expects a negative reply, *BDF,* 427, 2. Though, as we shall see, the author often allows the opponents of Jesus to expect negative answers to their questions while we know the opposite is true, it seems unlikely that the evangelist would transfer this device to Jesus. Nor does it seem likely that Jesus is working an ironic deceit, clearly implying that they will not leave, yet knowing that they will. It is more likely here that the intention of the expected negative is to encourage the Twelve and theologically to affirm that as verse 70 says, they are in fact chosen, and that "no one shall snatch them from my hand" (10:29–30; cf. 17:12). Rudolf Schnackenburg, *The Gospel According to St. John,* trans. Cecily Hastings, et al. (New York: Seabury Press, 1980), II, 75.

²⁵Gill, "Jesus, Irony and the New Quest," 139–151; Jónsson, *Humour and Irony in the New Testament,* 90–199; Henri Clavier, "La méthode ironique dans l'enseignement de Jésus," *Études*

théologiques et religieuses 4 (1929), 224–241, 323–344; "L'ironie dans l'enseignement de Jésus," *Novum Testamentum* 1 (1956), 3–20; André de Robert, "L'ironie et la Bible," *Études théologiques et religieuses* 55 (1980), 5–7; Robert H. Stein, *The Method and Message of Jesus' Teachings* (Philadelphia: The Westminster Press, 1978), 22–23; W. F. Stinespring, "Irony and Satire," *Interpreter's Dictionary of the Bible,* ed. George A. Buttrick (Nashville: Abingdon Press, 1962), II, 726; Elton Trueblood, *The Humor of Christ* (New York: Harper & Row, 1964), 53–67. It is unfortunate that none of these studies reflects much critical understanding of what irony is and is not. Definitions tend to be loose or faulty; the goal often seems to be to soften some hard saying by imagining Jesus with a grin. Typical are Gill's treatment of Jesus' conversation with the Syro-Phoenecian woman, 145, and Trueblood's conclusion that when Jesus said, "Not one jot or tittle of the law will pass away," "He was joking," 65.

[26]Alfred Plummer, *A Critical and Exegetical Commentary on the Gospel According to St. Luke,* ICC (Edinburgh: T & T Clark, 1928), 507, here speaks of Jesus' "sad irony."

[27]Twenty-three Synoptic dialogues are isolated by Rudolf Bultmann in *The History of the Synoptic Tradition,* trans. John Marsh, rev. ed. (New York: Harper & Row, 1963), 39–55. In no less than eighteen of these Jesus' reply includes a question: Matthew 12:27 par.; 15:3; 19:45; Mark 2:9 par., 19 par.; 3:3 par., 23 par.; 10:3, 18, 38; 12:16b par., 24, 26 par.; Luke 10:26; 12:14; 13:2, 4, 15–16; 14:3, 5. A brief discussion of the questions of Jesus appears in Stein, *The Method and Message of Jesus' Teachings,* 23-25.

[28]Considering irony as an indication of the authenticity of a saying of Jesus has been suggested by Gill, "Jesus, Irony and the New Quest," esp. 139–140. David E. Garland, *The Intention of Matthew 23,* Supplements to *Novum Testamentum* 52 (Leiden: E. J. Brill, 1979), 88, regards the irony of the "woes" as the mark of Jesus' own consciousness. Irony was earlier explored as an indicator of the prophetic mind in James G. Williams, "Irony and Lament: Clues to Prophetic Consciousness," *Semeia* 8 (1977), 51–71; and as a criterion for authenticity in W. L. Holladay, "Style, Irony and Authenticity in Jeremiah," *Journal of Biblical Literature* 81 (1962), 44–54.

[29]C. H. Dodd, *Historical Tradition in the Fourth Gospel* (Cambridge: Cambridge University Press, 1963), 319, reminds us that the Johannine dialogue form seems to have been influenced by current popular philosophical/religious dialogues, which apparently had their beginnings in the Socratic dialogues of Plato. Interestingly, Clavier, "L'ironie dans le quatrième Evangile," 264–265, takes precisely the opposite position from mine, saying that Jesus is actually less Socratic in John than in the Synoptics. Such a conclusion is possible for Clavier because, in my judgment, he overreads the Synoptics for irony not clearly present, and he reduces irony in John to the theme of Jesus' inscrutability.

[30]In that respect they typify the position of the reader of the Gospel as well. For a discussion of the disciples' relation to the reader, and John's characterization of the disciples singly and as a group, see Culpepper, *Anatomy,* 115–125.

[31]It will be recalled that one measure of irony is the degree of swaggering, or confident unawareness (alazony) displayed by the victim. See Muecke, *Compass,* 30.

[32]See Barrett, *John,* 154; Brown, *John,* I, 83; Bultmann, *John,* 103–104, n. 7.

[33]Cf. 5:12; 7:42; 8:53; *BDF,* 427, 2.

[34]The most likely Old Testament proof text is Judges 13:7. There is some evidence that Matthew is here and elsewhere making use of some early-established Christian exegesis. Eduard Schweizer, *The Good News According to Matthew,* trans. David E. Green (Atlanta: John Knox Press, 1975), 42.

[35]In this kind of ironic reiteration, "the pattern of repetition shows who is in charge of the flow of linguistic transactions." The status of Jesus is thus mirrored in the form of this exchange. He selects, the disciples follow; Amante, "Ironic Speech Acts," 160. Francis J. Moloney, "From Cana to Cana (Jn. 2:1—4:54) and the Fourth Evangelist's Concept of Correct (and Incorrect) Faith," *Salesianum* 40 (1978), 831, 836–837, in another context suggests that such repetition in John signifies an enacted refusal of Jesus' words, a failure to *receive* the words and a consequent *returning* of them.

[36]The irony is noted by Barrett, *John,* 496; and Lindars, *John,* 513. Kim E. Dewey, "*Paroimiai* in the Gospel of John," *Semeia* 17 (1980),

82, agrees that the disciples' remark serves only to emphasize their misunderstanding. Interestingly, Dewey takes *paroimiai* to include all forms of indirect speech in John, including irony. In that case Jesus' ironic response to the disciples in verse 31 is further indication that the time for "figures" has not passed.

[37]Cf. 6:42; 7:27; 9:24, 29. In each case except 7:27 and the present passage, however, the emphatic pronoun is added *(hēmeis)* to heighten the victims' confidence. The disciples are here spared that hubris. It should be noted that *oidamen* may also have serious confessional usage in the Fourth Gospel (cf. 3:11; 9:31).

[38]Bultmann, *John*, 591, notes the omission. Robert Alter, *The Art of Biblical Narrative* (New York: Basic Books, 1981), 88–113, stresses the importance of noting the changes or omissions in biblical repetitions.

[39]Irony is located in 1:45 by Barrett, *John*, 184; by Bernard, *John*, I, 62; and by Leon Morris, *The Gospel According to John*, New International Commentary on the New Testament (Grand Rapids: William B. Eerdmans, 1971), 165.

[40]John Painter, *Reading John's Gospel Today* (Atlanta: John Knox Press, 1980), 56.

[41]Culpepper, *Anatomy*, 123–124.

[42]See Wead, *Literary Devices*, 55, and possibly Barrett, *John*, 394.

[43]For an account of Mark's ironic treatment of the disciples as insiders who become outsiders, see Werner H. Kelber, *Mark's Story of Jesus* (Philadelphia: Fortress Press, 1979), 30–42, 49–53, 75–77. Dan O. Via, Jr., *Kerygma and Comedy in the New Testament* (Philadelphia: Fortress Press, 1975), 137, elaborates their roles as *alazōnes*, citing Mark 9:36; 10:28, 35–39a; 14:29, 31.

CHAPTER 4. Local Irony: Words from the Dark

[1]That *houtos* is used here with some disparagement is noted by Brown, *John*, I, 270. On the lips of Jesus' opponents this word will almost always signal irony (cf. 7:15, 26, 27, 35, 36; 9:16, 24; 18:30).

[2]Culpepper, *Anatomy*, 92, lists 3:4, 9; 4:9; 6:42, 52; 7:15; 8:33; 9:10, 15, 16, 19, 21, 26; 12:34; 14:5.

[3]Barrett, *John*, 295; Morris, *John*, 370; Hoskyns, *The Fourth*

Gospel, 296; William Temple, *Readings in St. John's Gospel* (London: Macmillan, 1940), I, 90. Those manuscripts and versions which omit *kai tēn mētera* (ℵ* W it^b syr^c, s, arm geo^j) are apparently under the same conviction.

⁴Bultmann, *John,* 229, is only partially correct in this regard when he says, "The folly of the Jews does not consist in their being mistaken about Jesus' father, but in their refusal to allow that a man might be the Revealer." The issue, however, is not Jesus' humanity but John's claim that the Jews do not know the Father.

⁵The connection is noted by Brown, *John,* I, 270, 276. The greatest concentration of the verb *gogguzein* in the LXX is in Exodus 15–17, where the Israelites, immediately following liberation from Egypt, murmur repeatedly about hunger and thirst (cf. Exod. 15:24; 16:2, 7 (twice), 9, 11; 17:3).

⁶This is an expectation upon which the Fourth Gospel capitalizes in 1:26. See Dodd, *Historical Tradition,* 266–269. On the expectation itself see Sigmund Mowinckel, *He That Cometh,* trans. G. W. Anderson (New York: Abingdon, [n.d.]), 304–308. It is significant that when Justin deals with this expectation he chooses to argue more directly with proofs from Scripture (*Trypho,* VIII, CX), a tactic which John's irony persistently eschews.

⁷In the *Odyssey,* for example, a suitor named Melantheus insults and kicks Odysseus, who he thinks is a beggar, and in the same breath makes reference to "divine Odysseus," XVI, 57. Similarly, in Euripides' *Helen,* Teucer speaks to Helen, not knowing who she is, and discusses how different she is from Helen: "For though in form thou does resemble Helen, thy soul is not like hers, nay, very different," 160–161.

⁸Says Lindars, *John,* 293, "As usual, there is an irony here: the people know where he comes from in the literal sense, but his real origin goes unrecognized; hence Jesus *does* pass this test."

⁹The significance of Jesus' temporary absence is noted by Marinus de Jonge, "Jesus as Prophet and King in the Fourth Gospel," *Ephemerides Theologicae Lovaniensis* 49 (1973), 165; reprinted in his *Jesus: Stranger from Heaven and Son of God,* ed. and trans. John E. Steely, Society of Biblical Literature Sources for Biblical Study, 11 (Missoula: Scholars Press, 1977), 54.

[10]This broad chiasmus in 7:40–52 is noted by Wayne A. Meeks, "Galilee and Judea in the Fourth Gospel," *Journal of Biblical Literature* 85 (1966), 160. J. Louis Martyn, *History and Theology in the Fourth Gospel*, rev. ed. (Nashville: Abingdon, 1979), 104–111, 115, however, warns against making any neat split between the categories of the Prophet and the Messiah, and actually considers the retort of verse 42 as an argument against Jesus as a Mosaic Prophet-Messiah.

[11]Among those who favor John's knowledge of the Bethlehem tradition are Barrett, *John*, 330–331; Brown, *John*, I, 330; Bernard, *John*, I, 286; Culpepper, *Anatomy*, 170-171; Hoskyns, *John*, 234; Morris, *John*, 429; and Adolf Schlatter, *Der Evangelist Johannes* (Stuttgart: Calwer Verlag, 1948), 203. Those dissenting include Bultmann, *John*, 306, n. 6; Lindars, *John*, 302; de Jonge, "Jesus as Prophet," 165; Meeks, "Galilee," 168, and *The Prophet-King*, Supplement to *Novum Testamentum*, 14 (Leiden: E. J. Brill, 1967), 37–38. Those taking a neutral position include Dodd, *Interpretation*, 91, and Schnackenburg, *John*, II, 158–159.

[12]Wayne A. Meeks, *The Prophet-King*, 37, raises three objections to this interpretation. He says first that such a reading of this verse "presupposes that the readers could not understand John without thorough acquaintance with the synoptic tradition." This claim is misleading. Readers perceiving the irony will need to have heard a tradition that Jesus was born in Bethlehem; that is all. The fact that two Synoptic authors present greatly differing versions of such a tradition hardly implies that John or his readers know the Synoptics or their particular versions of this tradition. Second, Meeks points out that "other ambiguous or ironic 'misunderstandings' by Jesus' opponents in John are eventually exposed in the development of the gospel," while "David" and "Bethlehem" are never mentioned again. The problem here is a confusion of terms. The Johannine "misunderstandings" are indeed always unraveled; the Johannine ironies, however, are more than once left without explicit exposition in the text. There is irony, for example, whose referent is the spread of Christianity to the Diaspora and the Greeks (7:35), the Roman destruction of Jerusalem (11:48), and the martyrdom of a disciple (13:38), none of which receives any comment from the narrator,

which would only weaken the irony. (Ironic references to extra-textual events occasionally occur in classical drama, as evidenced by some of Agamemnon's unwitting remarks in *Hecuba* [883, 1291–1292], which have their referent in another play.) Thirdly, Meeks says that considering verse 42 a positive testimony to Jesus destroys its parallelism with verse 52, which grants no positive testimony. Aside from the fact that, as will be seen, there are elements of positive testimony in verse 52, it should be noted that perfect parallelism is hardly required between these two verses. At the same time, our interpretation provides a good formal parallel with 7:27, considered above. There as here, an open negative reference to Jesus ("We know where this one is from"/"Is the Christ to come from Galilee?") is followed by a tradition about the Christ ("no one will know where he comes from"/"the Christ is descended from David and comes from Bethlehem"), which proves to be true of Jesus, thus reversing the early negative remark.

[13]Barrett's position, *John,* 330–331, is the same: "We may feel confident that John was aware of the tradition that Jesus was born at Bethlehem. . . . But John's irony goes far deeper than this. The birth of Jesus is a trivial matter in comparison with whether he is ἐκ τῶν ἄνω or ἐκ τῶν κάτω (8:23), whether he is or is not from God."

[14]Martyn, *History and Theology in the Fourth Gospel,* 115, n. 175; and Brown, *John,* I, 325. See also E. R. Smothers, "Two Readings in Papyrus Bodmer II," *Harvard Theological Review* 51 (1958), 109–111; and Bruce M. Metzger, *The Text of the New Testament,* 2d ed. (New York: Oxford University Press, 1968), 40. Lindars, *John,* 305, is not convinced, suggesting instead that the variant may have resulted from a copyist's insertion from verse 40.

[15]These Old Testament and rabbinic sources are given by Lindars, *John,* 305; and Barrett, *John,* 333.

[16]Martyn's remark, *History and Theology,* 115, n. 75, that "The Mosaic Prophet is to come, of course, not from Galilee, but from the wilderness" seems more from inference than textual evidence. Lindars, *John,* 305, notes the absence of speculation regarding the Prophet's origin.

[17]Interestingly enough, a fragment of an unknown Gospel (Papyrus Egerton 2) combines Jesus' "You search the scriptures" (John 5:39)

with "it is Moses who accuses you" (5:45) and "the Jews'" response "We know well that God spoke to Moses, but as for you, we do not know where you come from" (9:29); see Lindars, *John,* 230.

[18]Lindars, *John,* 182–183, notes the literary significance of woman's elaboration. "Moreover, by mentioning the cattle (and Jacob had vast flocks and herds [Gen. 31–33]), the woman hints that it must be a very copious supply of water. This makes Jesus' claim seem even more impossible, but takes the irony further, for in fact his waters are inexhaustible. Thus what appears to be an artless allusion to the history of the site turns out to be a subtle step in the progress of the discourse."

[19]Jerome H. Neyrey, "Jacob Traditions and the Interpretation of John 4:10–26." *Catholic Biblical Quarterly* 41 (1979), 419–437, makes the interesting but doubtful suggestion that the conscious theme here is of Jacob the supplanter being supplanted by Jesus.

[20]Schlatter, *Der Evangelist Johannes,* 218, remarks of verse 52, "That Abraham died is the most conclusive proof for the inevitability of death." The indefinite *hostis* in verse 53 points to such an emphasis, making Abraham a singular type of mortal humanity; see *BDF,* 293, 2.

[21]A textual variant quite naturally arose to smooth over this error, which the Gospel's sophisticated author almost certainly intended as such. "Abraham has seen you [*eōraken se*]" is read by p[75] ℵ* 0124 syr[s] and three Coptic versions.

[22]So Brown, *John,* I, 312; and Lindars, *John,* 287. That 7:15 originally followed the reference to the *grammasin* of Moses in 5:47 (Bultmann, Bernard, Sanders, Schnackenburg) is a solution that is both untenable and unnecessary.

[23]Note the crucial, framing position of the last ascription of "Teacher" (20:16). It is the first word uttered by the first person who recognizes the resurrected Christ. One is tempted to wonder if John's repeated translations of such words as "rabbi" (and "Messiah") are less for clarity of meaning and more to emphasize the theological stress intended in these titles.

[24]Barrett, *John,* 319; Lindars, *John,* 290; Brown, *John,* I, 310, translates, "You're demented."

[25]So Bultmann, *John,* 277; and Schnackenburg, *John,* II, 133. Barrett, *John,* 319, and Lindars, *John,* 290, admit uncertainty. For a

general discussion of the relation between "the Jews" and "the crowd" see Culpepper, *Anatomy*, 131–132.

[26]Lindars, *John*, 290.

[27]If, in fact, they do not know that they will kill Jesus, the irony is not unlike that of Sophocles' *Oedipus*, in which the protagonist expends a great deal of energy asking who the murderer of his father is, when all along the murderer is himself. When first confronted with the fact of a defiling offender, Oedipus responds, "And who is the man, the miscreant thus denounced?", 102, or, as J. A. K. Thomson, *Irony: An Historical Introduction*, 64, translates, "The guilty—who is he?"

[28]The irony is noted by Barnabas Lindars, *Behind the Fourth Gospel*, Studies in Creative Criticism, 3 (London: SPCK, 1971), 45.

[29]Lindars, *John*, 331; and Barrett, *John*, 350. Barrett bases his opinion upon the fact that Jesus gives a single reply to the two accusations, an interpretation which overlooks Jesus' refusal to include "Samaritan" in his denial.

[30]Schlatter, *Der Evangelist Johannes*, 217; Bultmann, *John*, 225, n. 6; Brown, *John*, I, 358; and John Bowman, "The Fourth Gospel and the Samaritans," *Bulletin of the John Rylands Library* 40 (1958), 306.

[31]Hoskyns, *John*, 345.

[32]Bowman, "The Fourth Gospel and the Samaritans," 307, in view of the fact that "sons of the devil," is what a Samaritan might call the Jews; see also Bernard, *John*, II, 316.

[33]For example, George Wesley Buchanan, "The Samaritan Origin of the Gospel of John," *Religions in Antiquity*, ed. Jacob Neusner, Studies in the History of Religions, 14 (Leiden: E. J. Brill, 1968), 149–175; and Edwin D. Freed, "Samaritan Influence in the Gospel of John," *Catholic Biblical Quarterly* 30 (1968), 580–587.

[34]For discussions of recent opinions regarding the relationship of the Fourth Gospel and the Samaritans, see Robert Kysar, *The Fourth Evangelist and His Gospel* (Minneapolis: Augsburg Publishing House, 1975), 160–163; and Raymond E. Brown, *The Community of the Beloved Disciple* (New York: Paulist Press, 1979), 35–40. Says Brown, p. 37, of 8:48, "This suggests that the Johannine community was regarded by Jews as having Samaritan elements."

[35]Such irony has a marvelous parallel in the jibe reported in Matthew 11:19/Luke 7:34: "Friend of tax collectors and sinners!"

[36]For example, Barrett, *John*, 348; Brown, *John*, I, 357; Lindars, *John*, 212; Sanders, *John*, 230. Dodd, *Interpretation*, 260, stresses that it is only a possibility.

[37]Schnackenburg, *John*, II, 212, suggests that *hēmeis* could simply be in response to Jesus' *humeis* in verse 41, or it could mean *we* as opposed to our disloyal ancestors, or as Dodd, *Interpretation*, 260, n. 1, suggests, *we* Jews as distinct from the Gentile nations.

[38]Origen, *Against Celsus*, 1:28; and in Acts of Pilate 2:13 the Jews actually say, "You are born of fornication."

[39]For a helpful analysis of the delaying technique employed here by Jesus, see Lindars, *Behind the Fourth Gospel*, 44–45.

[40]Lindars, *John*, 373.

[41]Barrett, *John*, 384. The regularly ironic misunderstanding of the kind of *anthrōpos* Jesus is will be a subject of discussion in chapter 6.

[42]Severino Pancaro, *The Law in the Fourth Gospel*, Supplements to *Novum Testamentum* 42 (Leiden: E. J. Brill, 1975), 18. Pancaro, p. 29, phrases John's point of view this way: "the question is not 'Can Jesus be a man of God and notwithstanding that still work on the Sabbath?' but, 'As Son of God *must* Jesus not work also on the Sabbath?'"

[43]Brown, *John*, I, 373, lists four ways in which Jesus may be said to have skirted the law.

[44]This contrast is forcefully argued by Pancaro, *Law*, 19–20.

[45]Brown, *John*, I, 374, notes the possibility of double meaning here.

[46]See Pancaro, *Law*, 30–52, which contains a careful study of *hamartōlos* in the Fourth Gospel and elsewhere. Pancaro, pp. 51–52, points out that while John flatly denies that Jesus can be accused of sin, he allows the accusation of sinner to be made. He notes that Johannine Christians will have certainly borne this charge themselves, a charge which reaffirmed to them their faithfulness to Jesus.

[47]Martyn, *History and Theology in the Fourth Gospel*, 86–89, sensibly stresses that the author could have done this without being "analytically conscious" of it, and without "playing a kind of code-game."

[48]Wead's assessment, *Literary Devices,* 67, that the negative particle is used here as "cautious assertion," that the man actually hopes the Pharisees may become disciples, and that "Ironically his hopes are wrong," seems to me a serious misreading of John's ironic style.

[49]Bultmann, *John,* 336.

[50]Pancaro, *Law,* 24–25.

[51]Mary Douglas, "The Social Control of Cognition: Some Factors in Joke Perception," *Man* 3 (1968), 367.

[52]Schnackenburg, *John,* I, 334. Birger Olsson, *Structure and Meaning in the Fourth Gospel,* trans. Jean Gray (Lund, Sweden: CWK Gleerup, 1974), 61, n. 85, notes that the last speech in the Johannine dialogues, and usually the longest as is the case here, has an essential function. Particularly when a narrative ends with direct speech is the author's didactic interest apparent.

[53]A number of commentators note this ironic quality of the steward's remark. Clavier, "L'ironie dans quatrième Evangile," 270, deems it "a prophetic anticipation"; Westcott, *John,* 142, calls it "one of those unconscious prophecies"; Hoskyns, *John,* 189, says "correctly but unconsciously he states the point at issue." Irony is also noted by Dodd, *Interpretation,* 297, and Culpepper, *Anatomy,* 173. Even John Marsh, *The Gospel of John,* The Pelican Gospel Commentaries (London: Penguin Books, 1968), 146, who normally rushes by such things, reflects, "There is a world of silent comment in the sentence."

[54]Dewey, "*Paroimiai* in the Gospel of John," 86.

[55]Such sarcasm is suggested by Culpepper, *Anatomy,* 173. Giblin, "Suggestion, Negative Response, and Positive Action," 206–207, claims too much, I think, in pointing to an ironic force in their choice of the word *metabainein.*

[56]For overstatement as a method of irony or a clue to its presence, see chapter 2.

[57]Dodd, *Interpretation,* 351. The irony is also noted by Morris, *John,* 397, and by Clavier, "L'ironie dans le quatrième Evangile," 272, who remarks that this unwitting prediction that the *world* will see Jesus is doubly ironic in that it is spoken by his own *brothers,* who do not believe in him. It might be added that though certainly unintended

by the author, it is no less ironic that here the brothers of Jesus occupy precisely the same role as the Synoptic Satan, who invites Jesus to engage in open display of power in Jerusalem (Matt. 4:5–6/Luke 4:9–11). Brown, *John,* I, 308, however, sees the process working in reverse in all three temptations; the Synoptics mythologize what the Fourth Gospel reports as humanly inspired; see also his "Incidents That Are Units in the Synoptic Gospels, but Dispersed in St. John," *Catholic Biblical Quarterly* 23 (1963), 152–155.

⁵⁸See Lindars, *John,* 296; Brown, *John,* I, 318; Barrett, *John,* 269; Bultmann, *John,* 309.

⁵⁹Barrett, *John,* 325; Morris, *John,* 418. Brown, *Community,* 57, suggests that the irony of this prediction may constitute "a portrait of the Johannine community."

⁶⁰So Schnackenburg, *John,* II, 198. Suicide would be a sure means of exclusion from the future age.

⁶¹Wayne A. Meeks, "The Man from Heaven in Johannine Sectarianism," *Journal of Biblical Literature* 41 (1972), 64, says, "The Jews' statement represents the view of the voluntary death *ek tōn katō;* Jesus' statement, the view *ek tōn anō.*"

⁶²This pattern of a figure of speech turning out to be literal truth is common in ancient dramatic irony. In the *Odyssey,* Odysseus beseeches a stranger with a simile, "To thee I pray as to a god," (XIII, 230–1)—and the stranger is Athena. Likewise in the *Oedipus,* the king pledges to avenge the death of Laius "as though he were my sire" (264), which he literally had been. And in Tobit 5:16 Tobit uses a figure of speech to bless Tobias, who is standing ready to depart with a stranger: "May [God's] angel attend you"—and the stranger is Raphael.

⁶³Calvin's comment, *The Gospel According to St. John and the First Epistle of John,* trans. T. H. L. Parker, *Calvin's Commentaries,* 2 vols. (Grand Rapids: William B. Eerdmans, 1961), II, 35, is worth quoting, "For it is a sort of reproach of their slothfulness—as if they had said that the reason why the people revolted to Christ was their own excessive slowness and spinelessness." *Alazōnes* indeed, to suppose the "hour" has been waiting on them!

⁶⁴Muecke, *Compass,* 102.

⁶⁵Barrett, *John,* 405, comments on this "striking example of Johannine irony." John A. T. Robinson, *Redating the New Testament*

(Philadelphia: Westminster Press, 1976), 276, must ignore the weight of John's persistent ironic method and speak instead of "unfulfilled prophecy."

[66]Pancaro, *Law,* 121–122.

[67]Culpepper connects the irony of these two texts, *Anatomy,* 169.

[68]Pancaro, "'People of God,' in St. John's Gospel," 114–129.

[69]Westcott, John, p. 175; Pancaro, "People of God," 121.

[70]On the centrality of *tekna tou theou* here and elsewhere in the Fourth Gospel, see R. Alan Culpepper, "The Pivot of John's Prologue," *New Testament Studies* 27 (1980), 1–31.

[71]Demonstrated by C. H. Dodd, "The Prophecy of Caiaphas, John 11:47–53," *Neotestamentica et Patristica,* Supplements to *Novum Testamentum* 6 (Leiden: E. J. Brill, 1962), 139–140.

[72]That the author intends a reference to Son of man is argued by Dodd, *Interpretation,* 437; Meeks, *Prophet-King,* 70–71; Josef Blank, "Die Verhandlung vor Pilatus Jo 18:28—19:16 im Lichte johanneischer Theologie," *Biblische Zeitschrift* 3 (1959), 75; and C. F. Evans, "The Passion of John," *Explorations in Theology 2* (London: SCM Press, 1977), 60.

[73]Unless one considers the narrator's comment in 2:21–22 a clarification of the irony, as does Wead, *Literary Devices,* 55. As indicated above, the weight of these verses seems to me more to overshadow the irony.

[74]Thomas' ironic misunderstanding of suffering and death (11:16; cf. 20:24–25) is, of course, a uniquely Johannine approach to the subject, wherein the heresy refuted is not a crossless theology but a hopeless theology, grim and blind to the glory. It is difficult to find evidence of need for such correction in the later Johannine community.

CHAPTER 5. Extended Irony

[1]Booth, *A Rhetoric of Irony,* 33–39.

[2]See James D. G. Dunn, "The Washing of the Disciples' Feet in John 13:1–20," *Zeitschrift für die neutestamentliche Wissenschaft* 61 (1970), 246–252.

[3]Culpepper, *Anatomy,* 120.

[4]Ibid., 119. It is interesting that another situational irony has been

located in Mark's juxtaposition of Peter's denial and the trial before the high priest. Donald Juel, *Messiah and Temple,* Society of Biblical Literature Dissertation Series 31 (Missoula: Scholars Press, 1977), 71, 73, notes that at the very moment the high priest's minions mock Jesus as false prophet, Peter's denials in the courtyard below unfold precisely as Jesus had prophesied.

⁵Brown, *John,* I, 80, insists that there is no significance to the future tense and points to similar usage in the LXX of Genesis 17:5, 15; also Brown, Karl P. Donfried and John Reumann, eds., *Peter in the New Testament* (Minneapolis: Augsburg Publishing House, 1973), 131, n. 279; and Barrett, *John,* 182. Bultmann, *John,* 101, n. 5, wrongly identifies the future tense as a foretelling of another scene known to the readers (from Matt. 10:16?) in which Simon will actually receive the name Peter; Schnackenburg, *John,* I, 311–312, with good reason I think, considers Jesus' words as a more general prophecy of who Simon will become. That such a prophetic element is included need not rule out that the name itself is changed as of 1:42.

⁶For example, the disciples as a group in 16:29–30 betray the same overeagerness and failure to understand Jesus' death that Peter demonstrates throughout. His representative character is also evident in 6:68–69 and 13:22–24. Oscar Cullmann, *Peter: Disciple, Apostle, Martyr,* trans. Floyd V. Filson (London: SCM Press, 1953), 27–30, emphasizes Peter's representative role in John as in the Synoptics; see also Raymond F. Collins, "The Representative Figures of the Fourth Gospel," *The Downside Review* 94 (1976), 126–129.

⁷Culpepper, *Anatomy,* 120–121.

⁸Cf. Mark 3:19 par.; 14:10–11 par., 43 par.

⁹The contrast is noted by D. Bruce Woll, *Johannine Christianity in Conflict,* Society of Biblical Literature Dissertation Series 60 (Missoula: Scholars Press, 1981), 88.

¹⁰Barrett, *John,* 448, "though he no longer holds his place with the Eleven, he is instantly obedient to the word of Jesus and goes out as he is bidden."

¹¹Culpepper, *Anatomy,* 174.

¹²Ibid., 124–125.

¹³Unfortunately, the literary sensitivity of some scholars is diverted

here by the trivial fact that Judas' presence has already been mentioned. Brown, *John,* II, 810, calls it "a very awkward editorial insertion" and wonders if it echoes Synoptic tradition. Bultmann, *John,* 640, speaks of its derivation from the Passion source. Lindars, *John,* 541, on the other hand, takes note of the dramatic effect of the sentence and ties it to 13:19. Barrett, *John,* 520, cites the extravagant but insightful tradition that Judas was unable to move because stricken with blindness or paralysis.

[14]These three instances were structurally compared by Robert C. Culley, *Studies in the Structure of Hebrew Narrative* (Philadelphia: Fortress Press, 1976), 41–43. A more recent and detailed analysis is offered by Robert Alter, *The Art of Biblical Narrative,* 51–62. Alter calls this structure the "type-scene" of "betrothal at the well" and demonstrates its use as a convention. That the imagery of Christ as Bridegroom informs a portion of the dialogue with the woman (4:16–18) is self-evident; but surprisingly little has appeared on the story's structural affinities with the betrothal type-scenes. Jerome H. Neyrey, "Jacob Traditions" 425–426, discusses some similarities with Jacob's courtship of Rachel. Normand R. Bonneau, "The Woman at the Well: John 4 and Genesis 24," *The Bible Today* 67 (1973), 1252–1259, gives a much fuller account of structural similarities with Isaac's betrothal. Neither writer, however, does justice to this structure as a received literary convention; consequently neither writer gives attention to the expectations of the conditioned reader and the resultant irony.

[15]Alter, *The Art of Biblical Narrative,* 52–58; passive Isaac's well scene is enacted by his father's servant and a dominating Rebekah. Jacob, always associated with stones, must labor to remove the well cover for Rachel, whose hand in marriage will also require labor and whose womb will be slow to open. Moses the deliverer must drive away belligerent shepherds for Zipporah and her sisters.

[16]Ibid., 52.

[17]Brown, *John,* I, 170, notes the likely progression in the woman's use of *kurie* in verses 11, 15, 19.

[18]Walter Bauer, William F. Arndt, and F. Wilbur Gingrich, *A Greek-English Lexicon of the New Testament and Other Early Christian Literature,* 4th ed. (Chicago: University of Chicago Press,

1957), 460, which also cites secular examples. For earlier instances of this usage see Werner Foerster, "κύριος," *Theological Dictionary of the New Testament*, ed. Gerhard Kittel, trans. Geoffrey W. Bromiley (Grand Rapids: William B. Eerdmans, 1965), III, 1043.

[19]Alter, *The Art of Biblical Narrative*, 52.

[20]The disguised Odysseus addresses Penelope as *gunai* in the *Odyssey*, XIX, 165, 221, 336.

[21]It is quite common in dramatic irony that one character talks about a character thought to be absent, when in fact that character is the very one addressed. See *Odyssey*, XIV, 40–44, 145–147; Euripides, *Ion*, 313, 325; *Electra*, 245, 263, 283. A similar instance is a speech by Penelope to a servant concerning what will happen when Odysseus comes, while, unknown to her, Odysseus is already her houseguest, *Odyssey*, XVII, 538–540.

[22]Morris, *John*, 838.

[23]It is tempting to side with the imaginative authors who have found Edenic overtones in Mary's mistaking Jesus for "the gardener"—and so one of those ironies by unconscious testimony. See Edwyn Clement Hoskyns, "Genesis I—III and St. John's Gospel," *Journal of Theological Studies* 21 (1920), 214–215; and *The Fourth Gospel*, 542; R. H. Lightfoot, *St. John's Gospel*, ed. C. F. Evans (Oxford: Oxford University Press, 1956), 321–322.

[24]Again, it is not uncommon in dramatic irony for one character to speak to some stranger concerning the demise of a loved one, when the "stranger" is none other than the alleged deceased. Cf. Gen. 42:13; 44: 20, 28; *Odyssey*, XIV, 68, 137; *Ion*, 348; Luke 24:19–24.

[25]There is a steady ascendancy of *kurios* in chapter 20 (vss. 2, 13, 15, 18, 20, 25) until finally in verse 28 Thomas takes it to its zenith. J. N. Sanders and B. A. Mastin, *John*, 427.

[26]On the classic distinction between writing that *tells* and writing that *shows*, along with a healthy warning against distinguishing them too clearly, see Booth, *The Rhetoric of Fiction*, 2–20.

[27]Culpepper, *Anatomy*, 171.

[28]Barrett, *John*, 360, offers the paraphrase and adds that the Pharisees' implication is that Jesus is certainly not more than human.

[29]Culpepper, *Anatomy*, 171.

[30]p[66, 75], favored by Brown, *John,* I, 319; Barrett, *John,* 331; Bruce M. Metzger, *A Textual Commentary on the Greek New Testament* (n.p.: United Bible Societies, 1971), 219.

[31]Francis J. Moloney, *The Johannine Son of Man,* Biblioteca di Scienze Religiose, 14, 2d ed. (Rome: Libreria Ateneo Salesiano, 1978), 205.

[32]Josef Blank, "Die Verhandlung vor Pilatus," 60–81, followed by Wayne A. Meeks, *The Prophet-King,* 70-71; and Marinus de Jonge, *Jesus: Stranger from Heaven,* 75.

[33]Meeks, *The Prophet-King,* 70.

[34]Ibid, 71. Meeks cites Zechariah 6:12 as a likely source: "Behold a man whose name is the Branch."

[35]Blank, "Die Verhandlung vor Pilatus," 75. Further, as Moloney, *The Johannine Son of Man,* 206, notes, it has twice been said that the Son of man would be lifted up (8:28; 12:23, 32–34), the second reference revealing this to be the method of Jesus' death, i.e., crucifixion. Significantly, when "the man" is presented, "the Jews" respond, "crucify."

[36]See Ernst Käsemann, *The Testament of Jesus,* trans. Gerhard Krodel (Philadelphia: Fortress Press, 1968), 13.

[37]George W. MacRae, "Theology and Irony in the Fourth Gospel," 92, says that the pronouncement in 19:5 is "the most ironical and theologically profound assertion made in the Pilate trial."

[38]Barrett, *John,* 541; Moloney, *The Johannine Son of Man,* 207.

[39]It is well to deal at the outset with the issue of historicity. To say that any image in the Fourth Gospel is symbolic or ironic is not necessarily to discount its factuality. As Sandra M. Schneiders, "History and Symbolism in the Fourth Gospel," *L'évangile de Jean: Sources, Rédaction, Théologie,* Bibliotheca ephemeridum theologicarum lovaniensum, 44 (Louvain: Louvain University, 1977), 371, 375, has said, "There is not an inverse proportion between the historical and the symbolic in the Fourth Gospel." Noting scholarly debate about whether the darkness in 20:1 is symbolic or factual, she denies any necessity to choose. The two categories more than intersect. "Because history is used by John as symbolic material, the more historical it is seen to be, the more symbolic it is seen to be."

[40]At 3:1–2 John's symbols of light and darkness are as yet not fully

developed; and though their significance has been stated clearly in the prologue, the reader may not realize in a first reading that "night" in 3:2 has symbolic and ironic import. The cumulative weight of the Gospel, however, and particularly the repetition of this detail in 19:39, leaves little doubt of the symbolic/ironic intent of this verse. See Culpepper, *Anatomy*, 192. Lindars, *John*, 149, says, "It is a detail which only becomes meaningful when the whole piece has been read."

[41]Brown, *John*, I, 130; Lindars, *John*, 149. J. Louis Martyn, *History and Theology in the Fourth Gospel*, 116, points to the possibility that the detail signifies the fear of secret believers in the evangelist's day.

[42]Gerald Vann, *The Eagle's Word* (New York: Harcourt, Brace and World, 1961), 14.

[43]Raymond E. Brown, "The Passion According to John: Chapters 18 and 19," *Worship* 49 (1975), 127.

[44]Ibid., 128.

[45]C. F. Evans, "The Passion of John," 57.

[46]Cited by MacGreggor, *John*, 353.

[47]Brown, *John*, II, 960.

[48]Meeks, "The Man from Heaven in Johannine Sectarianism," 55; see also M. de Jonge, "Nicodemus and Jesus: Some Observations on Misunderstanding and Understanding in the Fourth Gospel," *Bulletin of the John Rylands Library* 53 (1971), 343; reprinted in his *Jesus: Stranger from Heaven*, 34.

[49]Cf. 10:22–23, where "winter," while an accurate notation of the season, may be mentioned by the narrator as symbolic indication that during Israel's celebration of the temple, someone walks through its porticoes whose rejection by Israel signals the death of the holy place. See Hoskyns, *John*, 386. There is also ironic imagery in the trial, to be discussed later.

[50]MacRae, "Theology and Irony in the Fourth Gospel," 89.

[51]"The foundational irony of the gospel is that the Jews rejected the Messiah they eagerly expected," Culpepper, *Anatomy*, 169.

[52]"The Jews'" initial innocuousness serves not only to show a progression of their rejection of Jesus, but permits the author to establish in the reader's mind who it is they reject. As Culpepper, *Anatomy*, 91, has shown, chapters 1–4 "have a powerful primacy

effect, i.e., they firmly establish the reader's first impression of Jesus' identity and mission. The reader is led to accept the evangelist's view of Jesus before the antithetical point of view is given more than passing reference."

[53]Meeks, "Man from Heaven," 58, notes this "very heavy" irony.

[54]Dodd, *Interpretation,* 90; the irony of the signs' ambiguity is also noted by MacRae, "Theology and Irony in the Fourth Gospel," 93.

[55]MacRae, "Theology and Irony in the Fourth Gospel," 94.

[56]Northrop Frye, *Anatomy of Criticism,* 162, places irony on a continuum between tragedy and comedy. Auspicious beginnings can swing down into tragic irony, or threatening circumstances can rise into comic irony.

CHAPTER 6. Sustained Narrative Irony: Two Case Studies

[1]D. Moody Smith, *John,* Proclamation Commentaries, ed. Gerhard Krodel (Philadelphia: Fortress Press, 1976), 40, notes that 1:9–13 take on "concreteness and specificity in light of this story."

[2]Brown, *John,* I, 376.

[3]See Martyn, *History and Theology in the Fourth Gospel,* 27–36, 129–151.

[4]Ibid., 26.

[5]George W. MacRae, *Invitation to John* (Garden City, N. Y.: Image Books, 1978), 124. I have altered his first scene, "Jesus and the disciples," to "Jesus and the blind man," because of the minor role played by the disciples and the enriched parallel of motif that results with such a change (see below).

[6]It is a theme not unique to John's irony, for one recalls the figure of blind Teiresias, who, taunted by Oedipus for his blindness, saw what the king would not see, especially that Oedipus would soon blind himself quite literally; *Oedipus,* 300–462. Teiresias also appears as a blind seer in *Antigone, Odyssey* XI, and Euripides' *Bacchae* and *The Phoenecian Women.*

[7]For this reason I think Robert Thomson Fortna's conclusion, *The Gospel of Signs,* Society for New Testament Studies Monograph Series, 11 (Cambridge: Cambridge University Press, 1970), 71, is misleading that "the issue of the man's sin has no importance in the

dramatic scenes which follow (only incidentally at vs. 34), where the principal issue is whether *Jesus* is a sinner." In fact, the subject of sin as it pertains to the man, the Pharisees, and Jesus constitutes one issue.

[8]Hoskyns, *John*, 355, quoting Quesnell, "He is no longer the same man."

[9]Schnackenburg, *John*, II, 497, n. 24, observes that the man's failure to mention spittle locates his version "as he experienced it when blind," an interesting instance of the author's attention to point of view (or point of no-view!).

[10]Henry George Liddell and Robert Scott, *A Greek-English Lexicon*, rev. ed. (Oxford: The Clarendon Press, 1940), I, 483.

[11]Schnackenburg, *John*, II, 248.

[12]Bultmann, *John*, 335.

[13]MacRae, *Invitation to John*, 126, finds this scene central because of its explanation of the synagogue ban. Though I include the ban as part of the centrality of the scene, I find even more important the point made here that "the Jews" are now in full knowledge of the fact of the healing.

[14]See above, page 78.

[15]The scene between Oedipus and blind Teiresias, which we have cited as paralleling John's narrative, has a similar development:

Oed.: Are these taunts to be indeed borne from *him?*—Hence, ruin take thee! Hence this instant! Back!—away!—avaunt thee from these doors!

Teir.: I had never come, not I, hadst thou not called me.——
(429–432)

[16]Bultmann, *John*, 337.

[17]Ibid., 339.

[18]See Martyn, *History and Theology*, 140–143. A good number of manuscripts reflect the same expectation.

[19]Dodd's remark, *Interpretation*, 358, is typically sensitive to the drama: "When he is 'cast out,' it is Christ whom the judges have rejected. Then comes the dramatic *peripeteia*. Jesus swiftly turns the tables on his judges. . . ."

[20]Brown, *John*, I, 337, gives a good summary of these movements.

[21]This now generally recognized structure was apparently first

identified by R. H. Strachan, *The Fourth Gospel*, 3d ed. (London: Student Christian Movement Press, 1941), 310.

[22]Dodd, *Historical Tradition*, 96; see also Ernst Haenchen, "History and Interpretation in the Johannine Passion Narrative," *Interpretation* 24 (1970), 206.

[23]For this reason we disagree with those scholars who seek to minimize Pilate's importance in the narrative. Pancaro, *Law*, 315, n. 31, says, "Pilate is . . . extraneous to the whole religious drama." Haenchen, "History and Interpretation," 207, says, "Pilate was important only insofar as he exonerated Jesus without finally understanding him." Pilate's centrality in the structure of the seven scenes and the author's subtle attention to his character points to a far more significant representative role.

[24]Blank, "Die Verhandlung," 63.

[25]Bultmann, *John*, 651; cf. Blank, "Die Verhandlung," 66.

[26]Brown, *John*, II, 866.

[27]Ibid., and Rudolf Schnackenburg, *Das Johannesevangelium*, Herders theologischer Kommentar zum Neuen Testament (Freiburg: Herder, 1975), III, 279.

[28]Brown, *John*, II, 867.

[29]De Jonge, *Jesus, Stranger from Heaven*, 68, 76, n. 69, says Pilate's line is not a question but a declaration, one of this Gospel's unconscious confessional statements. If so, Pilate means to mock Jesus—"So *you* are the King of the Jews!"—and inadvertently states the truth. Similarly, the NEB offers an alternative reading in which Pilate coolly says, "You are the King of the Jews, I take it." We do not find such an interpretation compelling, especially in view of the identical words in each of the Synoptics (although only the Synoptics specify that Pilate *asked*). John's keen eye for such ironies nevertheless forbids us to rule out the possibility.

[30]Barrett, *John*, 536.

[31]Wayne A. Meeks, "'Am I a Jew?'—Johannine Christianity and Judaism," *Christianity, Judaism and Other Greco-Roman Cults*, ed. Jacob Neusner (Leiden: E. J. Brill, 1975), I, 163.

[32]An ironic tone was noted here by B. F. Westcott, *John*, 260; see also David W. Wead, *Literary Devices*, 56; and Morris, *John*, 770. For

a helpful discussion of the possible meanings of *oukoun* here see
C. F. D. Moule, *An Idiom Book of New Testament Greek*, 2d ed.
(Cambridge: Cambridge University Press, 1959), 165.

[33]Westcott, *John*, 260.

[34]Bultmann, *John*, 654, n. 6, says Jesus' answer is affirmative.
Lindars, *John*, 559, takes it to mean "You say it in a political sense, but
my kingship is otherwise." Brown, *John*, II, 853, rightly I think, takes it
in the qualified sense: "It is you who say it, not I."

[35]Haenchen, "History and Interpretation," 211, n. 28.

[36]Francis Bacon, "Of Truth," *Bacon's Essays with Annotations*,
ed. Richard Whately (Boston: Lee and Shepard, 1880), 1.

[37]Pancaro, *Law*, 311, n. 19, is right in insisting that Pilate's
repeated announcement of Jesus' innocence does not so much reflect
the church's apologetic interest in exonerating Rome, as it reflects a
crucial theological theme in the narrative.

[38]Brown, *John*, II, 869.

[39]Meeks, *Prophet-King*, 68.

[40]Brown, *John*, II, 872.

[41]Ibid., 886–888.

[42]Ibid., 889.

[43]Meeks, *Prophet-King*, 69.

[44]Blank, "Die Verhandlung," 62.

[45]Moloney, *The Johannine Son of Man*, 205.

[46]Brown, *John*, II, 890.

[47]Bultmann, *John*, 659.

[48]Pancaro, *Law*, 319–323, ties 19:7 to the New Testament theme
of divine necessity (*dei*) for Jesus' death. The fulfillment of Scripture in
the death of Jesus is emphasized in 19:24, 28, 36, 37.

[49]Brown, *John*, II, 891.

[50]Says Culpepper, *Anatomy*, 174, "Having been arrested by those
less powerful than he, Jesus is tried by those with less authority than
himself."

[51]Morris, *John*, 798.

[52]Evans, "The Passion of John," 61.

[53]For a comprehensive argument for Jesus' presence on the *bēma*,
see I. de la Potterie, "Jesus King and Judge According to John 19:13,"
Scripture 13 (1961), 97–111; also Meeks, *Prophet-King*, 73–76; and

Haenchen, "History and Interpretation," 216. Scholars arguing against the likelihood of this interpretation include Brown, *John,* II, 881; Bultmann, *John,* 664, n. 2; Lindars, *John,* 570; Schnackenburg, *Johannesevangelium,* III, 305; Wead, *Literary Devices,* 58. That the evangelist might have intended a meaningful ambiguity is suggested by Barrett, *John,* 544. Interestingly, both the Gospel of Peter (3:7) and Justin (1:35–36) report that Jesus was placed on the judgment seat and mocked.

[54]Brown, *John,* II, 895.

[55]Blank, "Die Verhandlung," 62.

[56]Meeks, *Prophet-King,* 76–77, cites this hymn, admitting uncertainty as to the date that it became part of the Seder, but he believes it was used quite early in Palestine. Brown, *John,* II, 895, seems to agree.

[57]Lindars, *John,* 572.

[58]Heinrich Schlier, "Jesus und Pilatus—Nach dem Johannesevangelium," *Die Zeit der Kirche: Exegetische Aufsätze und Vortrage* (Freiburg: Verlag Herder, 1958), 73.

[59]Culpepper, *Anatomy,* 169.

[60]Bultmann, *John,* 669; Dodd, *Interpretation,* 371, 436.

[61]Wayne Booth, *A Rhetoric of Irony,* 28, n. 21, contrasts Mark's silence regarding the people's mockery of Jesus as king with this Johannine elaboration that "weakens" the irony. John's point, however, is the opposite of Mark's. Mark's "crowd" (and John's soldiers—19:3) is ignorant of Jesus' true identity, and therein is that irony. John's deeper tragedy and deeper irony lie in the fact that Pilate now *knows* something of the identity of this one he has betrayed; and "the Jews" themselves are nervous about the sign not only because it mocks them, but because they too, not at all blind, have *chosen* not to see.

[62]See Brown, *John,* II, 859.

CHAPTER 7. Irony and the Johannine Context

[1]One can consult summaries of the alternatives in Stephen S. Smalley, *John: Evangelist and Interpreter* (Greenwood, S. C.: Attic Press, 1978), 41–68; Robert Kysar, *The Fourth Evangelist and His Gospel,* 102–146; and his "Community and Gospel: Vectors in the Fourth Gospel Criticism," *Interpretation* 31 (1977), 362–364.

²See, for example, Brown, *John*, I, lii–lxiv; Lindars, *John*, 36–38; Schnackenburg, *John*, 119–135; C. K. Barrett, *The Gospel of John and Judaism*, trans. D. M. Smith (Philadelphia: Fortress Press, 1975); Martyn, *History and Theology;* D. Moody Smith, *John*, 9–10.

³George W. MacRae, "The Fourth Gospel and *Religionsgeschichte*," *Catholic Biblical Quarterly* 32 (1970), 13–24; see also Kysar, *The Fourth Evangelist*, 145–146.

⁴J. A. K. Thomson, *Irony*, 2.

⁵A spate of articles on the dramatic quality of John's Gospel appeared in earlier decades of this century. See F. R. M. Hitchcock, "The Dramatic Development of the Fourth Gospel," *The Expositor*, 7, vol. 4 (1907), 266–279, and his "Is the Fourth Gospel a Drama?" *Theology* 7 (1923), 307–317; Clayton R. Bowen, "The Fourth Gospel as Dramatic Material," *Journal of Biblical Literature* 49 (1930), 292–305; Hans Windisch, "Der johanneische Erzählungsstil," 'ΕΥΧΑΡΙΣΤΗΡΙΟΝ: *Studien zur Religion und Literatur des Alten und Neuen Testaments—Hermann Gunkel zum 60. Geburtstage* (Göttingen: Vandenhoeck & Ruprecht, 1923), III, 174–213; James Muilenburg, "Literary Form in the Fourth Gospel," *Journal of Biblical Literature* 51 (1932), 40–53; C. M. Connick, "The Dramatic Character of the Fourth Gospel, *Journal of Biblical Literature* 67 (1948), 159–169; E. L. Pierce, "The Fourth Gospel as Drama," *Religion in Life* 29 (1960), 453–455.

⁶The importance of John's prologue for laying the groundwork of the Gospel's irony is stressed by David W. Wead, "Johannine Irony as a Key to the Author-Audience Relationship in John's Gospel," *American Academy of Religion Biblical Literature: 1974,* comp. Fred O. Francis (Missoula: Scholars Press, 1974), 34, 36–37; and Culpepper, *Anatomy*, 87–89.

⁷See Lindars, *Behind the Fourth Gospel*, 43–60.

⁸Muilenburg, "Literary Form," 52.

⁹Cf. 2:23–25; 4:31–38. These texts are compared to the role of the Greek chorus by Francis J. Moloney, "From Cana to Cana," 828. 4:42 is similarly presented by C. H. Dodd, *Interpretation*, 315.

¹⁰This element of Greek drama is stressed by Thomson, *Irony*, 37–38; and by Harsh, *Handbook*, 29.

¹¹As did Bowen, "The Fourth Gospel as Dramatic Material," 296.

¹²Some would call the Apocalypse an exception, rivaling the Fourth Gospel in dramatic quality and influence by the Greek theater. See John W. Bowman, *The First Christian Drama: The Book of Revelation* (Philadelphia: The Westminster Press, 1955); and James L. Blevins, "The Genre of Revelation," *Review and Expositor* 77 (1980), 393–407. Though Revelation has some structural affinities with Greek drama, it lacks the finely focused development and irony that characterize both Greek drama and John's Gospel.

¹³The significance of Greek drama as a religious phenomenon is stressed by W. H. Auden, *The Portable Greek Reader* (New York: The Viking Press, 1948), 12–13. D. Moody Smith, "Johannine Christianity: Some Reflections on Its Character and Delineations," *New Testament Studies* 21 (1974), 227, notes that the purpose of *religionsgeschichtliche* studies of John's Gospel should be, rather than to explain its departure from Paul and the Synoptics, to "shed light on distinct and peculiar features of Johannine style and thought as they have developed in independence of other dominant forms of early Christianity."

¹⁴"Thus says the Lord of hosts, 'Behold, the man whose name is Branch: for he shall grow up in his place, and he shall build the temple of the Lord.'"

¹⁵Wead, "Johannine Irony," 41, is in agreement that Johannine irony substantiates a Jewish setting for the Gospel.

¹⁶Norman Friedman, *Form and Meaning in Fiction* (Athens, Ga.: The University of Georgia Press, 1975), 289; cited by Culpepper, *Anatomy*, 181.

¹⁷Philip Wheelwright, *Metaphor and Reality* (Bloomington: Indiana University Press, 1962), 93.

¹⁸Culpepper, *Anatomy*, 182.

¹⁹A point not understood by David Wead, *Literary Devices*, 85–86, who seems to consider metaphor and symbol mutually exclusive.

²⁰Wheelwright, *Metaphor and Reality*, 71.

²¹E. K. Brown, *Rhythm in the Novel* (Toronto: University of Toronto Press, 1950), 58–59; cited by Culpepper, *Anatomy*, 190.

²²These differences are noted by Wead, *Literary Devices*, 32, 73. His work on this subject also appears in "The Johannine Double Meaning," *Restoration Quarterly* 13 (1970), 106–120.

[23]Oscar Cullmann, "Der johanneische Gebrauch doppeldeutiger Ausdrücke als Schlüssel zum Verständnis des vierten Evangeliums," *Theologische Zeitschrift* 4 (1948), 367–368, considers *hudōr zōn* and other metaphors as instances of Johannine double meaning, as does Wead, *Literary Devices*, 37.

[24]See Herbert Leroy, *Rätsel und Missverständnis;* M. de Jonge, "Nicodemus and Jesus," 337–359; François Vouga, *Le cadre historique*, 15-36; Jürgen Becker, *Das Evangelium nach Johannes: Kapitel 1–10*, Ökumenischer Taschenbuch Kommentar zum Neuen Testament 4 (Gütersloh: Gerd Mohn, 1979), 135–136; D. A. Carson, "Understanding Misunderstanding in the Fourth Gospel," and Culpepper, *Anatomy*, 152–169.

[25]Culpepper, *Anatomy*, 152. Eighteen instances of this pattern exist in John.

[26]Luise Schottroff, "Johannes 4:5–15 und die Konsequenzen des johanneischen Dualismus," *Zeitschrift für die Neutestamentliche Wissenschaft und die Kunde Alteren Kirche* 60 (1969), 207.

[27]Culpepper, *Anatomy*, 164–165.

[28]See, for example, Raymond E. Brown, *Community;* Oscar Cullmann, *The Johannine Circle*, trans. John Bowden (London: SCM Press, 1975); R. Alan Culpepper, *The Johannine School*, Society of Biblical Literature Dissertation Series, 26 (Missoula: Scholars Press, 1975); J. Louis Martyn, "Glimpses into the History of the Johannine Community," *The Gospel of John in Christian History* (New York: Paulist Press, 1978), 90–121; and Kysar, "Community and Gospel," 355-366.

[29]See above, pp. 38–39.

[30]On the method and function of the Johannine "reliable narrator" see Culpepper, *Anatomy*, 32–33.

[31]Wayne Meeks, "The Man from Heaven," 69-70, refers to "the self-referring quality of the whole gospel," and concludes, "only a rare outsider would get past the barrier of its closed metaphorical system. It is a book for insiders." Leroy, *Rätsel und Missverständnis*, 45–47, takes the same position.

[32]See Booth's comments on irony as the mark of "real intimacy" and "the key to the tightest bonds of friendship," *A Rhetoric of Irony*, 13–14.

[33]Culpepper, *The Johannine School,* 271, 274–275.

[34]Frank Kermode, *The Genesis of Secrecy* (Cambridge, Mass.: Harvard University Press, 1979), 121.

[35]Werner H. Kelber, *The Oral and Written Gospel* (Philadelphia: Fortress Press, 1983), esp. 90–139.

[36]On the significant differences in consciousness between a primarily oral culture and a primarily alphabetic culture, see Walter J. Ong, *The Presence of the Word* (Minneapolis: University of Minnesota Press, 1967), 17–47.

[37]On the differences between oral-based irony and literary-based irony see pp. 31–32, and Walter J. Ong, *Interfaces,* 288–289.

[38]Good, *Irony in the Old Testament,* 30.

[39]Bishop Connop Thirlwall, cited by G. G. Sedgewick, *Of Irony,* 5.

[40]Martyn, *History and Theology,* passim.

[41]W. C. van Unnik, "The Purpose of St. John's Gospel," *Studia Evangelia I,* ed. Kurt Aland, et al., Texte und Untersuchungen, 73 (Berlin: Akademie Verlag, 1959), 382–411; and John A. T. Robinson, "The Destination and Purpose of St. John's Gospel," *New Testament Studies* 6 (1960), 117–131.

[42]See, for example, Brown, *Community,* 67–68; Smith, *John,* 76; Martyn, "Glimpses," 120; M. de Jonge, "The Beloved Disciple and the Date of the Gospel of John," *Text and Interpretation: Studies in the New Testament Presented to Matthew Black,* ed. Ernest Best and R. McL. Wilson (Cambridge: Cambridge University Press, 1979), 112. Wayne Meeks, "Am I a Jew?", 182, summarizes: "It seems clear that at the time of the composition of the Gospel the Johannine community is separate from 'the Jews' and no longer expects 'Jews' to convert."

[43]Most notably, Robert T. Fortna, *The Gospel of Signs,* see esp. 225. Fortna's hypothesis is affirmed by J. Louis Martyn, "Source Criticism and *Religionsgeschichte* in the Fourth Gospel," *Jesus and Man's Hope,* ed. David G. Buttrick, A Perspective Book, I (Pittsburgh: Pittsburgh Theological Seminary, 1970), 248, 253–254; and D. Moody Smith, "The Setting and Shape of a Johannine Narrative Source," *Journal of Biblical Literature* 95 (1976), 231–241. Bultmann's earlier delineation of a *semeia* source separate from a

passion account is understandable as a missionary tract to disciples of John the Baptist. See D. Moody Smith, "The Milieu of the Johannine Miracle Source: A Proposal," *Jews, Greeks and Christians,* ed. Robert Hammerton-Kelly and Robin Scroggs (Leiden: E. J. Brill, 1976), 164–180.

[44]See Vouga, *Le cadre historique,* 34–35. Consider, for example, the effect of such texts as 7:41–42, 52 and 19:5 if the reader is convinced that Jesus is a fraud.

[45]Søren Kierkegaard, *The Concept of Irony,* 273–274.

[46]Booth, *A Rhetoric of Irony,* 28.

[47]See Fortna, *The Gospel of Signs,* 197–199.

[48]Vouga, *Le cadre historique,* does not use the phrase of 20:31 but as a summary of the purpose of Johannine misunderstanding and irony. On 20:31 as addressed to prior believers, see Brown, *John,* II, 1056; Barrett, *John,* 575; and *The Gospel of John and Judaism,* 17; Bultmann, *John,* 698–699; Schnackenburg, *Das Johannesevangelium,* III, 403–404.

[49]Brown, *John,* lxxiii–lxxv, lxxvii, says the audience of the Gospel is both fully-believing Christians and those in the synagogue who believed but lacked the courage to confess. He calls the latter group "crypto-Christians" in *Community,* 71–73. Martyn discusses such a group in *History and Theology,* 76–89, 116–118.

[50]Brown, *Community,* 73.

[51]Ibid., argues that the crypto-Christians would have been offended by such anti-synagogue polemic as is found in chapter 9. If they are loyalists to the Pharisees, that would certainly be so. If they are more like the fearful parents of 9:22, the chapter would be liberating.

[52]Martyn, *History and Theology,* 116–128, finds Jesus' dialogue with Nicodemus a paradigm of countering midrashic overtures with the personal issue of election. He also cites 7:15–17 and chapter 6.

[53]See Martyn, "Glimpses," 109–115.

[54]Booth, *A Rhetoric of Irony,* 125.

[55]Culpepper, *Anatomy,* 179–180.

[56]See Jerry H. Gill, "Jesus, Irony and the New Quest," 150–151; Vouga, *Le cadre historique,* 36, also likens John's irony to Jesus' parables.

BIBLIOGRAPHY

Abrams, M. H. *A Glossary of Literary Terms*. 3d ed. New York: Holt, Rinehart and Winston, 1971.

Alter, Robert. *The Art of Biblical Narrative*. New York: Basic Books, 1981.

Amante, David James. "Ironic Speech Acts: A Stylistic Analysis of a Rhetorical Ploy." Unpublished Ph.D. Dissertation, University of Michigan, Anne Arbor, 1975.

Aristophanes. *Aristophanes*. Trans. Benjamin Rickley Rogers. The Loeb Classical Library. 3 vols. Cambridge, Mass.: Harvard University Press, 1924.

Aristotle. *The Nicomachean Ethics*. Trans. H. Rackham. The Loeb Classical Library. Cambridge, Mass.: Harvard University Press, 1926.

Auden, W. H., ed. *The Portable Greek Reader*. New York: The Viking Press, 1948.

Auerbach, Erich. *Mimesis: The Representation of Reality in Western Literature*. Trans. Willard R. Trask. Princeton: Princeton University Press, 1953.

Bacon, Francis. *Bacon's Essays with Annotations*. Ed. Richard Whately. Boston: Lee and Shepard, 1880.

Barrett, C. K. *The Gospel According to St. John*. 2d ed. Philadelphia: The Westminster Press, 1978.

———. *The Gospel of John and Judaism*. Trans. D. M. Smith. London: SPCK, 1975.

Bauer, Walter, William F. Arndt, and F. Wilbur Gingrich. *A Greek-English Lexicon of the New Testament and Other Early Christian Literature*. 4th ed. Chicago: University of Chicago Press, 1957.

Becker, Jürgen. *Das Evangelium nach Johannes: Kapitel 1–10.* Ökumenischer Taschenbuch Kommentar zum Neuen Testament, 4. Gütersloh: Gerd Mohn, 1979.

Bernard, J. H. *A Critical and Exegetical Commentary on the Gospel According to St. John.* Ed. A. H. McNeile. The International Critical Commentary in 30 vols. Vol. 29, pt. I–II. New York: Charles Scribner & Sons, 1929.

Blank, Josef. "Die Verhandlung vor Pilatus Jo 18: 28–19:16 im Lichte johanneischer Theologie." *Biblische Zeitschrift* 3 (1959), 60–81.

Blass, F., A. Debrunner, and R. W. Funk. *A Greek Grammar of the New Testament and Other Early Christian Literature.* Trans. and ed. Robert W. Funk. Chicago: University of Chicago Press, 1961.

Blevins, James L. "The Genre of Revelation." *Review and Expositor* 77 (1980), 393–407.

Bolinger, Dwight. *Degree Words.* Janua Linguarum, Series Maior, 53. The Hague: Mouton and Company, 1972.

Bonneau, Normand R. "The Woman at the Well: John 4 and Genesis 24." *The Bible Today* 67 (1973), 1252–1259.

Booth, Wayne C. *The Rhetoric of Fiction.* Chicago: University of Chicago Press, 1961.

——— . *A Rhetoric of Irony.* Chicago: University of Chicago Press, 1974.

Bowen, Clayton R. "The Fourth Gospel as Dramatic Material." *Journal of Biblical Literature* 49 (1930), 292–305.

Bowman, John. "The Fourth Gospel and the Samaritans." *Bulletin of the John Rylands Library* 40 (1958), 298–315.

Bowman, John W. *The First Christian Drama: The Book of Revelation.* Philadelphia: The Westminster Press, 1955.

Brooks, Cleanth. "Irony and 'Ironic' Poetry." *College English* 9 (1948), 231–237.

——— . "Irony as a Principle of Structure." *Literary Opinion in America.* Ed. Morton D. Zabel. Rev. ed. New York: Harper and Brothers, 1951, 729–741.

———. *The Well Wrought Urn: Studies in the Structure of Poetry.* New York: Regnal and Hitchcock, 1947.

Brown, E. K. *Rhythm in the Novel.* Toronto: University of Toronto Press, 1950.

Brown, Raymond E. *The Community of the Beloved Disciple.* New York: Paulist Press, 1979.

———. *The Gospel According to John.* Anchor Bible Series, 29, 29A. 2 vols. Garden City, N. Y.: Doubleday, 1966.

———. "Incidents That Are Units in the Synoptic Gospels, but Dispersed in St. John." *Catholic Biblical Quarterly* 23 (1963), 143–160.

———. "The Passion According to John: Chapters 18 and 19." *Worship* 49 (1975), 126–134.

———, Karl P. Donfried and John Reumann, eds. *Peter in the New Testament.* Minneapolis: Augsburg Publishing House, 1973.

Buchanan, George Wesley. "The Samaritan Origin of the Gospel of John." *Religions in Antiquity: Essays in Memory of Erwin Ramsdell Goodenough.* Ed. Jacob Neusner. Studies in the History of Religions, 14. Leiden: E. J. Brill, 1968, 149–175.

Bultmann, Rudolf. *The Gospel of John.* Trans. and ed. George R. Beasley-Murray. Philadelphia: The Westminster Press, 1971.

———. *The History of the Synoptic Tradition.* Trans. John Marsh. Rev. ed. New York: Harper and Row, 1963.

Caird, G. B. *The Language and Imagery of the Bible.* Philadelphia: The Westminster Press, 1980.

Calvin, Jean. *The Gospel According to St. John and the First Epistle of John.* Trans. T. H. L. Parker. Calvin's Commentaries. 2 vols. Grand Rapids: William B. Eerdmans, 1961.

Carson, D. A. "Understanding Misunderstanding in the Fourth Gospel." *Tyndale Bulletin* 33 (1982), 59–91.

Chambers, Ross. "Commentary in Literary Texts." *Critical Inquiry* 5 (1978), 323–337.

Chatman, Seymour. *Story and Discourse: Narrative Structure in Fiction and Film.* Ithaca: Cornell University Press, 1978.

Chevalier, Haakon. *The Ironic Temper: Anatole France and His Time.* New York: Oxford University Press, 1932.

Cicero. *On Oratory.* Trans. F. W. Sutton. The Loeb Classical Library. Cambridge, Mass.: Harvard University Press, 1942.

Clavier, Henri. "L'ironie dans l'enseignement de Jésus." *Novum Testamentum* 1 (1956), 3–20.

_____ . "L'ironie dans le quatrième Evangile." *Studia Evangelica* I (1959) Ed. Kurt Aland, et al. Texte und Untersuchungen, 73. Berlin: Akadamie Verlag, 1959, 261–276.

_____ . "La méthode ironique dans l'enseignement de Jésus." *Études théologiques et religieuses* 4 (1929), 224–241, 323–344.

Collins, Raymond F. "The Representative Figures of the Fourth Gospel." *The Downside Review* 94 (1976), 26–46, 118–132.

Connick, C. M. "The Dramatic Character of the Fourth Gospel." *Journal of Biblical Literature* 67 (1948), 159–169.

Cornford, Francis McDonald. *The Origin of Attic Comedy.* Ed. Theodor H. Glaster. Gloucester, Mass.: Peter Smith, 1968.

Culley, Robert C. *Studies in the Structure of Hebrew Narrative.* Philadelphia: Fortress Press, 1976.

Cullmann, Oscar. "Der johanneische Gebrauch doppeldeutiger Ausdrücke als Schlüssel zum Verständnis des vierten Evangeliums." *Theologische Zeitschrift* 4 (1948), 360–372.

_____ . *The Johannine Circle: Its Place in Judaism, Among the Early Disciples and in Early Christianity.* Trans. John Bowden. London: SCM Press, 1975.

_____ . *Peter: Disciple, Apostle, Martyr.* Trans. Floyd V. Filson. London: SCM Press, 1953.

Culpepper, R. Alan. *Anatomy of the Fourth Gospel: A Study in Literary Design.* Philadelphia: Fortress Press, 1983.

_____ . *The Johannine School: An Evaluation of the Johannine School Hypothesis Based on an Investigation of the Nature of*

Ancient Schools. Society of Biblical Literature Dissertation Series, 26. Missoula: Scholars Press, 1975.

──────. "The Pivot of John's Prologue." *New Testament Studies* 27 (1980), 1–31.

Dewey, Kim E. *"Paroimiai* in the Gospel of John." *Semeia* 17 (1980), 81–99.

Dodd, C. H. *Historical Tradition in the Fourth Gospel.* Cambridge: Cambridge University Press, 1963.

──────. *The Interpretation of the Fourth Gospel.* Cambridge: Cambridge University Press, 1953.

──────. "The Prophecy of Caiaphas, John 11:47–53." *Neotestamentica et Patristica: Eine Freundesgabe Herrn Professor Dr. Oscar Cullmann zu seinem 60. Geburtstag Uberreicht.* Ed. W. C. van Unnik and Bo Reicke. Supplements to *Novum Testamentum* 6. Leiden: E. J. Brill, 1962, 134–143.

Douglas, Mary. "The Social Control of Cognition: Some Factors in Joke Perception." *Man* 3 (1968), 363–375.

Dunn, James D. G. "The Washing of the Disciples' Feet in John 13:1–20." *Zeitschrift für die neutestamentliche Wissenschaft* 61 (1970), 246–252.

Dyson, A. E. *The Crazy Fabric: Essays in Irony.* New York: St. Martin's Press, 1965.

Euripides. *Euripides.* Trans. Arthur S. Way. The Loeb Classical Library. 4 vols. Cambridge, Mass.: Harvard University Press, 1912.

Evans, C. F. "The Passion of John." *Explorations in Theology 2.* London: SCM Press, 1977, 50–66.

Foerster, Werner. "Κύριος." *Theological Dictionary of the New Testament.* Ed. Gerhard Kittel. Trans. Geoffrey W. Bromiley. Grand Rapids: William B. Eerdmans, 1965, III, 1039–1098.

Fortna, Robert Thomson. *The Gospel of Signs: A Reconstruction of the Narrative Source Underlying the Fourth Gospel.* Society for New Testament Studies Monograph Series, 11. Cambridge: Cambridge University Press, 1970.

Freed, Edwin D. "Samaritan Influence in the Gospel of John." *Catholic Biblical Quarterly* 30 (1968), 580–587.

Friedman, Norman. *Form and Meaning in Fiction*. Athens, Ga: The University of Georgia Press, 1975.

Frye, Northrop. *Anatomy of Criticism*. Princeton: Princeton University Press, 1957.

Garland, David E. *The Intention of Matthew 23*. Supplements to *Novum Testamentum* 52. Leiden: E. J. Brill, 1979.

Giblin, Charles H. "Suggestion, Negative Response, and Positive Action in St. John's Portrayal of Jesus (John 2:1–11; 4:46–54; 7:2–14; 11:1–44)." *New Testament Studies* 26 (1980), 197–211.

Gill, Jerry H. "Jesus, Irony and the New Quest." *Encounter* 41 (1980), 139–151.

Good, Edwin M. *Irony in the Old Testament*. Philadelphia: The Westminster Press, 1965.

Haenchen, Ernst. "History and Interpretation in the Johannine Passion Narrative." *Interpretation* 24 (1970), 198–219.

Harsh, Philip Whaley. *A Handbook of Classical Drama*. Stanford University: Stanford University Press, 1944.

Highet, Gilbert. *The Anatomy of Satire*. Princeton: Princeton University Press, 1962.

Hitchcock, F. R. M. "The Dramatic Development of the Fourth Gospel." *The Expositor*. Ser. 7, vol. 4 (1907), 266–279.

––––––. "Is the Fourth Gospel a Drama?" *Theology* 7 (1923), 307–317.

Holladay, W. L. "Style, Irony and Authenticity in Jeremiah." *Journal of Biblical Literature* 81 (1962), 44–54.

Homer. *The Odyssey*. Trans. A. T. Murray. The Loeb Classical Library. 2 vols. Cambridge, Mass.: Harvard University Press, 1942.

Hoskyns, Edwyn Clement. *The Fourth Gospel*. Ed. Francis Noel Davey. 2d ed. London: Faber and Faber, 1947.

_____ . "Genesis I—III and St. John's Gospel." *Journal of Theological Studies* 21 (1920), 210—218.

Hutchens, Eleanor N. "The Identification of Irony." *ELH,* 27 (1960), 352–363.

Jonge, Marinus de. "The Beloved Disciple and the Date of the Gospel of John." *Text and Interpretation: Studies in the New Testament Presented to Matthew Black.* Ed. Ernest Best and R. McL. Wilson. Cambridge: Cambridge University Press, 1979, 99–114.

_____ . "Jesus as Prophet and King in the Fourth Gospel." *Ephemerides Theologicae Lovaniensis* 49 (1973), 160–177.

_____ . *Jesus: Stranger from Heaven and Son of God—Jesus Christ and the Christians in Johannine Perspective.* Ed. and trans. John E. Steely. Society of Biblical Literature Sources for Biblical Study, 11. Missoula: Scholars Press, 1977.

_____ . "Nicodemus and Jesus: Some Observations on Misunderstanding and Understanding in the Fourth Gospel." *Bulletin of the John Rylands Library* 53 (1971), 337–359.

Jónsson, Jakob. *Humour and Irony in the New Testament Illuminated by Parallels in Talmud and Midrash.* Reykjavik, Iceland: Bókaútgáfa Menningarsjóts, 1965.

Juel, Donald. *Messiah and Temple: The Trial of Jesus in the Gospel of Mark.* Society of Biblical Literature Dissertation Series, 31. Missoula: Scholars Press, 1977.

Kaiser, Walter C., Jr. *Toward an Exegetical Theology.* Grand Rapids: Baker Book House, 1981.

Käsemann, Ernst. *The Testament of Jesus: A Study of the Fourth Gospel in Light of Chapter 17.* Trans. Gerhard Krodel. Philadelphia: Fortress Press, 1968.

Kelber, Werner H. *Mark's Story of Jesus.* Philadelphia: Fortress Press, 1979.

_____ . *The Oral and Written Gospel.* Philadelphia: Fortress Press, 1983.

Kermode, Frank. *The Genesis of Secrecy: On the Interpretation of Narrative.* Cambridge, Mass.: Harvard University Press, 1979.

Kierkegaard, Søren. *The Concept of Irony, with Constant Reference to Socrates.* Trans. Lee M. Capel. London: Collins, 1966.

Knox, Norman. "On the Classification of Ironies." *Modern Philology* 70 (1972), 53–62.

Kysar, Robert. "Community and Gospel: Vectors in the Fourth Gospel Criticism." *Interpretation* 31 (1977), 355–366.

_____. *The Fourth Evangelist and His Gospel: An Examination of Contemporary Scholarship.* Minneapolis: Augsburg Publishing House, 1975.

Léon-Dufour, Xavier. "For a Symbolic Reading of the Fourth Gospel." *New Testament Studies* 27 (1981), 439–456.

Leroy, Herbert. *Rätsel und Missverständnis: Ein Beitrag zur Formgeschichte des Johannesevangeliums.* Bonn: Peter Hanstein Verlag, 1968.

Lightfoot, R. H. *St. John's Gospel.* Ed. C. F. Evans. Oxford: Oxford University Press, 1956.

Liddell, Henry George and Robert Scott. *A Greek-English Lexicon.* Rev. ed. Oxford: The Clarendon Press, 1940.

Lindars, Barnabas. *Behind the Fourth Gospel.* Studies in Creative Criticism, 3. London: SPCK, 1971.

_____. *The Gospel of John.* New Century Bible. Grand Rapids: William B. Eerdmans, 1972.

MacGreggor, G. H. C. *The Gospel of John.* The Moffatt New Testament Commentary. London: Hodder and Stoughton, [n. d.].

MacRae, George W. "The Fourth Gospel and *Religionsgeschichte*." *Catholic Biblical Quarterly* 32 (1970), 13–24.

_____. *Invitation to John: A Commentary on the Gospel of John with Complete Text from the Jerusalem Bible.* Garden City, N. Y.: Image Books, 1978.

_____. "Theology and Irony in the Fourth Gospel." *The Word and the World: Essays in Honor of Frederick L. Moriarty.* Ed. Richard

J. Clifford and George W. MacRae. Cambridge, Mass.: Weston College Press, 1973, 83–96.

Marsh, John. *The Gospel of John*. The Pelican Gospel Commentaries. Baltimore: Penguin Books, 1968.

Martyn, J. Louis. "Glimpses into the History of the Johannine Community." *The Gospel of John in Christian History*. New York: Paulist Press, 1978.

––––––. *History and Theology in the Fourth Gospel*. Rev. ed. Nashville: Abingdon, 1979.

––––––. "Source Criticism and *Religionsgeschichte* in the Fourth Gospel." *Jesus and Man's Hope*. Ed. David G. Buttrick. A Perspective Book, I. Pittsburgh: Pittsburgh Theological Seminary, 1970, 247–273.

Meeks, Wayne A. "'Am I a Jew?'—Johannine Christianity and Judaism." *Christianity, Judaism and Other Greco-Roman Cults*. 4 vols. Ed. Jacob Neusner. Leiden: E. J. Brill, 1975, I, 163–186.

––––––. "Galilee and Judea in the Fourth Gospel." *Journal of Biblical Literature* 85 (1966), 159–169.

––––––. "The Man from Heaven in Johannine Sectarianism." *Journal of Biblical Literature* 41 (1972), 44–72.

––––––. *The Prophet-King: Moses Traditions and the Johannine Christology*. Supplements to *Novum Testamentum* 14. Leiden: E. J. Brill, 1967.

Metzger, Bruce M. *The Text of the New Testament: Its Transmission, Corruption, and Restoration*. 2d ed. New York: Oxford University Press, 1968.

––––––. *A Textual Commentary on the Greek New Testament*. [N.P.]: United Bible Societies, 1971.

Miranda, José Porfirio. *Being and the Messiah: The Message of St. John*. Trans. John Eagleson. Maryknoll, N. Y.: Orbis Books, 1977.

Moloney, Francis J. "From Cana to Cana (Jn. 2:1—4:54) and the Fourth Evangelist's Concept of Correct (and Incorrect) Faith." *Salesianum* 40 (1978), 817–843.

———. *The Johannine Son of Man.* 2d ed. Biblioteca di Scienze Religiose, 14. Rome: Libreria Ateneo Salesiano, 1978.

Morris, Leon. *The Gospel According to John.* New International Commentary on the New Testament. Grand Rapids: William B. Eerdmans, 1971.

Moule, C. F. D. *An Idiom Book of New Testament Greek.* 2d ed. Cambridge: Cambridge University Press, 1959.

Mowinckel, Sigmund. *He That Cometh.* Trans. G. W. Anderson. New York: Abingdon, [n. d.].

Muecke, D. C. *The Compass of Irony.* London: Methuen, 1969.

———. *Irony.* The Critical Idiom, 13. Ed. John D. Jump. London: Methuen, 1970.

Muilenburg, James. "Literary Form in the Fourth Gospel." *Journal of Biblical Literature* 51 (1932), 40–53.

Neyrey, Jerome H. "Jacob Traditions and the Interpretation of John 4:10–26," *Catholic Biblical Quarterly* 41 (1979), 419–437.

Olsson, Birger. *Structure and Meaning in the Fourth Gospel: A Text-Linguistic Analysis of John 2:1–11 and 4:1–42.* Trans. Jean Gray. Lund, Sweden: CWK Gleerup, 1974.

Ong, Walter J. *Interfaces of the Word.* Ithaca: Cornell University Press, 1977.

———. "Irony, Dead and Alive." Unpublished paper 1980.

———. *The Presence of the Word: Some Prolegomena for Cultural and Religious History.* Minneapolis: University of Minnesota Press, 1967.

Painter, John. *Reading John's Gospel Today.* Atlanta: John Knox Press, 1980.

Pancaro, Severino. *The Law in the Fourth Gospel: The Torah and the Gospel, Moses and Jesus, Judaism and Christianity According to John.* Supplements to *Novum Testamentum* 42. Leiden: E. J. Brill, 1975.

———. "'People of God' in St. John's Gospel." *New Testament Studies* 16 (1969), 114–129.

Pickard-Cambridge, A. W. *Dithyramb*. Oxford: The Clarendon Press, 1927.

Pierce, E. L. "The Fourth Gospel as Drama." *Religion in Life* 29 (1960), 453–455.

Plato. *The Dialogues of Plato*. Trans. B. Jowett. 4 vols. Oxford: The Clarendon Press, 1953.

Plummer, Alfred. *A Critical and Exegetical Commentary on the Gospel According to St. Luke*. The International Critical Commentary. Edinburgh: T & T Clark, 1928.

Potterie, I. de la. "Jesus et Nicodemus: de necessitate generationis ex Spiritu (Jo 3, 1–10)." *Verbum Domini* 47 (1969), 193–214.

———. "Jesus King and Judge According to John 19:13." *Scripture* 13 (1961), 97–111.

———. "Naître de l'eau et naître de l'Esprit." *Sciences Ecclésiastiques* 14 (1962), 428-430.

Quintilian. *The Institutio Oratio of Quintilian*. Trans. H. E. Butler. The Loeb Classical Library. 4 vols. Cambridge, Mass.: Harvard University Press, 1953.

Robert, Andre de. "L'ironie et la Bible." *Études théologiques et religieuses* 55 (1980), 3–30.

Robinson, John A. T. "The Destination and Purpose of St. John's Gospel." *New Testament Studies* 6 (1960), 117–131.

———. *Redating the New Testament*. Philadelphia: The Westminster Press, 1976.

Salmon, George. *A Historical Introduction to the Study of the Books of The New Testament*. London: John Murray, 1885.

Sanders, J. N. and B. A. Mastin. *A Commentary on the Gospel According to St. John*. Harper's New Testament Commentaries. New York: Harper and Row, 1968.

Schlatter, Adolf. *Der Evangelist Johannes*. Stuttgart: Calwer Verlag, 1948.

Schlier, Heinrich. "Jesus und Pilatus—Nach dem Johannesevangelium." *Die Zeit der Kirche: Exegetische Aufsätze und Vortrage*. Freiburg: Verlag Herder, 1958, 56–74.

Schnackenburg, Rudolf. *The Gospel According to St. John.* Trans. Cecily Hastings, et al. 3 vols. New York: Seabury Press, 1982.

Schneiders, Sandra M. "History and Symbolism in the Fourth Gospel." *L'évangile de Jean: Sources, Rédaction, Théologie.* Bibliotheca ephemeridum theologicarum lovaniensum, 44. Louvain: Louvain University, 1977, 371–376.

Schottroff, Luise. "Johannes 4:5–15 und die Konsequenzen des johanneischen Dualismus." *Zeitschrift für die Neutestamentliche Wissenschaft und die Kunde Alteren Kirche* 60 (1969), 199–214.

Schweizer, Eduard. *The Good News According to Matthew.* Trans. David E. Green. Atlanta: John Knox Press, 1975.

Sedgewick, G. G. *Of Irony, Especially in the Drama.* Toronto: University of Toronto Press, 1935.

Sharpe, Robert Boies. *Irony in the Drama: An Essay on Impersonation, Shock, and Catharsis.* Chapel Hill: The University of North Carolina Press, 1959.

Smalley, Stephen S. *John: Evangelist and Interpreter.* Greenwood, S. C.: Attic Press, 1978.

Smith, D. Moody. "Johannine Christianity: Some Reflections on Its Character and Delineations." *New Testament Studies* 21 (1974), 224–244.

_____. *John.* Proclamation Commentaries. Ed. Gerhard Krodel. Philadelphia: Fortress Press, 1976.

_____. "The Milieu of the Johannine Miracle Source: A Proposal." *Jews, Greeks and Christians: Religious Cultures in Antiquity— Studies in Honor of William David Davies.* Ed. Robert Hammerton-Kelly and Robin Scroggs. Leiden: E. J. Brill, 1976, 164–180.

_____. "The Setting and Shape of a Johannine Narrative Source." *Journal of Biblical Literature* 95 (1976), 231–241.

Smothers, E. R. "Two Readings in Papyrus Bodmer II." *Harvard Theological Review* 51 (1958), 109—122.

Sophocles. *Sophocles.* Trans. F. Storr. The Loeb Classical Library. 2 vols. Cambridge, Mass.: Harvard University Press, 1951.

Spencer, Aida Besançon. "The Wise Fool (and the Foolish Wise). A Study of Irony in Paul." *Novum Testamentum* 23 (1981), 349–360.

Stählin, G. "νῦν (ἄρτι)." *Theological Dictionary of the New Testament.* Ed. Gerhard Kittel. Trans. and ed. Geoffrey W. Bromiley. Grand Rapids: William B. Eerdmans, 1967, IV, 1106–1123.

Stein, Robert H. *The Method and Message of Jesus' Teachings.* Philadelphia: The Westminster Press, 1978.

Stinespring, W. F. "Irony and Satire." *Interpreter's Dictionary of the Bible.* Ed. George A. Buttrick. 3 vols. Nashville: Abingdon Press, 1962, II, 726–728.

Strachan, R. H. *The Fourth Gospel: Its Significance and Environment.* 3d ed. London: Student Christian Movement Press, 1941.

Temple, William. *Readings in St. John's Gospel.* 2 vols. London: Macmillan, 1940.

Thirlwall, Bishop Connop. "On the Irony of Sophocles." *The Philological Museum,* 2 vols. Cambridge, Mass.: Deightons, 1833.

Thompson, Alan Reynolds. *The Dry Mock: A Study of Irony in Drama.* Berkeley: University of California Press, 1948.

Thomson, J. A. K. *Irony: An Historical Introduction.* London: George Allen and Unwin, 1926.

Trueblood, Elton. *The Humor of Christ.* New York: Harper and Row, 1964.

Unnik, W. C. van. "The Purpose of St. John's Gospel." *Studia Evangelica I.* Ed. Kurt Aland, et al. Texte und Untersuchungen, 73. Berlin: Akademie Verlag, 1959, 382–411.

Vann, Gerald. *The Eagle's Word.* New York: Harcourt, Brace, and World, 1961.

Vawter, Bruce. "The Gospel According to John." *Jerome Biblical Commentary.* 2 vols. Ed. Raymond E. Brown, et al. Englewood Cliffs, N. J.: Prentice Hall, 1968, II, 414–466.

Vellacott, Philip. *Ironic Drama.* Cambridge: Cambridge University Press, 1975.

Via, Dan O., Jr. *Kerygma and Comedy in the New Testament: A Structuralist Approach to Hermeneutic.* Philadelphia: Fortress Press, 1975.

Vouga, François. *Le cadre historique et l'intention théologique de Jean.* Paris: Éditions Beauchesne, 1977.

Wead, David W. "The Johannine Double Meaning." *Restoration Quarterly* 13 (1970), 106–120.

――――. "Johannine Irony as a Key to the Author-Audience Relationship in John's Gospel." *American Academy of Religion Biblical Literature: 1974.* Comp. Fred O. Francis. Missoula: Scholars Press, 1974, 33–50.

――――. *The Literary Devices in John's Gospel.* Theologischen Dissertationen, IV. Ed. Bo Reicke. Basel: Friedrich Reinhart Kommissionsverlag, 1970.

Westcott, B. F. *The Gospel According to St. John.* Reprint. Grand Rapids: William B. Eerdmans, 1978.

Wheelwright, Philip. *Metaphor and Reality.* Bloomington: Indiana University Press, 1962.

Wilder, Amos N. *The Language of the Gospel.* New York: Harper & Row, 1964.

Williams, James G. "Irony and Lament: Clues to Prophetic Consciousness." *Semeia* 8 (1977), 51–71.

Wimsatt, W. K., Jr. and Monroe C. Beardsley. *The Verbal Icon.* Lexington, Ky.: University of Kentucky Press, 1954.

Windisch, Hans. "Der johanneische Erzählungsstil." 'EYXAPIΣTH-PION: *Studien zur Religion und Literatur des Alten und Neuen Testaments—Hermann Gunkel zum 60. Geburtstage.* Göttingen: Vandenhoeck & Ruprecht, 1923, III, 174–213.

Woll, D. Bruce. *Johannine Christianity in Conflict: Authority, Rank, and Succession in the First Farewell Discourse.* Society of Biblical Literature Dissertation Series, 60. Missoula: Scholars Press, 1981.

Worcester, David. *The Art of Satire.* Cambridge, Mass.: Harvard University Press, 1940.

INDEX OF AUTHORS

211

INDEX OF SCRIPTURE REFERENCES

OLD TESTAMENT